# AN ANTHROPOLOGY OF FUTURES AND TECHNOLOGIES

This book examines emerging automated technologies and systems and the increasingly prominent roles that each plays in our lives and our imagined futures. It asks how technological futures are being constituted and the roles anthropologists can play in their making; how anthropologists engage with emerging technologies within their fieldwork contexts in research which seeks to influence future design; how to create critical and interventional approaches to technology design and innovation; and how a critical anthropology of the way that emerging technologies are experienced in everyday life circumstances offers new insights for future-making practices. In pursuing these questions, this book responds to a call for new anthropologies that respond to the current and emerging technological environments in which we live, environments for which thinking critically about the possible, plausible, and impossible futures are no longer sufficient. Taking the next step, this book asserts that anthropology must now propose alternative ways, rooted in ethnography, to approach and engage with what is coming and to contest dominant narratives of industry, policy, and government, and to respond to our contemporary context through a public, vocal, and interventional approach.

**Débora Lanzeni** is Research Fellow at Monash University, Australia.

**Karen Waltorp** is Associate Professor – Promotion programme at University of Copenhagen, Denmark.

**Sarah Pink** is Professor at Monash University, Australia.

**Rachel C. Smith** is Associate Professor at Aarhus University, Denmark.

# AN ANTHROPOLOGY OF FUTURES AND TECHNOLOGIES

*Edited by Débora Lanzeni, Karen Waltorp, Sarah Pink, and Rachel C. Smith*

Routledge
Taylor & Francis Group

LONDON AND NEW YORK

Cover image: copyright: Christian Vium (www.christianvium.com)

First published 2023
by Routledge
4 Park Square, Milton Park, Abingdon, Oxon OX14 4RN

and by Routledge
605 Third Avenue, New York, NY 10158

*Routledge is an imprint of the Taylor & Francis Group, an informa business*

ISBN: 9781350144927 (hbk)
ISBN: 9781350144910 (pbk)
ISBN: 9781003084471 (ebk)

DOI: 10.4324/9781003084471

Typeset in Bembo
by Newgen Publishing UK

# CONTENTS

# ACKNOWLEDGEMENTS

Each chapter acknowledges the specific funding sources that have supported the contributors' different research projects and positions. We would additionally like to acknowledge the support for our work as editors as follows: the European Association of Social Anthropologists has generously supported the work of and given a home to our Future Anthropologies Network; Débora Lanzeni's and Sarah Pink's work is intellectually and practically supported by the Emerging Technologies Research Lab at Monash University, Australia; Sarah Pink's conceptual and editorial work and contribution to the introduction of this book is also supported by her role as a Chief Investigator in the Australian Research Council Centre of Excellence for Automated Decision-Making and Society (CE200100005) (2020–2027); Karen Waltorp wishes to thank the Department of Anthropology for intellectual support, and the Danish Research Council, as especially the intellectual work going into the introduction is supported through her role as PI of the DigiSAt: Digital everyday lives far from Silicon Valley: Technological Imaginaries and Energy Futures in a South African Township (DFF-1130-00019B 2021–2024).

We thank our Routledge editors for their support and unending patience as we edited this international book through the many challenges of a global pandemic, and our contributors for their commitment to this project during such a complicated time.

# CONTRIBUTORS

**Simone Abram** is Professor in Anthropology at Durham University, UK, and is a director of the Durham Energy Institute. Recent publications include *Ethnographies of power* (Eds T. Loloum, S. Abram, N. Ortar), *Electrifying Anthropology* (Eds S Abram, B. R. Winthereik, T. Yarrow), and a chapter on Electricity in *The Palgrave Handbook of the Anthropology of Technology* (Eds M. H. Bruun et al).

**Maja Hojer Bruun** is Associate Professor at the Department of Educational Anthropology, Aarhus University, and convenor of the Danish research network for the Anthropology of Technology (AnTech). Her research centres on emerging digital technologies, spanning robots, drones, urban living labs, and data encryption infrastructures, and in her work, she explores collaborative, interventionist, and experimental ethnographic methods. In her current research project, she is interested in the forms of knowledge, organisation, and government through which cities are turned into living labs and sites of experimentation. She is co-editor of *Palgrave Handbook of the Anthropology of* Technology (2022).

**Nathan Crilly** is Professor of Design in the Engineering Department at the University of Cambridge. He employs an interdisciplinary approach to studying how people undertake creative activities. His work, and that of his group, has been published in peer-reviewed journals, such as *Design Studies, Design Issues, Journal of Creative Behavior* and *International Journal of Design, Creativity and Innovation*.

**Elizabeth de Freitas** is Professor at Adelphi University. Her research explores innovative data methodologies in the social sciences, anthropological and philosophical investigations of digital life, and cultural-material studies of mathematical practices in complex learning environments. Her work has been funded by the Canada Council for the Arts, the Ontario and Toronto Arts Council, the US National Science Foundation, and the UK Economic and Social Research Council.

**Harry Ferguson** is a Professor of Social Work at the University of Birmingham. He has conducted many empirical research projects into social work, child protection, and child welfare practices and been at the forefront of using social science to develop theory for social work and new understandings of practices. Over the past decade, he has used ethnographic methods to get close to practice to study embodied practices and interactions between social workers and service users and has used digital ethnography to make sense of these encounters during the COVID-19 pandemic. His books include *Child Protection Practice* (Palgrave Macmillan).

**Vaike Fors** is Professor in Design Ethnography at School of ITE at Halmstad University in Sweden. Her area of expertise lies in the fields of visual, sensory, and design ethnography. In her pursuit to contribute to further understandings of contemporary conditions for learning, she has studied people's interaction with new and emerging technologies in various research projects. Fors is an experienced project leader of international scientific, applied, and collaborative research projects. Recent publications include the book *Imagining personal data. Experiences of Self-Tracking* (Routledge, 2020).

**Christopher Gad**, is Associate Professor in the research group *Technologies in Practice* at the IT University of Copenhagen. He is the chair of the Danish Association for Science and Technology Studies. His current research interests include how hopes and dreams of digitalisation affect the relationship between state and citizens and how the proliferation of digital technologies and computer science thinking affect renegotiations of social issues and concerns, such as trust.

**Bastian Jørgensen** holds a PhD from the IT University of Copenhagen. He wrote his dissertation about the vision of the Danish Customs and Tax Administrations to become a data-driven organisation. His main interest is in how work is being reconfigured around data infrastructures in public organisations. Bastian is currently employed in the Danish Customs and Tax Administration, where he works as a data engineer.

**Laura Kelly** is Lecturer in Criminal Justice at the University of Birmingham. Laura is a sociologist with experience in researching work with children and young people in a number of settings. She was a Research Fellow on the Child Protection and Social Distancing project, led by Professor Harry Ferguson with Professor Sarah Pink. This research was funded by the Economic and Social Research Council, as part of the UK Research and Innovation call for studies that could help understand and alleviate the social impact of the COVID-19 pandemic.

**Débora Lanzeni** is Research Fellow in the Emerging Technologies Research Lab and member of the Faculty of Information Technology at Monash University, Australia. She has co-convene the EASA Future Anthropologies Network since 2016. Her research, located at the nexus between anthropology and Science and Technology Studies, focuses on the development and design of emerging technologie, Data, Digital, tech developers, and the future of work. Her publications include the books *Design Ethnography: Research, Responsibilities and Futures* (2022) and *Designing Digital Materialities* (2016). She is the co-director of the Urban Computing Lab at Monash.

**Peter Lutz** is a post-doctoral researcher at the Department of Intelligent Systems and Digital Design (ISDD), and School of Information Technology, Halmstad University, Sweden. He holds advanced degrees in sociocultural anthropology with extensive research experience in the domains of technology design, healthcare, media, and education. His current research and teaching interests attend to the human-centric study of future mobility including autonomous vehicles and sustainable modes of transportation.

**Maggie MacLure** is Professor Emerita in the Education and Social Research Institute (ESRI), Manchester Metropolitan University, UK. She has a long-standing interest in the development of theory and methodology in social research. She is co-founder with Elizabeth de Freitas of the Manifold Lab at MMU and Founder-Director of the International Summer Institute in Qualitative Research, where researchers engage with the latest issues in theory and methodology in dialogue with leading theorists.

**Roxana Moroşanu Firth** is a social anthropologist working in the fields of computing, sustainability, and innovation. Her work has been published in numerous peer-reviewed journals, such as *Design Studies*, *The Cambridge Journal of Anthropology* and *Cultural Anthropology*. She is the author of *An Ethnography of Household Energy Demand in the UK: Everyday Temporalities of Digital Media Usage* (Palgrave Macmillan, 2016).

**Katalin Osz** is Senior User Experience Researcher with a Design Anthropology and strategic design focus in Volvo Cars UX organisation and an affiliated Design Researcher in the School of Information Technology at Halmstad University, Sweden. Her work focuses on applying and developing future-focused ethnographic methods for strategic experience design and emerging technologies.

**Sarah Pink**, PhD, FASSA, is Professor and Director of the Emerging Technologies Research Lab at Monash University, Australia, and Associate Director of Monash Energy Institute. She is also a Chief Investigator in the Australian Research Council Centre of Excellence for Automated Decision-Making and Society, where she co-leads the People Programme and leads the Transport Mobilities Focus Area. Her recent books include *Emerging Technologies: life at the edge of the future* (2022), *Everyday Automation* (2022), *Energy Futures* (2022) and *Design Ethnography* (2022).

**Dan Podjed** is Research Associate at the Research Centre of the Slovenian Academy of Sciences and Arts, Associate Professor at the University of Ljubljana's Faculty of Arts, and Senior Advisor at the Institute for Innovation and Development of the University of Ljubljana. He was Convenor of the EASA Applied Anthropology Network from its inception in 2010 until 2018 and continues to be active as one of the Network's Executive Advisors. In 2013 he was the founder and until 2018 the main organiser of the annual event *Why the World Needs Anthropologists*, which has become the most important meeting place for applied anthropologists in Europe and beyond.

**Ajda Pretnar Žagar** holds a PhD in anthropology from the University of Ljubljana. She is a researcher at the Laboratory for Bioinformatics, Faculty of Computer and Information Science, and the Institute of Contemporary History. Her research focuses on the methodology of interdisciplinary and multidisciplinary research as well as the uses of machine learning and data mining in the humanities and social sciences. She teaches at the Higher School of Economics in Moscow, Russia.

**David Rousell** is an artist and social researcher based in Naarm/Melbourne, Australia. He is a director of the Creative Agency Lab for transdisciplinary studies of creativity at RMIT, and a core member of the Digital Ethnography Research Centre (DERC). He is also a Visiting Research Fellow in the Education and Social Research Institute (ESRI) at Manchester Metropolitan University. David's research is invested in a more-than-human re-imagining of educational cultures, theories, and environments and often involves artful collaborations with children, young people, and their wider ecological communities. His recent monograph is titled *Immersive Cartography and Post-Qualitative Inquiry* published with Routledge in 2021.

**Minna Ruckenstein** works as Professor at the Consumer Society Research Centre, University of Helsinki. She directs The Datafied Life Collaboratory that studies processes of digitalisation/datafication by highlighting emotional, social, political, and economic aspects of current and emerging data practices. Currently funded research projects focus on re-humanising automated decision-making, algorithmic culture, and everyday engagements with algorithmic systems in Helsinki and in Shanghai and Hangzhou.

**Antti Silvast** is Associate Professor at the Technical University of Denmark, DTU Management, Division for Responsible Innovation and Design. He is an editor of the journal *Science & Technology Studies*. His recent publications include *Sociology of Interdisciplinarity* (with C. Foulds), "On Theory-Methods Packages in Science and Technology Studies" (with M. J. Virtanen), and a chapter on "Producing the User in

Smart Technologies" (with R. Williams, S. Hyysalo, K. Rommetveit, and C. Raab) in the *Routledge Handbook on Smart Technologies* (Eds H. Kurz et al).

**Rachel Charlotte Smith** is Associate Professor of Design Anthropology at the Department for Digital Design and Information Studies, Aarhus University. Her research focuses on relations among culture, design, and technology, specifically on social change and transformation through emerging digital technologies. Exploring and developing theoretical and methodological approaches of research in and through design, among social anthropology, participatory design, and interaction design, her work has contributed to the development of design anthropology as a transdisciplinary field of academic research. Smith is co-founder of the international Research Network for Design Anthropology and co-editor of Design Anthropology: Theory and Practice (2013), Design Anthropological Futures (2016), and Design Studies Special Issue on Design Anthropology (2022).

**Sonja Trifuljesko** is a social and cultural anthropologist and a post-doctoral researcher at the Centre for Consumer Society Research of the University of Helsinki and the Datafied Life Collaboratory. She is particularly interested in how large-scale transformation processes, including digitalisation, datafication, and algorithmisation, affect the dynamics of social relations. Her ongoing research focuses on the ethics of automated decision-making accountability and revolves around the notions of trust, transparency, and risk.

**Karen Waltorp** is Associate Professor – Promotion Programme, Department of Anthropology. University of Copenhagen, where she heads the Ethnographic Exploratory, and coordinates the Researcher Group Technē. She is convener of the EASA Future Anthropologies Network since 2016 and serves on the Editorial Board of Cultural Anthropology and Visual Anthropology. Waltorp is the author of *Why Muslim Women and Smartphones* (Routledge 2020), co-editor of *Energy Futures* (de Gruyter 2022), and has published widely on multimodal and digital methodologies, technologies, gender, migration, and representation. She was Co-PI on ARTlife (2017–2020) and is PI on DigiSAt: Digital Everyday Lives and Energy Futures – www.digisatproject.com (DFF 1130-00019B) (2021–2024).

**Brit Ross Winthereik** is Professor in the Research Group Technologies in Practice at the IT University of Copenhagen where she directs the Center for Digital Welfare. Her book *Monitoring Movements in Development Aid: Recursive Infrastructures and Partnerships* with Casper Bruun Jensen came out with MIT Press in 2013. She has co-edited several volumes at the interface of anthropology and Science and Technology Studies: *Electrifying Anthropology* (Bloomsbury, 2019), *Energy Worlds in Experiment* (Mattering Press, 2021), and *Experimenting with Ethnography* (Duke, 2021), as well as *Handbook for the Anthropology of Technology* (Palgrave, 2022).

# INTRODUCTION

## An anthropology of futures and technologies

*Karen Waltorp, Débora Lanzeni, Sarah Pink and Rachel C. Smith*

What does an Anthropology of Futures and Technologies look like? What does it seek to achieve? And what does it contribute; to whom – and why? This edited volume addresses these questions as we examine empirically and theoretically how people and technologies participate in constituting futures that cannot be predicted or necessarily imagined. The book as a whole argues and demonstrates that anthropologists need to have a role to play in shaping this world as it comes about and proposes a critical role for anthropology that contests dominant narratives of industry, policy and government existing and promoted within futures and technologies. There are growing concerns and questions about how anthropology and anthropologists should engage with machine learning and other increasingly prevalent technologies and their many implications as we move forward. The present moment invokes a fundamental question about what is next – both for anthropology and for diverse groups of people in their everyday worlds?

Our environment and sociality can be said to be changing at high speed and in fundamental ways with technologies; but techno-solutionism and -determinism stand in the way of imagining technological futures otherwise (Escobar 1995, 2007, Chan 2014, Duclos et al. 2017, McTighe & Raschig 2019, Pink et al. 2022a,b, Waltorp et al. 2022). This book takes a step towards opening that up in utopian, speculative and at the same time empirically grounded and concrete ways, which the anthropological approach and refigured ethnographic methodologies allow for. The contributors advance a *future anthropologies* agenda (www.easaonline.org/netwo rks/fan/), which seeks to respond to our contemporary context through a public, vocal and interventionist anthropology that confronts the contingency and uncertainty of our futures (see also Pink et al. 2022a,b, Smith 2022). The chapters collectively show how technologies emerge *in* and *with* societies and people's everyday practices and stakes a claim for anthropology to be at the centre of debates about our technological futures.

DOI: 10.4324/9781003084471-1

Significant work has been done around questions of how technology, its design and use is part of society and everyday life in the existing research fields of Science and Technology Studies, anthropology of technology and digital anthropology. Here, however, we call for a new anthropological approach and response to the current and emerging technological environment in which we live – where humans, other species and technologies develop alongside each other, shaped by, and shaping the planetary environment. The participation of anthropologists in contexts of the design, development, legislation and use of new automated, connected and intelligent emerging technologies is creating new opportunities as well as generating ethical challenges.

*An Anthropology of Futures and Technologies* demonstrates how technological futures are being constituted anthropologically and the roles anthropologists are playing in their making. The arguments of this book are rooted in in-depth ethnographic research undertaken across the world. Its contributors draw on both the classic anthropological immersive, micro-scale fieldwork traditions, and on multi-sited fieldwork (Marcus 1995), novel short-term ethnography practices, design anthropological collaboration (Smith et al. 2016, Drazin 2021), and on more recent assemblage ethnography focusing across scales, sites and practices (c.f. Fischer 2018, Wahlberg 2022). Bringing together such diverse approaches demonstrate how anthropological theory and practice can help us to rethink anthropology for a contemporary digitalised world. Moreover, they collectively address how technological futures are constituted and imagined in the discourses and practices of professionals in the domains of technology and design; how anthropological and technology-based research can be combined to create new insights into the social, cultural and experiential aspects of emerging technologies and their design; how people live with- and adopt emerging technologies into their everyday practices, making them part of continuously unfolding lives and environments; how innovation and development happens in the field of technology research and design; and simultaneously, how an interventional anthropology can disrupt and contribute to making such processes socially and environmentally sustainable and responsible.

Throughout, the contributors to this book seek to explore ethnographically, from a very tangible and situated perspective, how we live with emerging technologies. They reflect on how new technologies come about and/or are experienced in everyday life scenarios in the process of their emergence. There is an explicit emphasis on an anthropology of emergence working *with* and *within* such settings, as well as *looking at* how imagined and developed technologies 'meet' specific people's everyday worlds, in concrete empirical contexts. From an ethnographic stance, they look to the world focusing on its creative possibilities of making and shaping new and different practices and societies, which should be, to some extent, part of the anthropological project (Fischer 2018, Graeber & Wengrow 2021). The temporality and timing in/of various field sites, and the timing of anthropological knowledge and intervention, is part of this, as the authors study technologies and the imaginaries and worlds that they come with and that come with them

(Ferguson 1990, Sneath et al. 2009): focusing on engineering in/and modelling labs, artificial intelligence (AI) and machine-learning algorithms, automated cars and drones, sensor technologies, smartphones, as well as practices and conceptually fraught notions of 'data work', 'smartness' and 'innovation'. In the case of the latter, the authors investigate these concepts as objects of knowledge and social inquiry as well, concepts that order our understanding of the contemporary world and what future is possible (c.f. Roitman 2013). Technology has long been a foundational concept for how we perceive our world, and we turn to this below.

## An anthropology of technologies

The uncertainty related to the new spectra of insecurities in today's world as relates to climate, health, political crisis – and technologies across and entangled in these – is often seen as potentially controlled by prediction, prognosis and ever smarter technologies. Depending on perspective, technologies and AI can be viewed as offering solutions, and as problematic as well, in that they reproduce the biases that already exist in society (Benjamin 2019, Sadowski 2020, Strengers 2013). With new opportunities come the questions of who should engage with these new technologies and for what purposes. The political is entwined with science and technology and 'telling stories of the future is always a social, material, and political practice'. It always has effects; it is always non-innocent (Watts 2008: 188, see also Haraway 1988). However, it is not necessarily clear *how*: very different visions and images abound in terms of what our future societies should look like, they emerge from these layers of uncertainty, possible solutions and new problems. Envisioned futures tend to differ radically from how they eventually unfold in the situatedness of people's lives (Bell & Dourish 2007).

The questions addressed in *An Anthropology of Futures and Technologies* draw on foundational questions for the discipline, rendered new in our contemporary situation. Turning to early works in the field, it raises questions about our relation to technology; it concerns our futures with both specific technologies and questions the 'essence' of technology as what, through our relationship to it, becomes a specific 'enframing' in Martin Heidegger's term, something that dominates how we perceive the world (Heidegger 2008/1953). The often taken-for-granted, dominant techno-solutionist scaffolding or 'enframing' 'endangers the human in its relation to itself and everything that exists' (Heidegger 2008: 322–3), especially if this way of 'revealing' what is, is the only one available; the only frame through which reality appears, and thereby closing down possible or alternative futures. Seventy years ago, Heidegger posited technology as a way of 'revealing' the world – so pervasive and fundamental in his time that one could not 'opt for' technology or 'opt out' of it (Heidegger 2008). It is arguably the same today where technology as an all-encompassing framing appears to be inevitable. As Heidegger implored, we should ask about – *question* – technology, to draw out our relation to it. Technology's 'essence', as he termed it, is neither technical nor machinic alone, but a way in which the world reveals itself to us, and thus this enframing works as a kind of scaffolding which orders our understanding of what exists in the world. Departing from Heidegger's understanding, in this volume, we question and critically examine dominant understandings of technology and intervene into the ongoing processes of technological progress. We insist on paying attention to how that relationship and perception of the technological world comes about, and how that looks in various empirical settings and the often mundane everyday processes of use, development, design, implementation, and legislation.

To work collaboratively towards desirable and democratic technological futures, implies ethnographic work across all of the settings where technologies are imagined, modelled, tested, legislated about, funded, and adapted (to). Both various technological imaginaries, the abstract and concrete utopias, and the very tangible technologies are part of an anthropology of futures and technologies. It is imperative that we critically and constructively question our relation to technology and anthropologists have long since started to do so. This has been done, for instance, by examining and intervening in how technology development and design happens (Pink & Lanzeni 2018), exploring human–digital relations and new technological forms across anthropology, design and politics (Geismar & Knox 2021), collaboratively engaging in understanding and co-designing new digital futures (Cizek et al. 2019, Smith 2022), and calls for a new futures-focused anthropology that moves forward with people, planet and technology (Pink 2022) and by opening up the possibility of imagining our relation to technology, as well as to specific technologies, otherwise (Waltorp et al. 2022). *Anthropos* (Greek: Human) and *techne* (Greek: art, craft, technique or skill) are inseparable when it comes to the study of humans and their societies. Heidegger pointed back to this nuanced understanding of all the aspects of techne/technology to illuminate what it really is, and to understand our relation to it.[1] From its very origins as a discipline, anthropology has recorded and researched human-technology interfaces in efforts to account for and understand forms of social organisation and practice as well as systems of belief and meaning throughout the world. Whether approached in terms of the tools and dexterous capabilities that were seen to separate humans from other species or the technical systems that allowed for subsistence and the reproduction of society, human ingenuity and practice involving the development and use of various kinds of technologies has been a definitive object of ethnographic inquiry (see Bruun & Wahlberg 2022).

While 'exact' or natural sciences reconstruct nature as forces that can be calculated; as resources to provide energy that can be stored, social sciences and humanities on the other hand offer alternative framings to the anthropos-techne relation. Perceiving the environments, we inhabit as spaces to be conquered or as 'standing reserves' has imminent dangers for human, non-humans and the planet alike (Heidegger 2008, Waltorp et al. 2022). This is not to say that we should have another 'science war', rather the opposite, that we need both natural and social sciences and a multiplicity of framings and perspectives on technology and our relation to it, to be able to unsettle the reified dominant view and imagine otherwise. Following Donna Haraway in *Situated Knowledges* from 1988, we are not after radical social constructionism any more than we are ready to accept the God-eye view of a supposedly neutral, objective, positivism (1988: 577). What we want is akin to 'feminist objectivity' or critical empricism as defined by Haraway (ibid: 580), where the situatedness and partial nature of all knowledge is the starting point.

From an anthropological perspective, Lucy Suchman (2011) has critically questioned the localised optimism and hubris associated with design and technologies, arguing instead for the acknowledgement of these as just one among many figures and practices of transformation. Building on her early foundational work of Plans and Situated Action (1987), she sees technology as *both* stimulating and productive as a fetish of the new, as well as depressing and augmenting the unequal distribution and tempi at which technological worlds can be inhabited; Ruha Benjamin (2019) shows how technologies are materially imbued with values and views which are racist (2019), and Henrik Vigh (2009) how geography, class and neo-coloniality makes the young men he works with in Guinea-Bissau perceive only technological *voids*, a technological world that is forever out of their reach. A continuation of the anthropological engagement in such contexts, and across them, is part of the contributions to this book where the imagined and projected worlds and emerging technologies become part of mundane work environments and everyday living with various effects, feedback loops and future-making opened up for study and debate.

## A future-oriented anthropology

A future-oriented anthropology is concerned with what horizons are opened up, and what concrete impacts can be traced, often with unforeseen implications. It builds on both ethnography and anthropological theorisation (Crapanzano 2004, Escobar 2007, Ferguson 1999, Fischer 2009, Guyer 2007, Halse 2013, Hannerz 2015, Miyazaki 2004, Nielsen 2014, Rabinow 2007), which the editors' work departs from and engages in various ways (Pink et al. 2022a,b, Pink & Lanzeni 2018, Salazar et al. 2017, Smith 2022, Waltorp 2017, Waltorp & Halse 2013). With *Marking Time: On the Anthropology of the Contemporary*, Paul Rabinow (2007) extended 'the analytical gaze to encompass the near future, still with the aim of critical engagement with the present. Such non-linear understandings of time and causality generally render the present contingent, and imply that things could be different' (cf. Smith et al. 2016: 2). We attend to how specific orientations to the future impact the ways in which academics, politicians and industry conceptualise the future(s), and to how such orientations shape dominant and contested ways of thinking about the future(s) that are being forged or worked towards.

As the discipline of anthropology traditionally focused on studying so-called primitive peoples and cultures far away from the Euro-American centre both geographically and in terms of time (Fabian 1983), we earned a reputation for being concerned with the past and present, rather than the future (Waltorp & Halse 2013, Pink & Salazar 2017). There has, however, always been a focus on the varied ways to think and relate to time and temporality among people (c.f. Fabian 1983, Munn

1992, Otto & Smith 2013), as well as technologies and technical skills have been part and parcel of the discipline since its inception (Gell 1992, Bruun and Wahlberg 2022, Mauss 2006/1941).

Future-oriented anthropology clearly stakes the claims for a refigured anthropology, which not only relies on documenting and analysing the past but also confronts and intervenes in the challenges of contested and controversial (technological) futures (FAN manifesto 2014 in Salazar et al. 2017: 3) and there is a strong case for an anthropology, which works forwards rather than retrospectively (Pink 2022). These foundations, as mentioned above, already exist, and as stated in the EASA Future Anthropologies Network Manifesto:

> Anthropology of the future is accretive. It builds on traditions, reflects on (fraught) pasts to foster a politics of listening attuned to a diversity of voices and we tell stories that are imaginative, illustrative and informative. We are ethical, political and interventionist, and take responsibility for interventions.
> *FAN Manifesto 2014 in Salazar et al. 2017*

This conceptual and empirical work already takes place across fields and is pivotal in opening up to imagining our relation to technology/ies and futures otherwise: The fields of applied anthropology and design anthropology – and as mentioned above, in STS, anthropology of technology, digital anthropology, and also environmental anthropology. Across these fields are inspirations towards an interventional anthropology that puts at its core a theoretical and practical consideration of futures, and the possible ways they might be conceptualised and played out (Abram et al. 2022).

By 'interventional' anthropology, we mean a collaborative anthropology that encompasses but goes beyond the application of anthropology to resolve questions and support solutions for others; a public anthropology that critically reveals the issues in ways that are globally and locally sensitive, equitable and ethical. An anthropology that gets involved with what matters, what happens, and the events and experiences that participants in fieldwork as well as the wider world we inhabit are implicated in. The manifesto stipulates that we are critical ethnographers engaged with confronting and intervening in the challenges of contested and controversial futures; de-centring the human, embracing larger ecologies and technological entanglements (FAN manifesto 2014 in Salazar et al. 2017: 4). Interventional anthropology (Pink 2022), like design ethnography and anthropology (Pink et al. 2022a,b, Smith et al. 2016), refers to an engaged discipline which 'has the power and possibility to engage its audiences through critical, incisive and disruptive narratives and to mobilise dynamic future-focused questions in society' – both locally and globally (Pink 2021: 232). While not all of the projects described in this book have necessarily achieved all these components of an interventional anthropology, they form part of a journey through which they collectively shape and form elements of a growing anthropological engagement with futures and technologies that seeks to shift the terrain of the discipline and of broader societal understandings and practices.

A future-oriented anthropology is both imaginative and grounded in the empirical. Again, such issues have long since been part of scholarships. German philosopher Ernst Bloch (1986) discerned between abstract utopias and concrete utopias. Abstract ones emerge in daydreams and wishful thinking whereas concrete utopias take their point of departure in reflections about the human- and societal needs and possibilities for change. Concrete utopias thus gather energy and direction from people's collective actions towards changed circumstances and praxis to arrive at a better society. The abstract utopias of daydreams are stringed together with researching *with* people who design, develop, legislate and those who live with emerging technologies. *An Anthropology of Futures and Technologies* thus invites speculation and engagement across scales – with a grounding in the empirically concrete, not in a generic sense but emerging from situated contexts. As argued by Rachel C. Smith and Ton Otto (2016: 19), anthropological approaches to ongoing processes of research and intervention 'involves defining and inventing the ethnographic field or design space, and even to an extent the ethnographic subject(s), as well as acting situationally to produce various cultural agendas through the research and design process'. This makes the question of how we position ourselves as researchers pivotal. Future-oriented anthropologists make a commitment to exploring and researching in a new space, and in doing so departing from certain conventions – particularly those who oriented previous anthropologies towards the past. A future-oriented anthropology leaves behind the illusion of disinterested social science and promotes an accountable anthropology rather, in terms of how the knowledge created is active in the world – insisting on a critical, ethical and engaged practice (read the manifesto in full at the EASA Future Anthropologies network: www.easaonline.org/networks/fan/).

Leaving behind the illusion of a disinterested social science and anthropology relates in interesting ways to 'the moral economy of anthropology'. Hanne Mogensen, Birgitte Hansen and Morten A. Pedersen theorise the moral economy of anthropology as the perceived divide between 'pure' basic research and applied anthropology (Mogensen et al. 2021). The authors zoom in on a distinction between what they call 'anthropology as an identity' and 'anthropology as a tool' (ibid: 28), where a specific self-disciplining and moral economy cultivated means identifying very strongly with the discipline of anthropology and spending considerable time and energy on maintaining and patrolling boundaries towards other professions inside and outside the academy. (ibid: 24). This, they argue, is informed by the idea of a particular 'mission' and ability of anthropologists to serve as a 'moral corrective' in society (ibid: 11). While agreeing that the questions of *to whom* anthropologists are responsible (interlocutors, 'consumers', institutions, companies, the university or discipline, or the client paying for results) and under what circumstances is ever-relevant, we also agree that this moral economy of anthropologists is quite unreflective and at times even arrogant. Paradoxically this might stand in the way of one of our most important contributions: to provide empirical and theoretical insights, question enframings and thereby point to new openings, knowledges, and approaches and thus solutions beyond the dominant paradigms, towards democratic debate, the environment and equality. This work can be done from the positions of an insider as well as outsider, as Pink and colleagues (2017) have discussed, presenting ways in which theoretical research has been incorporated into the practices of anthropologists outside of academia. In this volume's Chapter 3, Roxana Firth and Nathan Crilly address some of the negative implications of this attitude and warn against falling into the trap of anthropology's 'exceptionalism'. Rather they propose working with the natural sciences according to the model they have conceptualised during fieldwork in 'multi-engineering'. Their approach takes seriously the truth claims of those we work with as being what some anthropologists have called 'epistemic partners' (Holmes & Marcus 2008, Estalella & Criado 2018). This involves an approach to anthropology that devises inquiry and research *with* rather than *about* people, as has long been the practice of visual and sensory ethnography (explained in Pink 2021, Waltorp 2020) and design anthropology (Cizek et al. 2019, Smith 2022, Waltorp 2021, Waltorp & ARTlife Film Collective 2021). We return to this below, as we look at the book's chapters, and the various ways in which the contributors in this book have collaborated and experimented in ways that diverge from the traditional role of the anthropologist, always with the relations and commitments through which people create knowledge and the implied philosophical and ethical debates part and parcel of this, remembering that 'transnational, global and nation state networks and institutions, guide, control and govern how and what kind of knowledge is valued, created, distributed and managed' (Grønsleth & Jospehides 2017: 2).

We believe in the ability and imperative of future-oriented anthropologists to militate for (technological) futures that have both social responsibility and environmental sustainability at the top of the agenda. It is about behaving ethically in the situations we find ourselves in, and asking continually about to whom and under what circumstances we are responsible. In this approach, ethical questions are never settled, but part of ongoing processes and dialectics between uncertainty and possibility (Akama et al. 2018), productively addressed and debated as part of how humans, other species and technologies develop alongside each other, shaped by, and shaping the planetary environment. There is not just one way to be a future-oriented anthropologist, and indeed the ways in which we work are continuously shaped by the very circumstances that frame our projects, the collaborators or stakeholders with whom we become co-invested and the participants in research who guide us and invite us into their future imaginations, visions and experiences.

## Methods for anthropologies of futures and technologies

Both futures and technologies present anthropologists with new opportunities regarding the sites and methods of their research. Futures imply seeking field sites which engage with temporalities and imaginaries, beyond the ethnographic present and into future possibilities. Research that decentres the human, to consider our relationality to technologies and environments, and which might even consider technologies as other 'species' (Pink et al. 2022a,b), shifts the subject matter of our fieldwork and our own positionality within it.

As the contributors to this book reveal, the sites in which possible or imagined futures become evident can be qualitatively different to the sites of both traditional anthropology and contemporary anthropology. On the one hand, much of the research discussed in this book did not involve the researchers going elsewhere but was undertaken close to where they lived and worked and in cultures they were familiar with. Sometimes this meant doing ethnography with engineers and designers – which is demonstrated in relation to the fieldwork discussed in Chapters 1–3 – by Débora Lanzeni and Sarah Pink, Simone Abram and Antti Silvast and Roxana Moroşanu Firth and Nathan Crilly. Lanzeni's relationships with her techie participants spanned years, and she continued to learn, collaboratively, with them over this period, in a process of what Lanzeni and Pink in Chapter 1 call co-visioning, which enabled insights for both Lanzeni and her participants; an ethnographic practice which encompasses the futures narrated by technological systems to the *possibles* that unfold from the smallest shared visions. Simone Abram and Antti Silvast bring us to the practices of energy forecasters, in Chapter 2, whose work we might both understand anthropologically and engage with constructively. Concepts and practices grasped from the field and masterfully theorised as *model* in this chapter becomes a receiver of both imaginaries and temporalities. The authors take us ethnographically into the sites where energy modelling is practised and demonstrate the logics of forecasting and the uncertainties it involves. Simultaneously we connect with the careers and dilemmas of energy modellers, as their trajectories as academics are likewise visible. Roxana Moroşanu Firth and Nathan Crilly introduce the concept of 'multi-engineering' in Chapter 3, whereby different engineering disciplines come together in a flat, rather than hierarchical mode of collaboration, each bringing different expertise, to suggest that anthropologists might also participate in such processes. The practices and experimental imaginaries of scientists become a rich reference point for ethnographies of contemporary – and future – worlds in these chapters. Entrepreneurial startups, corporate innovation labs, even whole areas such as Silicon Valley are often seen as privileged centres of innovation; similarly, science, engineering and design labs are described as privileged spaces for inventing 'the new' (Smith et al. 2016: 3). Each of the Chapters 1–3 shows how collaborative modes of doing anthropology are coming about, and how they can depart from the anthropology *of* others and *of* futures, towards new modes of interdisciplinarity and connections outside academia, including interventional ethnographies.

A Future Anthropologies promote refiguring approaches – methodologies and epistemologies with the world both in responsive ways and as experimentally alongside and in ways that take seriously that researching the world is also world-making. As the very methodological core of anthropology was inaugurated by Bronislaw Malinowski being stuck on the Trobriand Islands during World War 2 and inventing long-term, immersive fieldwork (Malinowski, 1961/1922), and the Manchester school invented the extended case-studies as a response to an accelerated change in Africa South of Sahara (Evans & Handelman 2006, Gluckman 1958), so the current moment of the COVID-19 pandemic has propelled the methodological innovation regarding mediated and digital methods as an addition to the ethnographic toolbox. However, as we see in the history of the discipline, these shifts with the world and with the technologies available to us are more than additions to a toolbox: methodology and epistemology are closely related, and these shifts impact what we are able to know and how we are able to intervene. Indeed, the COVID-19 pandemic created sites and moments of disruptive and rapid change, such as that discussed by Sarah Pink, Harry Ferguson and Laura Kelly in Chapter 4. In some cases, doing ethnography 'at home' and during the COVID-19 pandemic meant doing online ethnography. Online ethnography in itself is not necessarily a facet of doing futures anthropology. However, the reality is that it was during the COVID-19 pandemic that online ethnography became a necessity and simultaneously evolved into a new mode of being with people in lives which they themselves were similarly living with new technologies. Pink and colleagues immersed themselves in the lives of social workers and families experiencing a dramatic and rapid shift in the way they related and worked in the United Kingdom. Their participants began using video and voice calls in a new situation where the anticipatory practices of social workers needed to shift along with new work practices. In parallel the practices of the researchers, for whom in-person fieldwork in homes had in the past been so important also meant that their fieldwork site was online, using the same video and voice calls.

The mundane present also offers us a site from which to contemplate possible futures, and through which to contest predicted futures suggested in dominant narratives. The meanings and values of automated decision-making (ADM) systems, as Minna Ruckenstein and Sonja Trifuljesko discuss in Chapter 5, are constantly negotiated with the changing imaginaries of the benefits and dangers of implementing them. Looking at implications of credit-scoring systems documented for AlgorithmWatch, specifically biases and discriminatory qualities, they argue for an analytical approach that combines 'broken world thinking' with the notion of the 'unsettled sense of care'. They argue that in order to explore ADM futures we need to be 'thinking with care', as they demonstrate in the chapter and commit to concerns that are currently neglected. Ruckenstein and Trifuljesko graph data in a case that composes institutions, software and singular aspects of a human trajectory resulting in unsettling our sociological common sense (Wacquant & Bourdieu 1992) of what an algorithm is for. In between social segmentations challenging algorithmic imaginaries to re-thinking where and when automation meets race and gender in Chapter 5 to smart materialities that encode sterile desires of human well-being in Chapter 7, we have Chapter 6 taking us into the elusive character of work (turned into code). In this chapter, Bastian Jørgensen, Christopher Gad and Brit Ross Winthereik look at implications of implementing AI, in their ethnographic case, into the work undertaken in the Danish Tax and Customs Administration (SKAT). With Lucy Suchman's *work* as a frame, the authors point to how public sector organisations direct attention towards machine-learning algorithms, and risk losing sight of the practical work this technology is imagined to support in the process. Customs officers express that they once 'trained their nose' when building experience of which packages should be selected for inspection, whereas now this sense (nose) is lost as it has been taken over by an algorithm. Bringing the customs officers into the dialogue could be part of the development process, the authors suggest. As the customs officers do not understand how or why the algorithm works – and selects – in the way it does, they do not gain or build experience alongside the technology and cannot work *with* it: the machine-learning algorithm is hyped from managers but creates distance in the formal organisations of work, and it is even the case that 'work' is not represented. Data work is valued over practical, situated work which the algorithm is supposed to support. Chapter 7 by Ajda Pretnar Žagar and Dan Podjed likewise provides an analysis of what happens in the interplay of technology as imagined and when encountered by people in practice. The ethnographic site and case is that of a building at the University of Ljubljana in Slovenia, one of the largest infrastructural investments of recent years. It was designed as an automated building, with approximately 20,000 input and output signals coming from sensors into the monitoring system every second. Žagar and Podjed show how this state-of-the-art building and sensor technology does not guarantee the well-being and satisfaction of its occupants. On the contrary, the 'smartness' of the building has often proven to be a source of discontent and disappointment, especially when it tries to appropriate agency from the people and make independent choices regarding their needs and wants. The authors show how people tend to find innovative solutions for outsmarting the building and 'taking back control' and demonstrate the necessity of highlighting the needs, analyse the expectations and study the habits and practices of people *before* designing smart buildings. In this way, one might truly make sense of the thousands of sensors and the data collected by them.

In Chapter 8, Karen Waltorp and Maja Hojer Bruun shed light on privacy concerns among the Danish population in relation to increased use of drones. They look at interfaces that are not 'in place' but moving around us in an increasingly shared human-machine environment. A collaboration with the Danish Ministry of Transport, Construction and Housing Authority made it clear how drones offer an apt illustration of the changing technological environment, and of institutions and people adapting to, modifying, and legislating *as* it emerges. The environments we inhabit change rapidly as digital technologies and infrastructures become ubiquitous, involving major changes in the ways people consume, produce and re-circulate digital media content. This becomes a backdrop to understanding how the people in this study instantly related the drone with a camera, and with image-circulation on the Internet, what the authors term a 'drone-assemblage'. They show how the drone emerges as a specifically gendered matter of concern in the material, tying into already existing norms of female modesty and the male gaze. This goes to show that the technology always emerges and merges with(in) already existing sociocultural contexts. Waltorp and Bruun suggest that the anthropological empirical approach and collaborative problematisation can serve to make apparent the discrepancies between people developing technology, those making policies and legislation to regulate the emerging world, and differently situated people whose perspective ought to make up part of these processes. In Chapter 9, Sarah Pink, Vaike Fors and colleagues critically engage with another (semi)-autonomous technology – that of the future automated mobilities systems that are often imagined in industry and government narratives, through their ethnographic research undertaken with people living in a diverse neighbourhood in Sweden. This fieldwork, also undertaken online during the COVID-19 pandemic, enabled them to surface the real everyday stories that so often contest the assumptions about human-technology futures that prevail in media, industry and governmental narratives of technological solutionism.

The book's final chapter, Chapter 10 by Elizabeth de Freitas, Maggie MacLure and David Rousell, ties back into Chapter 1 and the importance of 'vision'. Whereas the term 'co-visioning' is offered in Chapter 1 to describe the work that the anthropologist carries out with and alongside her interlocutors, in Chapter 10, it is a co-visioning with sensor technologies that the authors propose. They describe an experiment with young people in Manchester, UK, wearing sensors when visiting the Whitworth Art Gallery's *Thick Time*-exhibition by South African artist William Kentridge. As the authors argue, sensing is now distributed across an increasingly complex array of digital devices, bodies, architectures and built environments, with digital sensors emplaced within buildings, embedded in smartphones, worn on bodies, mounted on rooftops, orbiting in satellites, submerged in soil, flying through air and connected to plant and animal life. Rather than a conventional ethnographic study, they share an experiment where sensors and digital devices are engaged with as *ecological agents*, in the framework of Gilles Deleuze and Felix Guattari, tracking intensive flows, layering affect, ramifying insight and entangling concepts through playful inversion, pursuing what they frame as a 'surreal participation'. They draw on the surrealist impulse or 'minor tradition' within ethnography and visual anthropology interfacing with surrealism and inspired by this open up to thinking differently about what sensor technology can be and how we can be with, kursiv reframing our relation to technology in a small-scale playful experiment.

## Horizons for the anthropology of futures and technologies

What does an anthropology of Futures and Technologies look like? What is it after? And what does it contribute? We began our introduction with these questions and have discussed how we approach futures and technologies, ethics and world-making, and not least the roles that anthropologists can take up in this as we move forward. As the chapters in this volume demonstrate, it is the anthropologist's imperative and opportunity to point to technological futures otherwise, not from a position of arms-length distance, but as involved, engaged, and interventional. As the FAN manifesto suggests, we are striving, failing and striving again, self-critically and reflectively getting our hands dirty.

Orientation affects how we think about what we are aiming for; about how researchers are placed towards technologies and its forms. This book is not about technology as much as it is about how we approach it, how we live with it, how we imbricate it in other sets of values and, above all, how we account for it in our descriptions of the world we study. Throughout the chapters, the authors play out notions of what 'futures' could be in an anthropology that looks closely to actual, current and vibrant technologies. These come out of social, political and material processes in constellation with technologies, and carefully crafted research that allows us to elaborate situated research problems to be addressed ethnographically. To grasp what a situated future experience with emerging technologies would look like, this book expands and brings into life new concepts to address futures and technology (in all its forms). Complicating futures for a better understanding of the phenomena at hand travels across all of the chapters in this volume, making use of now classic conceptual tools to address futures, overcoming techno-binarisms such as technological determinism vs possibilism (Suchman 2011, Lanzeni & Ardevol 2017), the methods developed engage creatively with the urgent matter of thinking social sciences in coalition with other disciplines and stakeholders – usually understood as antagonistic. Doing this, two movements occur, one of them towards ethnographic analysis as the specific domain where we seek to challenge the dominant narratives about the already set technological path to the future for different social worlds; another movement towards a new theoretical opening up of the relationship between temporality and social theory, where the category of the future is no longer stagnant. We take an assertive position on intervention as a figure that not only emerges from ethnography but also from its conceptual anchorage in Anthropology. Thinking critically about technologies and possible, plausible and impossible futures is not enough, anthropology must propose alternative ways to approach and engage with what is new and is coming (Graeber 2001, 2011) in order to remain faithful to its knowledge project. This is what *An Anthropology of Futures and Technologies* want, and steps towards it are demonstrated in this volume.

## Note

1  In Heidegger's example, he uses the 'bringing-forth' of a silver chalice to explain how all of these are part of technology as it assembles 1. Causa materialis (the material); 2. Causa formalis (the form or outline the material takes); 3. Causa finalis (the goal or purpose, what the chalice is to be used for) and 4. Causa efficiens (those who/that which brings it forth – the silver smith in the case of a silver chalice, and his embodied skill set). This is an assemblage of the four causes together making possible the bringing-forth of, in this case, a silver chalice (2008: 313–4).

## References

Akama, Y., Pink, S., & Sumartojo, S. (2018). *Uncertainty and Possibility: New Approaches to Future Making in Design Anthropology*. London: Bloomsbury Publishing.

Bell, G. & Dourish, P. (2007). Yesterday's tomorrows: notes on ubiquitous computing's dominant vision. *Personal and Ubiquitous Computing,* Vol. 11, 133–143.

Benjamin, R. (2019). *Race After Technology: Abolitionist Tools for the New Jim Code*. Hoboken, NJ: John Wiley & Sons.

Bloch, E. (1986) *The Principle of Hope*. Cambridge, MA: MIT Press.

Bruun, M. H., & Wahlberg, A. (2022). The Anthropology of Technology: The Formation of a Field. In Bruun, M. H., Wahlberg, A., Douglas-Jones, R., Hasse, C., Hoeyer, K., Kristensen, D. B., & Winthereik, B. R. (eds.), *The Palgrave Handbook of the Anthropology of Technology* (pp. 1–33). London: Palgrave Macmillan.

Chan, A. S. (2014). *Networking Peripheries: Technological Futures and the Myth of Digital Universalism*. Cambridge, MA: MIT Press.

Cizek, K., Uricchio, W., Anderson, J., Carter, M. A., Detroit Narrative Agency, Harris, T., Maori Holmes, M., Lachman, R., Massiah, L., Mertes, C., Rafsky, S., Stephenson, M., Winger-Bearskin, A., & Wolozin, S. (2019). *Collective Wisdom Co-Creating Media within Communities, across Disciplines and with Algorithms*. Boston, MA: MIT Press.

Crapanzano, V. (2004). *Imaginative Horizons: An Essay in Literary-Philosophical Anthropology*. Chicago, IL: University of Chicago Press.

Drazin, A. (2021). *Design Anthropology in Context: An Introduction to Design Materiality and Collaborative Thinking*. London: Routledge.

Duclos, V., Criado, T. S., & Nguyen, V. K. (2017). Speed: An Introduction. *Cultural Anthropology*, 32(1): 1–11.

Escobar, A. (1995). Anthropology and the Future. New Technologies and the Reinvention of Culture. *Futures*, 27(4): 409–421.

Escobar, A. (2007). Worlds and Knowledges Otherwise. *Cultural Studies*, 21(2–3): 179–210, DOI: 10.1080/09502380601162506

Estalella, A., & Criado, T. S. (eds.) (2018). *Experimental Collaborations: Ethnography through Fieldwork Devices*. London: Berghahn Books.

Evens, T. M. S., & Handelman, D. (eds.) 2006. *The Manchester School: Practice and Ethnographic Praxis in Anthropology*. Oxford and New York: Berghahn.

Fabian, J. (1983). *Time and the Other: How Anthropology Makes Its Object*. New York: Columbia University Press.

Ferguson, J. (1990). *The Anti-Politics Machine: 'Development', Depoliticization and Bureaucratic Power in Lesotho*. Cambridge: Cambridge University Press.

Ferguson, J. (1999). *Expectations of Modernity. Myths and Meaning of Urban Life on the Zambian Copperbelt*. Berkeley, Los Angeles, London: University of California Press.

Fischer, M. J. (2018). *Anthropology in the Meantime*. New York: Duke University Press.

Fischer, M. M. J., & Dumit, J. (2009). *Anthropological Futures*. New York: Duke University Press.

Geismar, H., & Knox, H. (eds.) (2021). *Digital Anthropology*, 2nd edition. London: Routledge.

Gell, A. (1992). *The Anthropology of Time: Cultural Constructions of Temporal Maps and Images*. Oxford, Washington, DC: Berg.

Gluckman (1958 [1940]). Analysis of a Social Situation in Modern Zululand. In *Rhodes – Livingstone Paper Number 28*. Manchester: Manchester University Press. (Rhodes-Livingstone Papers).

Graeber, D. (2001). *Toward an Anthropological Theory of Value: The False Coin of Our Own Dreams*. New York: Palgrave

Graeber, D. (2011). *Revolutions in Reverse*. London: Minor Compositions.

Graeber, D., & Wengrow, D. (2021). *The Dawn of Everything: A New History of Humanity*. London: Penguin UK.

Grønseth, A. S., & Josephides, L. (2017). Introduction. The Ethics of Knowledge Creation Transactions, Relations and Persons. In Josephides, L., & A. S. Grønseth (eds.), *The Ethics of Knowledge Creation*, pp. 1–26. New York: Berghahn Books.

Guyer, J. (2007). Prophecy and the Near Future: Thoughts on Macroeconomic, Evangelical, and Punctuated Time. *American Ethnologist*, 34(3): 409–421.

Halse, J. (2020/2013). Ethnographies of the Possible. In Gunn, W., Otto, T., & Smith, R. C. (eds.), *Design Anthropology: Theory and Practice*, pp.180–196.

Hannerz, U. (2015). Writing Futures. *Current Anthropology*, 56(6), 797–818. doi:10.1086/684070.

Haraway, D. (1988). Situated Knowledges: The Science Question in Feminism and the Privilege of Partial Perspective. *Feminist Studies*, 14(3): 575–599.

Heidegger, M. (2008/1953). The Question Concerning Technology. *Basic Writings*, pp. 307–342. London: Harper Perennial.

Holmes, D. R., & Marcus G. E. (2008). Collaboration Today and the Re-Imagination of the Classic Scene of Fieldwork Encounter. *Collaborative Anthropologies*, 1(1): 81–101.

Lanzeni, D., & Ardèvol, E. (2017). Future in the Ethnographic World. In Salazar, J. F., Pink, S., Irving, A., & Sjöberg, J. (eds.), *Anthropologies and Futures. Researching Emerging and Uncertain Worlds*, pp. 116–31. London: Bloomsbury Academic.

Malinowski, B. (1961/1922). *Argonauts of the Western Pacific*. Long Grove: Waveland Press.

Marcus, G.E. (1995). Ethnography in/of the World System: The Emergence of Multi-Sited Ethnography. *Annual Review of Anthropology*, 24: 95–117.

Mauss, M. (2006) [1941]. *Techniques Technology and Civilisation*. New York: Durkheim Press/Berghahn Books.

McTighe, L., & Raschig, M. (2019). An Otherwise Anthropology. Theorizing the Contemporary, Fieldsights. *Cultural Anthropology*. https://culanth.org/fieldsights/series/an-otherwise-anthropology

Miyazaki (2004). *The Method of Hope: Anthropology, Philosophy, and Fijian Knowledge*. Redwood City, CA: Stanford University Press.

Mogensen, H. O., Gorm Hansen, B., & Pedersen, M. A. (2021). Introduction: An Ethnography and Anthropology of Anthropologists. In H. Mogensen, & B. G. Hansen (Eds.), *The Moral Work of Anthropology: Ethnographic Studies of Anthropologists at Work*, pp. 1–38. Berghahn Books.

Munn, N. (1992). The Cultural Anthropology of Time: A Critical Essay. *Annual Review of Anthropology*, 21: 93–123.

Nielsen, M. (2014). A Wedge of Time: Futures in the Present and Presents Without Futures in Maputo, Mozambique. *Journal of the Royal Anthropological Institute*, 20(S1): 166–182.

Otto, T., & Smith, R. C. (2013). Design Anthropology: A Distinct Style of Knowing. In Gunn, W., Smith, R. C., Otto, T. (eds.), *Design Anthropology. Theory and Practice*, pp. 1–30. London: Bloomsbury.

Pink, S. & Lanzeni, D. (2018). Afterword: Refiguring Collaboration and Experimentation. In Estalella, A., & Sánchez-Criado, T. (eds.), *Experimental Collaborations: Ethnography through Fieldwork Devices*, pp. 201–212. London: Berghahn Books.

Pink, S. (2021). *Doing Visual Ethnography*, 4th edition. London: Sage.

Pink, S. (2022). *Emerging Technologies / Life at the Edge of the Future*. Oxford: Routledge.

Pink, S., & Lanzeni, D. (2018). Future Anthropology Ethics and Datafication: Temporality and Responsibility in Research. *Social Media + Society*, vol. 4, 1–9.

Pink, S., Fors, V., Lanzeni, D., Duque, M., Sumartojo, S., & Strengers, Y. (2022a). *Design Ethnography: Research, Responsibilities and Futures*. Oxford: Routledge.

Pink, S., Ortar, N., Waltorp, K. and Abram, S. (2022b). Imagining Energy Futures: An Introduction. In Abram, S., Waltorp, K. Ortar, N., & Pink, S. (eds.), *Energy Futures: Anthropocene Challenges, Emerging Technologies and Everyday Life* (pp. 1–24). Berlin: De Gruyter.

Rabinow, P. (2007). *Marking Time: On the Anthropology of the Contemporary*. Princeton, NJ: Princeton University Press.

Roitman, J. (2013). *Anti-Crisis*. Durham: Duke University Press.

Sadowski, J. (2020). *Too Smart: How digital capitalism is extracting data, controlling our lives, and taking over the world*. Cambridge, MA: MIT Press.

Salazar, J. F., Pink, S., Irving, A., & Sjöberg, J. (2017). *Anthropologies and Futures. Researching Emerging and Uncertain Worlds*. London: Bloomsbury Academic.

Simone, A., Waltorp, K., Ortar, N., & Pink, S. (2022). *Energy Futures: Anthropocene Challenges, Emerging Technologies and Everyday Life*. Berlin and Boston: De Gruyter.

Smith, R. C. (2022), Design Anthropology (Editorial, Special Issue). *Design Studies – The Interdisciplinary Journal of Design Research*, 80, https://doi.org/10.1016/j.destud.2022.101081

Smith, R. C., & Otto, T. (2016). Cultures of the Future: Emergence and Intervention in Design Anthropology. In Smith, R. C., Vangkilde, K., Kjærsgaard, M. G., Otto, T., Halse, J., & Binder, T. (eds.), *Design Anthropological Futures*, pp. 19–36. London: Routledge.

Smith, R. C., Vangkilde, K. T., Kjærsgaard, M. G., Otto, T., Halse, J., & Binder, T. (eds.) (2016). *Design Anthropological Futures*. London: Bloomsbury.

Sneath, D., Holbraad, M., & Pedersen, M. (2009). Technologies of the Imagination: An Introduction. *Ethnos*, 74: 5–30.

Strenger, Y. (2013). Resource Man. In Strenger, Y (ed.), *Smart Energy Technologies in Everyday Life. Smart Utopia?* (pp. 34–52). London: Palgrave Macmillan.

Suchman, L. (1987). *Plans and Situated Actions – the Problem of Human-Machine Communication*. New York: Cambridge University Press.

Suchman, L. (2011). Anthropological Relocations and the Limits of Design. *Annual Review of Anthropology*, 40(1), 1–18.

Vigh, H. (2009). Wayward Migration: On Imagined Futures and Technological Voids. *Ethnos*, 74(1), 91–109, DOI: 10.1080/00141840902751220.

Wacquant, L. J., & Bourdieu, P. (1992). *An Invitation to Reflexive Sociology*. Cambridge: Polity.

Wahlberg, A. (2022). Assemblage Ethnography: Configurations Across Scales, Sites and Practices. In Bruun, M. H., Wahlberg, A., Douglas-Jones, R., Hasse, C., Hoeyer, K., Kristensen, D. B., Winthereik, B. R. (eds.), *The Palgrave Handbook of the Anthropology of Technology* (pp. 125–144). London: Palgrave Macmillan.

Waltorp, K. (2017). Digital Technologies, Dreams and Disconcertment in Anthropological World-Making. In Salazar, J., Pink, S., Irving, A., & Sjöberg, J. (eds.), *Anthropologies and Futures: Researching Emerging and Uncertain Worlds*, pp. 101–116. London: Bloomsbury.

Waltorp, K. (2018). Fieldwork as Interface: Digital Technologies, Moral Worlds and Zones of Encounter. In Estalella, A., & Sánchez Criado, T. (eds.), *Experimental Collaborations: Ethnography through Fieldwork Devices*, pp. 114–131. London: Berghahn Books.

Waltorp, K. (2020). *Why Muslim Women and Smartphones: Mirror Images*. London and New York: Routledge.

Waltorp, K. (2021). Multimodal Sorting: The Flow of Images Across Social Media and Anthropological Analysis. In Ballestero, A., & Winthereik B. R. (eds.), *Experimenting with Ethnography* (pp. 133–150). Durham: Duke University Press.

Waltorp, K., & ARTlife Film Collective (2021). Isomorphic Articulations: Notes from Collaborative Film-Work in an Afghan-Danish Film Collective. In Martinez, F., Puppo, L. D., & Frederiksen M. D. (eds.), *Peripheral Methodologies: Unlearning, Not-Knowing and Ethnographic Limits* (Anthropological Studies of Creativity and Perception) (pp. 115–130). London and New York: Routledge.

Waltorp, K. & Halse, J. (2013). Introduction. In Dresner, J., Halse, J., Johansson, V., Troelsen, R., & Waltorp, K. (eds.), *Question Waste: Experimental Tactics between Design and Ethnography* (pp. 1–10). Copenhagen: Det Kongelige Danske Kunstakademis Skoler.

Waltorp, K., Dale, R., Fonck, M., & du Plessis, P. (2022). Imagining Energy Futures beyond Colonial Continuation. In Abram, S., Waltorp, K., Ortar, N., & Pink, S. (eds.), *Energy Futures: Anthropocene Challenges, Emerging Technologies and Everyday Life* (pp. 169–214). Berlin: De Gruyter.

Watts, L. (2018). *Energy at the End of the World: An Orkney Islands Saga.* Cambridge: The MIT Press.

# 1

# COMPLICATING FUTURES

*Débora Lanzeni and Sarah Pink*

## Introduction

In recent years, a focus on futures has become increasingly central to the theory and practice of anthropology. It has been engaged to open up discussions about how we do ethnography and the purpose of contemporary anthropology (Salazar et al. 2017, Collins 2021), to propose a new orientation in the anthropology of time (Bryant and Knight 2019), and to advance the ethnographic practice (Pink 2022, Pink et al. 2022). This means that the temporalities of anthropological methods, and the epistemology and ethical commitments of ethnographic practice, are being reshaped through a focus on futures (Pink et al. 2017). This shift to a futures-focused anthropology has begun to have a significant impact within the discipline. This, we argue, needs to also be further connected to the role of anthropology as an interventional and engaged discipline.

In other words, we can no longer justify an anthropology that simply reflects on itself, its theory and its methodology, with the aim of advancing the discipline. Rather we need to apply and consolidate the new futures focus in anthropology as an interventional practice.

There are two dimensions of this shift that require particular attention. First the question of how new anthropological conceptualisations of, and practices of investigating, futures shape research design, fieldwork encounters and the ethnographic alliances we make with participants and stakeholders in our research. Second, we need to ask how these shifts create possibilities for anthropologists to intervene conceptually, and we must consider the implications this has for our capacity to 'complicate' the very futures we investigate. In discussing these questions, we also call for attention to the conceptual foundations of future-focused anthropology and their implications for the interventional role of anthropology and anthropologists in generating what we refer to as 'possibility'. By labelling this practice as one of

DOI: 10.4324/9781003084471-2

generating possibility, we emphasise the ability of anthropology to enliven alternative future visions by creating new pathways through which to imagine and generate plausible and realistic possible futures, instead of predicting supposedly likely futures.

In this chapter, we make this practice of generating possibility visible. To develop our discussion, we draw on insights from ethnographic research involving processes of co-envisioning possible futures with qualified tech workers. We first outline how anthropology has been implicated in the visioning of the future. We then explain the process of visioning in tech design. We next show how, differently, a co-envisioning approach, whereby an interventional anthropologist is implicated, can play out. In doing so, we discuss two ethnographic processes in which an interventional approach was developed, between Débora Lanzeni and techies within the ethnographic encounter. As we argue, within these processes, technology engineering and the possibilities it creates offer continually evolving 'anticipatory infrastructures' (Pink et al. 2022), through which possible futures can become accessible. These anticipatory infrastructures, engaged in relation to interventional ethnographic practices of co-envisioning, we argue, constitute a transformative mode of interventional ethnographic engagement within the processes of technological development.

## Visions of technological future(s)

Technological visions of the future have been explored through diverse social science disciplines and their corresponding theoretical frames, including in geography (Kitchin and Dodge 2011, Anderson 2007, Kinsley 2012, Zook and Graham 2007, Thrift and French 2002), sociology (Mau and Bell, 1971), anthropology (Suchman et al. 2008, 2012; Gell 1992, Strathern 2006, Wallman 1992, Heilbrorner 1967, Nielsen 2011, Maurer y Schwab 2006), human-computer-interaction studies (Dourish and Bell 2011, Mackenzie 2012, Star and Bowker 2006) and in science and technology studies (STS) (Novotny et al. 2001, Williams 1990, Wajcman 2008). Between these fields of research, a dynamic empirical landscape emerges, where STS scholars have emphasised the relations between socio-technical future visions and the production of technology and scientific knowledge, whereby particular possible future scenarios are promoted above others, through alignments between the sites where technologies and markets are produced and constituted, within science-and-technology dominated value systems. These critical perspectives are valuable in terms of offering interpretations of how dominant narratives are interconnected with science, technology, innovation systems and flows of power, capital and knowledge. What they show is a system in gridlock, where the existing status quo is maintained by a never-ending techno-solutionist (Morozov 2013) vision of futures, whereby new technological innovation is always needed to solve the problems of an always imperfect process. Yet, as we argue in this chapter, there are other possibilities and potentials for change, other future visions and other ways of moving forward. We next examine two of these. First, the importance of a theory of ethnographic attention to the everyday as a site for future technology visioning. Second, the need to go beyond critique, to actively participate in ethical, responsible and inclusive future visioning, in the form of an interventional anthropology of emerging technologies.

Research on the ground, in real everyday worlds, as opposed to the study of the representational world of discourse, reveals other stories. For example, studies in geography and anthropology have viewed this situation through ethnographic research, which has attended to how future visions are generated in the everyday life sites of design, creativity and production of digital technologies. As the geographer Kinsley points out, future concerns are articulated in many ways and we must be careful not to miss the subtleties through which futures are spoken of (Kinsley 2012: 1562). There is a long history of anthropological studies of technology design, historically by anthropologists such as Suchamn (2008), and more recently including the work of Seaver (2017), Canay Ozden Schilling (2015), and ourselves (Pink et al. 2018, Lanzeni and Pink 2021, Lanzeni 2016). As this work demonstrates, we need to frame 'future visions' more broadly, beyond the processes of technology design and creation, capital and power relations, to instead interrogate the human activity through which other future visions come about.

To explore how future visions are articulated in human activity, we draw on the notion of anticipatory practices (Anderson 2007), which suggests a focus on what people do in the present as they move towards possible futures. In the context of technology development, anticipatory practices are oriented to a future which can be 'caught up with'. That is, it involves practitioners taking specific actions which review and demonstrate the viability and possibility of imagined futures associated with what Dourish and Bell (2011) have referred to as the 'proximate future'. The proximate future is a close temporality, which is reachable through anticipatory practices. For instance, Nielsen (2011) has drawn on an analysis of anticipatory practices in house building in Maputo, Mozambique, to propose the concept of 'durational time', meaning circumstances where different temporalities converge, rather than happening linearly (2011: 399). Drawing on the work of Strathern, Nielson proposes a vision of anticipatory action, whereby 'possible worlds' (or futures) are taken seriously, in the sense that while they are not visibly present, they nevertheless inform people's everyday actions (2011: 398).

Thus, such future visions become the spatio-temporal bridge that connects people's actions and beliefs in the present with possible futures which are known sensorially, but for which their coming about and knowing them might not follow a linear trajectory. Such anticipatory actions and the ways of knowing that are inseparable from them are therefore differently constituted, experienced and manifested to the anticipatory knowledge which pertains to a measurable and visible version of the future. In this latter mode of anticipation, the future is made apprehendable in the present, through a process of generating documentable knowledge (Anderson 2007; Kinsley 2012; Adam y Groves 2007). Anticipatory practices as we attend to them here are therefore concerned with ways of knowing in possibility, rather than through measurable certainties. For us this means engaging ethnographically.

Indeed, recent anthropological characterisations imply the liveliness of the imagination and invoke its power to actively bring things to the world we live in. Over the last decade, such ideas have progressively inhabited the work of scholars across a range of fields of anthropology: in design anthropology in the form of 'ethnographies of the possible' whereby possible futures might be invoked, materialised and performed in mundane everyday situations (Halse 2013); in feminist anthropology through the notion of the imagination as field of action (Benjamin 2019); and for anthropologists interested in the concept of technologies of the imagination, where the imagination is situated as an ongoingly emergent, indeterminate and relational element of everyday worlds and practices (Sneath et al. 2009). This work has invited anthropologists to question the temporality of the discipline and to conceptualise futures through a focus on the imagination, usually developed through a dialogue between ethnography and theory.

Scholars working in the field of STS have dedicated significant effort to surface and show the relevance of what have been called socio-technical imaginaries (Jasanoff and Kim 2013). Recently, critical sociologists and STS scholars have become interested in understanding shared social or societal socio-technical imaginaries (Taylor 2002) produced and crystallised in and by institutions (Castoriadis 1997). This approach has resonated with other scholars who are critical not only of the socio-technical visions of the future that narratives taken up by government, industry and institutions, but also of how these frame and allocate value to the production of scientific knowledge (Novotny et al. 2001, Williams 1990, Wajcman 2008). Such narratives and the socio-technical imaginaries and visions attached to them are regarded as performative, culturally produced and promoting certain possible future scenarios. They are problematised both in terms of the correlation they have with the creation of artefacts and the constitution of markets and for the ways in which they and the power relationships in which they are enmeshed involve shaping the value systems that inform much of the business, governance and funding of technology, engineering, development and design. This body of work describes a context in which it is all the more necessary for us to intervene. Indeed, often such critical theoretical scholars call for change.

Yet what is striking about these approaches to and accounts of social and socio-technical imaginaries is that their chief objective appears to be to analyse, expose and critique the limitations of imaginaries that are constituted through capitalist neoliberal societies, governments and institutions. While of course we do not dispute that this is a good thing, it leaves two gaps, meaning that we need: further attention to imagination as a facet of the everyday (as opposed to being an institutional or political vision); and an interventional agenda and practice (which acknowledges but goes beyond critical impulse of theoretical approaches to socio-technical imaginaries in sociology and STS, as indicated by the Futures Anthropologies Manifesto [in Salazar et al. 2017]). Filling these gaps, for us, involves creating an interventional and engaged extension of the growing interest in the imagination as an emergent and contingent facet of everyday worlds. This might be thought of as an externally engaged approach to the anthropology of the imagination and imagnaries, which rather than simply focusing its interest in how possible futures are imagined and envisioned, in relation to anthropological debate and critique, instead employs a methodology of intervention, situated in the fieldwork encounter and played out as a relational practice. Here the anthropologist is always and inevitably implicated in the shaping of possibility with participants in research, through the ongoingly emergent state of affairs that characterise immersive anthropological ethnography.

Our proposal raises new questions not only about the practical orientation of anthropology but the question of how to practice responsible and ethical anthropology. In the technology industry, accountability often falls on the side of the engineers – the techies – alleviating the other actors that enable and make the technological design processes malleable to such responsibility. This is reinforced by the tendency for techies to be characterised, and often described or caricatured ironically or humorously, while entrepreneurs or business people tend to be described, or treated as the incarnation of contemporary neoliberalism, or the new capitalist technology ethos. In contrast, while it has been argued that anthropologists have an important role to play in the world, as interventional scholars and researchers (e.g. Podjed et al. 2020), it is less often argued that academic anthropologists who work with techies should themselves shoulder some accountability. An exception is when anthropologists are actually employed in leading roles in the technology industry. For instance, anthropologists like Genevieve Bell, who is well known for her work at Intel Corporation, and Melissa Cefkin, currently at Waymo, and previously at companies including Nisssan and Xerox, have been involved in working closely and influentially in technology development within large and powerful research, design and innovation organisations. However, when not situated as such, with an institutional brief to actually intervene, the interventional academic anthropologist who is engaged in smaller-scale tech projects is less visible.

The different strands of disciplinary, theoretical and empirical research discussed above have produced some excellent work, which has highlighted and situated the dominant socio-technical imaginaries or techno-solutionist narratives which frame emerging technologies societally and has shown how they can be studied ethnographically in the sites of technology design and development. In this chapter, we want to push these practices of research further, towards a more interventional agenda. This means departing from the conventional structures and practices of anthropology as a bounded critical discipline, to shift anthropology towards as an open interventional and co-creative practice. We need a new anthropology which can engage with, take responsibility for and co-create visions of possible futures (see also Pink 2022). In the next section, we explain ethnographically how such practices emerge within fieldwork.

## Ethnographic co-envisioning

The ethnographic examples we discuss in this chapter are based on Débora Lanzeni's long-term immersion in the world of techies in Barcelona, London and Melbourne, for approximately a decade, since 2012. Research participants include software designers, mechanical engineers, firmware and hardware engineers, procurement and operation engineers and quality assurance experts, all working at different stages of the design process of Internet of Things (IoT) projects. We examine examples of ethnographic and participant/stakeholder practices and narratives of 'focusing on the future' or 'sketching the future' of the labour market for technology workers. We focus specifically on the emergence of an imaginary concerning the dramatic changes that artificial intelligence (AI) (in particular machine learning) could bring, as emerging technologies evolve and AI-assisted tools and services expand into new domains. Adapting and absorbing the evolution of the technology and the tools themselves is already a challenge that requires the full attention of engineers in this field; AI implies greater velocity, both in the evolution of their tools and in terms of arriving at the distant future in the technology itself. They need to adapt to these new AI-assisted tools in the present as well as potentially to their application in future products and services in new domains to which they are not used to connecting.

This imaginary was generated in a context where currently, most of the technological development in AI and IoT happens in the internal technology market, meaning where the clients of technology engineers are not end users themselves but companies who make end-user products. This means provider companies are leading the field by creating the technology and end-user services are following by applying it. For tech workers who work in this situation, a shift to new circumstances, where machine learning would be applied to new domains such as smart infrastructure, was daunting, as one participant put it: 'AI is not easy when your clients are other than engineers'.

Ethnographic co-envisioning involves being and collaborating with people in shared practices of visioning or creating imaginaries of possible futures. The significance of ethnographic co-envisioning lies not solely in the insights we can draw from in the form of research findings, but in its relevance as a practice of engagement through which technology developers and designers allow the ethnographer to think and engage with them in various ways. This includes: accompanying them as they unfold their visions in the everyday life of technology design; as well as collaborating with them to analyse the bigger questions and narratives (or the dominant societal visions noted above) that characterise the technological promise or predictions that underpin the premises, investment and funding for much technology design and development.

It is tempting, when approaching the world of tech design, to consider it as a whole, as if it was an entire thing, a 'world' or culture of its own, and particularly as a world separate from, and with different values to, anthropology. The dominance of concepts such as the 'sociotechnical', as something we need to either critically unravel through research (Latour 1999) or that we are obliged to re-constitute with anthropological principles, has set an agenda for anthropological studies of technology, that have exacerbated this image of the separateness of the world of technology design and engineering from anthropology. In this approach, the tech world is thus figured as an object of anthropological study, rather than as a site for collaboration. Ethnographic co-envisioning, we argue, offers an alternative and new way forward, because it seeks to dissolve this division and the ways in which it hinders an engaged anthropology.

Co-envisioning implies a type of collaboration that moves research beyond the conventions of academic practice. Collaboration in anthropology has been broadly understood as happening mainly in the ethnographic and dissemination processes, including writing and media outlets, and with the 'others' (Rappaport 2016) that take part in the research. It has enduringly been grounded in the ethics and poetics of grounding our ways of knowing informants'/consultants' participation in the co-creation of what will ultimately become anthropological knowledge and will respect and be committed to making participants visible.

Co-envisioning departs from these conventional modes of collaboration. It constitutes a shared body of knowledge established through ethnographic fieldwork, and which might follow different trajectories: it may become part of anthropological research knowledge and publications, while it is also the basis of an exploration of the socially transformative possibilities of the technical project at hand, and thus part of the very technology process that 'traditionally' the anthropologist would have simply been studying.

Ethnographic co-envisioning is not the only methodology which has centred collaborative thinking and making with participants in technology research. For instance, Sanchez Criado developed a fieldwork practice of making wheel chairs with disabled people (2020) and Knox (2020) developed an anthropological workshop practice involving making speculative energy devices with people, and Akama et al.'s (2017) workshop created a series of speculative technologies. However ethnographic co-envisioning takes a different tack, in that rather than having as its objective the making of a particular practical or speculative thing or product, it does not have specific outcomes. Instead, co-envisioning is a processual practice, which is dialogic, and open ended. It does not have an end where it is analysed and closed down but rather is as dynamic as life itself, in the ways it weaves through ethnographic encounters and through the years. It is a mode of practising interventional anthropological ethnography, rather than a method designed to produce a specific or predetermined output. In the next sections, we develop two ethnographic examples through which to demonstrate how co-envisioning plays out in practice.

### Catalysing co-envisioning

In the middle of the second decade of the twenty-first century, the idea that AI and IoT would live alongside us, rather than being separated from everyday life in a kind of technological bubble, was just a promise. At the time, workers in the field of emerging technologies believed that AI had the potential to change and enhance the way infrastructures and systems work. Today, that potential remains, while simultaneously the aspirations of technology designers to make AI a disruptive technology are receding. In this example, we show how these shifts can be understood through the prism of ethnographic co-envisioning over a period of five years.

Débora's ethnographic co-envisioning fieldwork was undertaken in two different settings, with the same participants, but five years apart. We argue that future visions that implicate AI fuel both the design of technologies and the ways that technological imaginaries become associated with markets. In what follows, we demonstrate how engaging ethnographically with visions when they are vibrantly being shaped – that is the method of co-envisioning – can enable anthropologists to actively take part in how technologies are oriented towards futures.

Franck works in a company that makes sensors and platforms for the industrial and urban sectors. He leads a team of engineers dedicated to developing firmware architectures. When we met for the first time at his office (the engineering department occupies almost the entire level twelve of a three level company), with long, dark hair, he looked young and serious to Débora.

A more recent scene from our long-term collaboration happened in 2021, in the context of a fortnight meet up to discuss a science fiction film along with a podcast about philosophical theories related to that film. Débora's participation in these events was by invitation. Some of the techies, who had been involved in her ethnographic fieldwork in the past, organised the meeting and invited Débora to participate. Some of the topics discussed ranged from issues relating to human free will, to the question of the right of technologies to live. One of the movies, *Contact* (1997) kicked off a discussion about the connivance of science and beliefs in scientific practice. The conversation, which had pivoted around a critique of dogmatic thinking, then moved on to discuss some of the participants' feelings about the dogmatism entailed in the filmmakers' attempts to use gender-fluid inclusive language in the film. This was particularly relevant since the participants were Catalan and Spanish speakers, and these languages are explicitly gendered, making any shifts towards gender-fluid language unambiguous in their intention, but complicated to apply practically. Frank, the organiser of the meeting, had strong opinions around this issue. To be clear, Frank supported the principle that language should be inclusive or gender fluid, but rather his approach was practical. Throughout the meeting, he kept coming back to the point that the 'problems' that the application of inclusive language entailed made the attempt to apply it nonsensical because it had no 'practical solution'. This meant that from his perspective, it was impossible to apply any formulation of gender-fluid language in Spanish or Catalan to everyday life situations, since all attempts to achieve this were complex and incoherent in relation to conventional logics. Thus, following his perspective, any attempt at inclusive language would be doomed, in that it would *not work perfectly* and was therefore *not worth trying*. In the heat of the discussion, Franck escalated more and more in the defence of his argument: it is not possible to totally correct the language, therefore it is not an effective practice and it should stop. Some of the participants felt that his argument seemed 'carved in stone', so they did not engage in the discussions; others, among whom was Débora, posed the counterargument that it was not necessary for the inclusive language to work perfectly, and that attempting to apply it was worth it. Paul, an ex-co-worker and friend of Franck, played the role of mediator during most of the discussion. However, in what he saw as a direct attack on Franck, a group of the other participants accused Franck of being too much of an 'engineer' in his analysis of this topic. Suddenly Paul tried to defend Franck: 'I believe what he is trying to say is there are *no solutions*, and we are not prepared to operate in life without *solutions*, right Débora?' said waiting for a comment. The comment came from another participant, Julius, a hardware engineer, and another of Franck's co-workers, reinforcing Franck's logic to assert: 'what's the point of technology if it doesn't solve anything?'. Indeed five years earlier some of the participants in this discussion had been together at a Smart City Congress, where they had participated in a public debate around the question of what the point of smart technology was. Then, after listening to a talk on future water systems presented by the chief of innovation (CIO) of a digital infrastructure company, while walking among the conference stands in search of a food truck, Frank suggested that the talk was 'bubble tech'. Meaning that the CIO had delivered a presentation that was not accurate and was about something that it would be impossible to do.

Back then Smart Technologies were at the edge of the brownfield. Brownfield refers to the implementation of new systems to resolve IT problem areas while accounting for established systems (see technopedia). At the time governments and companies desperately wanted the integration of every new piece of tech into a technological mash, let us say the city (Balestrini et al. 2017). But some techies resisted relinquishing the possibility of future technological perfection for the sake of supplying and integrating already existing but undeveloped pieces of tech (Pink et al. 2018). In contrast, others believed that the purpose of tech is to do the task even when it doesn't work perfectly. Thus presenting a debate around the 'orientation to solve problems' (Lanzeni 2016) as a technological imperative. At that moment the importance of this rested on what Joana, a software engineer working on a smart city agenda in Portos City council in Portugal, told Debora: 'to innovate we (the techies) need to have a problem to solve… everything else will follow'. Indeed all the engineers who participated in the discussion at the conference agreed that solving a problem is indispensable, mandatory and rooted in the very core of technological making.

Débora asked Paul and two other engineers who were walking with them: 'What would happen if there was no problem to solve? If clients asked you to do things that are not based on anything that already exists?' This question catalysed a process of discussion between Débora and the techies that endured over the five years, up to the ethnographic example with which we opened this section. Ethnographically, it invoked the question of 'how people deal with the A-logical parts of everyday life' (Wright and Ceriani Cernadas 2007), and in techie terms, it asked 'how to clean up the bullshit'. For most of the engineers in the IoT industry most of what surrounded the tech making (business models, investors rounds and product management) is populated by, what they call, 'needed bullshit'. Narratives about the potentialities of the tech at hand or a company to produce impact in the scene are always built upon what could fit into a possible emerging market. An image of a market coming from plans and discursive imaginaries made by financial and governmental sectors.

Techies believe these narratives do not represent what is *possible* for technology or the current state of a company. There is no alignment between how the tech designers envision a 'technological success' and how those discursive imaginaries draw the possibilities for them in a new market. This gap makes the techies quite sceptical of the technological market and places it very far away from where they are: the design process. It is in these terrains where engineers, product owners, evangelists, the CEO and the ethnographer move and where the different visions of tech futures are crucial.

The conversations about what a market should be is what allowed participants to envision a common path for all the elements of it they were interested in. This entailed going beyond simply including others' points of view, to rather incorporate an understanding of the permeability of the visions of the future and how malleable they are.

As articulated in the ethnographic scene described at the beginning of this section, this example reveals how the practice of co-envisioning is not about a specific topic or technology at hand. Rather it is woven through lines that connect technological approaches as well as being embedded in understanding the common logic that techies operate with while navigating their professional, personal and social life. Co-envisioning is not unidimensional and tailored to a specific question. However, co-envisioning does aim to articulate possibilities rooted in the design process; possibilities for emerging markets and social relations, possibilities of intervention for those at the core of the technology, in realms that software and hardware engineers usually exclude themselves because they imagine them to be distant and written in a code foreign to theirs.

In this example, co-envisioning implies attuning many visions in a new imaginary that is inclusive and reachable. In this case, co-envisioning in the ethnographic encounter brings greater flexibility to imaginaries that dominant narratives and logics of innovation would fix as points on a distant horizon that only certain actors can reach (see Forsythe 2001, Lindtner 2015).

We next present a second ethnographic example of co-envisioning, to demonstrate how the practice emerged within and as part of the fieldwork encounter over five years.

## 5 stars

'IoT Stars' is a European contest that happens before the *IoT solutions world congress* (along with *The Things Conference* it is the most prominent gathering of IoT). In this contest, new start-ups and initiatives present what they are developing and what must happen for them to succeed. In this edition, 2019, the atmosphere was flooded with a triumphant halo, the event had received twice the budget of previous years and the hosts had agreed on a brewery as the venue. Many big names were attending; the organisers knew about some of them being there to invest in new promising start-ups. Along with the big tech companies were also high-profile emergent small companies that still run as start-ups for market purposes but they have strong investing capitals. Almost all of them have an employee as a member of the jury. The contest consists of three rounds of 10-minute showcases for each 'product', which is evaluated by an industry expert jury. Between the rounds, the attendees relax, having a drink and talking for at least 15 minutes. The punctuation system is based on five stars. One being the poorest qualification and five being the maximum possible. Originally, the stars were equivalent to numbers but with time, tacitly, the system became a more sophisticated way to qualify according to the evolution of the IoT market. As an example of this, certain aspects such as *feasibility* and *quality* intrinsically bond with the engineering ethos (Forsythe 2001, Özden-Schilling 2015) slowly banished from speech and the punctuation system.

While other notions like *fit into* and *reliability* found a place in speeches. This shift in the discourse, for the engineers working in IoT companies and regulars of the IoT Stars, does not happen unnoticed.

> First star means the *effort is there*; the second star means the project has some highlights that are valuable to keep trying; the third star adds to the previous two in that your work is demonstrating some success; the fourth star is given to those that already have a clear outcome; the last one is reserved for the projects that could *attract money* in the emergent markets.

'This is not about tech anymore, this is to be pleasant with the CEOs' explained Jordan to Débora after being on the jury for the first round. IoT used to be a label that catalysed all the technological possibilities around connecting things (stuff and hardware) to the Internet but lately it had come to represent an emerging market that has the business model as its main focus. One of the participants in this 'IoT Stars' edition was Laura, the CEO of an established start-up dedicated to designing and producing sensors for the maker and Do-it-Yourself market.

'All this week preparing the presentation was such work in vain' said Laura when she came back to the bottom of the room where Débora and her partners were sitting, after she gave the presentation. Next to her was Daniel, one of the hosts of the night's event, he asked her what had gone wrong, sounding alarmed. There was no obvious reason, as Daniel would later comment to Débora, for Laura to be 'pissed off'. Laura, an engineer and CEO with an extensive career in IoT had just presented, in her words, a 'product outline' with an investment of 5 million euros that had been scored five stars. For her, having gotten the maximum grading was evidence of something Débora had heard before, the 'profanity of the engineering quality stone value' which was happening in the IoT market. The people who do the hands-on technology design and production were finding themselves in a situation where the promises about what an IoT device can do are made by the business units. Laura, like many other engineers, rejected this blending of business and the craft of working with technology.

For David (and the other hosts) the paradox of Laura's anger is that she is the one who runs the business in her company: the one who contacts investors, goes to business meetings and talks with governments. However, for her, it is offensive that the effort and craftsmanship that making a technology represents are evaluated only with short-term market values.

The co-envisioning here happened after this event in the following way: aware that the ethnographer had been capable of receiving Laura's words, capable of understanding her and at the same time understanding the bewilderment of the hosts. They invited her to think and redesign the scoring system so that it strikes a balance between the expectations of the start-ups when they participate in it and the business that the 'IoT Stars' event is itself – a funded tool to bring up an intangible market located in an uncertain future.

In this ethnographic story, the invitation *to contribute* – something that happens in many anthropological fieldworks (Faubion and Marcus 2009, Marcus 1997) – instead of leading an actual contribution to the matter under discussion allowed the ethnographer to create a conceptual bridge which could to make meanings from shared and unshared imaginaries together with the participants.

Co-envisioning always implies an invitation to take part in something that is happening and which *matters*. But it does not necessarily matter on the same terms, levels of importance or impact that it would have in an ethnographic analysis. In this example, what mattered for participants was clear and this led to co-envisioning which was shaped as a more concrete intervention in what might seem like a mundane activity: it involved redesigning a scoring system that was perceived by start-up techies as under-representing them and the tech design processes.

## Co-envisioning as anthropological practice

As a collaborative ethnographic practice, co-envisioning involves bringing together different modes of know-how – and in the cases described above, it combined that of engineering and that of anthropology. As we have outlined, co-envisioning is a deliberate but not determinate practice. That is, to undertake it, the ethnographer needs to be open to its occurrence, or even perhaps see its occurrence as inevitable, or at least always possible, while not planning it. It is likewise a collaborative act, but not a structured mode of collaboration, making it what has been coined as an invisible side of ethnographic collaboration. It falls into the category of those ethnographic practices 'which are invisible to us as outside readers, except in those instances in which they are cast as "ethnographic facts"' (Rappaport 2016-17: 9), and subsequently abstracted into anthropological knowledge.

Yet, these local forms of sharing entail circumstances where the findings of research come into play as part of encounters which could never have happened had ethnographic past encounters and anthropological knowledge not been part of the situation. As for instance, in the discussion of the film described above, Débora and the participants were not simply in a lineally determined bubble, but rather in a sequence of events that spanned five years, and which 'gathered' and drew together different moments of encounter around similar questions and logics. Here, collaboration came about as Débora's research knowledge was invoked and called on by Paul, as a way to continue to moderate a discussion, as well as to work *with* the participants in understanding a problem space. As such research was harnessed to the work of culture-making, itself a type of contemporary politics. Such encounters cannot be predetermined as 'research', and often they are hard to identify, or become 'invisible' because they are so interactive and embedded, so distinct from a published book or article, that they appear as what is 'already there' (Rappaport 2016-17: 9).

While co-envisioning is an almost invisible and unpredictable practice, there are ways to make it visible, detectable, and to ensure that an ethnographic process is open to it. This involves creating, or at the least becoming aware of, the infrastructures that make this, otherwise difficult to view and plan for, activity possible. We define infrastructures anthropologically, following Larkin (2013), as things that make other things possible, and as constituting the relations between things and processes. In the case of ethnographic co-visioning, they are also the foundations that are apparent, while co-visioning itself appears as something that happens along the course of what was happening anyway.

Conventionally anthropologists would make visible the narratives that inform the ways engineers think and practice. For example, Canay Özden-Schilling (2015) demonstrates how narratives of supply and demand dominate the ways that energy engineers imagine markets and futures. Likewise above, we have shown how a problem-solution paradigm dominated the ways that the software engineers with whom Débora collaborates understand not only their professional roles, but also what kinds of futures are possible more broadly. However, co-envisioning goes beyond this analytical and descriptive mode of doing anthropology, that is it exceeds the convention of moving from the ethnographic encounter, to description, to abstraction. Instead, co-envisioning maintains the analytical thread and story in dialogue with and *in* the ethnographic encounter, as an ongoing state of affairs. It introduces alternative possible futures into dialogues with participants and keeps them there, present in their worlds. Thus creating a reflexive mode of knowing within the fieldwork context, whereby there are moments when visions are surfaced and at specific times made visible to all. We can crystallise a moment in fieldwork for analysis and define narratives, visions and practices that are at play, and indeed we must do this to participate in anthropological debate. However, when we acknowledge that the understandings that are represented in such work are the outcomes of co-visioning, a reflexive engagement with the practice enables us to emphasise that the narratives we surface are not fixed or readily on the surface of the worlds we write about, but rather they are buoyant, living in co-visioning fieldwork in a realm of possibilities.

So what kinds of things are infrastructures for co-envisioning, or put differently what modes of participation and collaboration make us open to co-envisioning occurring? In this chapter, we have discussed two related events which happened at opposite ends of five years of fieldwork. The first was sparked by an IoT event, where participants began to question two things – first how realistic other speakers' visions were and the ways that business perspectives underpinned the evaluation of technology development. In this case, these events created the infrastructure that opened the possibilities for response that is there were circumstances in which the participants' visions momentarily surfaced and became visible. It was in this moment that Débora could not only document them for future analysis, but rather the circumstances also meant that she could begin to dialogue with them, making them visible not just to herself and other readers of her work but to participants. Once visions have surfaced as such, for the ethnographer, they are always present, even if not immediately visible, and they can inform our understanding of many other elements of the ethnographic encounter. But there will also be other moments where they manifest. Our second example, five years later, is an ideal case, where a different event created the infrastructure that made this possible, by creating the opening for the discussion, in the form of a film screening and discussion. By this time, we see not only how participants surfaced their visions, but also that they surfaced Débora's own visions back to her, thus showing how such co-envisioning enables the invisible presence of not only the visions of those 'studied' to participate under the surface of life and fieldwork, but also that the visions of the anthropologist can equally become part of their world.

It is in this last sense that we argue that co-envisioning is an interventional practice. Because, as we have argued above, its characteristics include being both invisible and processual, it is not interventional in the sense of involving a determined 'intervention', which is planned beforehand, intended to have certain outcomes and subsequently reported on. Instead it is emergent from the circumstances of fieldwork, it happens because we make ourselves open to it. It has no certain outcomes, but rather its effects are contingent and may be neither immediately obvious nor play out in a defined temporality. Finally, it does not necessarily produce tangible visible outcomes or changes that can be looked for, but rather its outcomes become evident over time, when clues as to how anthropological visions have intervened.

## Conclusion

Existing academic work, as we have shown, has begun to form a coherent story of how futures are imagined and anticipated in relation to technology engineering, development and design. However, the picture of future imaginaries and anticipatory modes painted in existing scholarship tends to reflect its traditional ambitions to produce critical arguments and participate in disciplinary debate, rather than in developing an interventional practice. By this, we mean that even though such scholarship seeks to portray futures and ways of looking forward that pertain to technology development, engineering and design, it treats futures *as an object of study* which can only be encountered academically *through the analysis of the techie or other institutional actors*. In contrast, the approach we advocate and have demonstrated in Débora's fieldwork practice in this chapter is one where the techie and their imagination is not the object of study, but rather techies are active participants with the anthropologist, in the co-envisioning of possibility. This means that what can be 'seen' ethnographically and analytically is different because it *brings possibilities into view.*

If ethnography is more than a process that is oriented towards the production of tangible or measurable outcomes (publications, conference talks and such like) then it necessarily entails forms of knowledge production that cannot be encapsulated within a finished ethnographic product. Such forms of knowledge, rather, emerge and evolve within fieldwork and can be thought of as co-emergent with, and never completely separable from, the circumstances and participants with whom they came about. They are, however, vital as interventions through which the ways futures are imagined, and courses that futures take may shift; precisely because co-envisioning creates modes of relationality between ways of knowing and makes them part of the sites of our ethnographic encounters.

## References

Adam, B. & Groves, C. (2007). *Future matters: Action, knowledge, ethics.* Leiden and Boston: Brill.

Anderson, B. (2007). "Hope for nanotechnology: anticipatory knowledge and the governance of affect". *Area 39*(2), 156–165.

Akama, Y., Moline, K., & Pink, S. (2017). Disruptive interventions with mobile media through Design+ Ethnography+ Futures. In *The Routledge companion to digital ethnography* (pp. 484–495). London: Routledge.

Balestrini, M., Rogers, Y., Hassan, C., Creus, J., King, M., & Marshall, P. (2017, May). A city in common: a framework to orchestrate large-scale citizen engagement around urban issues. In Proceedings of the 2017 CHI Conference on Human Factors in Computing Systems (pp. 2282–2294).

Bell, W. & Mau, J. (eds.). (1971). *The sociology of the future. Theory, cases, and annotated bibliography.* New York: Russell Sage Foundation.

Benjamin, R. (2019). "Assessing risk, automating racism". *Science, 366*(6464), 421–422.

Bryant, R., & Knight, D. M. (2019). *The anthropology of the future.* Cambridge University Press.

Brown, N. & Michael, M. (2003). "A Sociology of expectations: Restrospecting prospects and prospecting retrospect". *Technology Analysis and Strategic Management, 15*(1), 3–18.

Castoriadis, C. (1997). *The imaginary institution of society.* Cambridge, MA: MIT Press.

Collins, S. G. (2021). *All tomorrow's cultures.* New York: Berghahn.

Criado, T. S. (2020). "Anthropology as a careful design practice?". *Zeitschrift für Ethnologie, 145*(1), 47–70.

Dourish, P. & Bell, G. (2011). *Divining a digital future: Mess and mythology in ubiquitous computing.* Cambridge, MA: MIT Press.

Faubion, J. D. & Marcus, G. E. (2009). Fieldwork is not what it used to be. Learning Anthropology's Method in a Time of Transition. Cornell University Press. Ithaca and London. Tecnopedia acceded on 15th of March of 2022: www.techopedia.com/definition/24409/brownfield

Fergnani, A. (2019). Corporate foresight: A new frontier for strategy and management Academy of Management perspectives, 2020-02-19.

Forsythe, D. (2001). *Studying those who study us: An anthropologist in the world of artificial intelligence.* Stanford, CA: Stanford University Press.

Gell A (1992). *The anthropology of time: Cultural constructions of temporal maps and images.* Oxford: Berg.

Halse, J. (2013). Ethnographies of the Possible. In *Design anthropology* (pp. 180–196). London: Routledge.

Heilbroner, R. L. (1967). "Do machines make history?". *Technology and Culture, 8*(3), 335–345.

Jasanoff, S. & Kim, S. H. (2013). Sociotechnical imaginaries and national energy policies. *Science as Culture, 22*(2), 189–196.

Kinsley, S. (2012). "Futures in the making: Practices for anticipating ubiquitous computing". *Environment and Planning A, 44*(7), 1554–1569.

Kitchin, R. & Dodge, M. (2011). *Code/Space, software and everyday life.* Cambridge: The MIT Press.

Knox, H. (2020). Digital Devices. 102–114. In Carroll, T., Walford, A., & Walton, S. (eds.). (2021). *Lineages and advancements in material culture studies: Perspectives from UCL anthropology.* London: Taylor & Francis.

Lanzeni, D. (2016). Smart global futures: Designing affordable materialities for a better life. In *Digital materialities* (pp. 45–60). London: Routledge.

Lanzeni, D. & Pink, S. (2021). Digital material value: Designing emerging technologies. *New Media & Society, 23*(4), 766–779.

Latour, B. (1999). *Pandora's hope: essays on the reality of science studies.* Harvard University Press.

Larkin, B. (2013). The politics and poetics of infrastructure. *Annual Review of Anthropology, 42*(1), 327–343.

Lindtner, S. (2015). Hacking with Chinese characteristics: The promises of the maker movement against China's manufacturing culture. *Science, Technology, & Human Values, 40*(5), 854–879.

Mackenzie, A. (2012). "Set". In Lury, C. & Wakeford, N. (eds.). *Inventive methods, the happening of the social.* London: Routledge

Marcus, G. E. (1997). The uses of complicity in the changing mise-en-scene of anthropological fieldwork. *Representations, 59*, 85–108.

Maurer, B. & Schwab, G. (eds.). (2006). *Accelerating possession: Global futures of property and personhood.* New York: Columbia University Press.

Morozov, E. (2013). *To save everything, click here: The folly of technological solutionism.* New York: Public Affairs.

Nielsen, M. (2011). "Futures within: Reversible time and house-building in Maputo, Mozambique". *Anthropological Theory, 11*(4), 397–423.

Novotny, H. Scott, P., & Gibons, M. (2001). *Re-thinking science: Knowledge and the public in an Age of Uncertainty.* Cambridge: Polity Press.

Rappaport, J. (2016). Rethinking the meaning of research in collaborative relationships. *Collaborative Anthropologies, 9*(1), 1–31.

Özden-Schilling, C. (2015). Economy electric. *Cultural Anthropology, 30*(4): 578–588. https://doi.org/10.14506/ca30.4.06.

Pink, S. & Lanzeni, D. (2018). Future anthropology ethics and datafication: Temporality and responsibility in research. *Social Media+ Society, 4*(2), 2056305118768298.

Pink, S., Lanzeni, D., & Horst, H. (2018). Data anxieties: Finding trust in everyday digital mess. *Big Data & Society, 5*(1), 2053951718756685.

Pink, S. (2022). *Emerging technologies/life at the edge of the future.* Oxford: Routledge.

Pink, S., Fors, V., Lanzeni, D., Duque, M., Sumartojo, S., & Strangers, Y. (2022). *Design ethnography.* Oxford: Routledge.

Podjed, D., Gorup, M., Borecký, P., & Guerrón-Montero, C. M. (Eds.). (2021). Why the World Needs Anthropologists. Abingdon & New York: Routledge.

Salazar, J. F., Pink, S., Irving, A., & Sjoberg, J. (eds.). (2017). *Anthropologies and futures: Techniques for researching an uncertain world.* Oxford: Bloomsbury.

Sneath, D., Holbraad, M., & Pedersen, M. A. (2009). Technologies of the imagination: An introduction. *Ethnos, 74*(1), 5–30.

Suchman, L., Danyi, E., & Watts, L. (2008). *Relocating innovation: Places and material practices of future-making.* Lancaster, UK: Centre for Science Studies.

Suchman, L. (2012). *"Configuration".* In Lury & Wakeford (eds.). *Inventive methods: The happening of the social* (pp. 48–60). London: Routledge.

Star, S. L. & Bowker, G. C. (2006). How to infrastructure. In L. A. Lievrouw & S. Livingstone (eds.), *The handbook of new media* (pp. 230–245). London: Sage.

Strathern, M. (2006). "On space and depth". In: Law, J. and Mol, A. (eds.). *Complexities: Social studies of knowledge practices* (pp. 88–115). Durham: Duke University Press.

Seaver, N. (2017). Algorithms as culture: Some tactics for the ethnography of algorithmic systems. *Big Data & Society, 4*(2), 2053951717738104.

Thrift, N. & French, S. (2002). "The automatic production of space". *Transactions of the Institute of British Geographers, 27*(3), 309–335.

Taylor, C. (2002). Modern social imaginaries. *Public Culture, 14*(1), 91–124.

Wajcman, J. (2008). "Life in the fast lane? Towards a sociology of technology and time". *The British Journal of Sociology, 59*(1), 59–77.

Wallman, S. (ed.). (1992). *Contemporary futures: Perspectives from social anthropology.* London: Routledge.

Williams, R. H. (1990). *Notes on the underground: An essay on technology, society, and the imagination* (p. 1). Cambridge, MA: MIT Press.

Wright, P. G. & Ceriani Cernadas, C. (2007). Antropología simbólica: pasado y presente. *Relaciones de la sociedad argentina de antropología, 32*, 319–348.

Zook, M. A. & Graham, M. (2007). "Mapping DigiPlace: Geocoded Internet data and the representation of place". *Environment and Planning B: Planning and Design, 34*(3), 466.

# 2

# MODELLING THE FUTURE[1]

*Simone Abram and Antti Silvast*

## Introduction

What are research engineers doing when they develop models of the energy system? While modellers may or may not be designing specific technological interventions, their modelling activities play a crucial role in the progress of technological ideas and imaginaries. Contrary to the popular vision of inventors tinkering in workshops – an image promoted by appliance developers such as Dyson or Trevor Bayliss, the majority of significant engineering and infrastructure developments come out of research laboratories (including those commissioned by Dyson itself), through a lengthy process of detailed modelling. What is meant by modelling can vary extraordinary widely. Models may be calculative computing models of inputs and outputs or processes, they may be based on readings from real physical entities, simulated data generated mathematically from physical measurements, or actual material exemplars – even a whole house fitted with monitors that acts as a 'model' or archetype of building responses to environmental conditions or changes of use. Common to all such models is the measurement of something in the real world that is used for the production of mathematical data that can then be manipulated with the use of computing software, using programmes often designed and run by those researchers who we refer to, in shorthand, as modellers.

## What do modellers do?

This chapter is based on empirical research carried out under the auspices of the National Centre for Energy Systems Integration, a 5-year research centre project funded by the Engineering and Physical Sciences Research Council (EPSRC) UK and co-funded by industrial partners, including Siemens and others.[2] Our role in the project was to conduct an analysis of the energy systems modelling process

DOI: 10.4324/9781003084471-3

itself, and to contribute social science knowledge to the integration process. Antti Silvast spent a term in university modelling laboratories, interviewing around 30 engineering modellers, some of whom were directly engaged in the ESI project, others who were conducting PhDs in engineering on other, related topics, and Simone Abram participated in project meetings and interviews with modellers over three years prior to the pandemic in 2020.

The laboratory is a large open-plan office space in a large northern University known for its engineering excellence. Hidden in a middle floor of a multi-story building, the long rectangular space has windows onto an internal courtyard along one side, strip lighting along the ceiling, and a fibreboard and glass panelled meeting room jutting out from the inner wall, its windows obscured by venetian blinds. From the long window side of the room, pairs of L-shaped desks with low separators sit in serried ranks, each with a black wheeled office chair, computer screens, stacks of papers and books, and a motley collection of pens, books, calendars, files, jars of coffee, bags, jackets and even coffee machines clutter the desks. White vertical blinds keep sunlight off the many screens and obscure the visual connection with the outside world. Other than a clock, the walls are bare. A private office at the end of the room is the preserve of the senior academic, and this is full of books and papers; whiteboards on the walls show diagrams and equations in different coloured pen, and multi-coloured academic posters line the walls. Odd bits of equipment lie around in heaps, and wires are tangled behind a standing desk. Other low-level desks are cluttered with mugs, coffee jugs, plastic water bottles, lamps, rulers, university telephones, and on the cream-painted breezeblock walls behind them are dark green baize pinboards with old notices, phone number lists, campus maps and old yellow sticky-notes clinging on with assorted drawing pins. Under the desks are plastic and cardboard boxes bulging with papers. Overall, the impression is of a generic scientific office space, somewhat impersonal, that might be found in any of numerous British universities.

Modellers working in the office come from many different countries to do doctoral research here and are of diverse ages, from early 20s to mid-40s. All have or are conducting doctoral degrees and in this office they mostly have engineering or maths degrees, some economics. Under a third are women, which is a relatively high proportion in the context of UK engineering departments.

What is it that is going on in these offices? According to Antti's informants, those working here are engaged in diverse forms of modelling:

> Modelling is done to better understand an energy system in transition – i.e. a "future" energy system that is confronted by the impacts of climate change. This is very similar to some building models, while the model in this case is a large-scale energy-economy model.

In technical terms, they are mostly using coding packages such as Matlab, or Simulink, coding or recoding for new applications. Some models are economic models, some are physics or mechanical models, some are design-based, all aim to achieve a correspondence between the model and reality, at least to some degree (proprietary energy models, such as TIMES,[3] MARKAL, ARIMA, MonteCarlo, are rarely available to doctoral students, although some researchers have access to these systems). What interests us is the way that these modellers integrate assumptions about the world into their modelled systems, and what the eventual implications of such assumptions might be. This concern arises from an STS and feminist perspective that might be seen to suggest that identity politics plays a role in science. We are not suggesting that the social identity of the scientist necessarily directly directs the science that they conduct, but we are implying that the positionality or perspective of the modeller might be reflected in the judgements they make – often implicitly – in the modelling process. This is relevant in particular areas, including in the construction of the limits of the model, the characterisation of its uncertainties or doubts, the quality of the data and their evaluation of the significance of quality. We also make a further hypothesis, that these assumptions 'disappear' into the model, particularly when the model leaves the modeller's desk(top) and is taken up by others, as we outline below.

## Uncertainties and temporalities

When climate change modelling is mentioned, our interest is piqued, since we are familiar with the work of philosopher Wendy Parker on the ethics of climate modelling (Parker 2018, Parker and Winsberg 2018). Parker's work explores the nooks and crannies of modelling procedures, to expose the moments when modellers make decisions of ethical consequence. Parker shows how apparently technical evaluations around the setting of threshold criteria or tolerance levels in modelling processes can have dramatic effects on the visions generated with the use of modelling processes. Elements of personal judgement and cultural norm impinge on technical modelling processes as the modellers make decisions about how to represent probabilities and uncertainties in the models or in the data qualities. Parker intervenes in a debate about evaluation of evidence that goes back to the 1950s arguments about whether science is, should or could be value-free. Richard Rudner argued that acceptance of a hypothesis should depend on what is at stake if the hypothesis is right or wrong:

> For instance, if people might die if a hypothesis turns out to be wrong we should accept it only if we have very strong reasons to believe that it is true: "How sure we need to be before we accept a hypothesis will depend on how serious a mistake would be." (Rudner 1953, p. 2) If nothing really important is at stake, the hypothesis can be accepted even if our level of confidence is a bit lower.
>
> *Peterson and Zwart 2014: 1*

In other words, in their models and theories, scientists depend on value-judgements of different kinds. Others argued that it was for practitioners to make such judgements, guided by subjective probabilities assigned to the utility of various outcomes caused by accepting a hypothesis (e.g. Jeffrey 1956). The significance of attributing probabilities to outcomes has only increased since then, and Bayesian methods to attribute figures to levels of uncertainty are now a widely accepted means of externalising doubt about models, whether those are theoretical models or measurements from trial-and-error prototypes. However, reducing uncertainty to a quantity may not account for the role of non-factual influences in models. If, as Peterson and Zwart argue, models are 'approximate representations of some target system', they are subject to 'a plethora of normative influences' (Ibid.: 2). Normative influences might derive from the definition of a phenomenon (what counts as 'poverty', say), may be shaped by whether modelling is for analysis or design, how multiple researchers collaborate on joint models, or how the entity modelled fits into a wider socio-technical system. Parker argues that models are subject to the priorities and interests of modellers:

> When it comes to model construction, for instance, purposes and priorities shape not just which entities and processes are represented in a model but also how they are represented, including which simplifications, idealizations and other distortions are more or less tolerable.
>
> *Parker 2018: 128*

And furthermore, estimates of probabilities in scientific models are themselves subject to the background knowledge and social values of the modellers: 'purposes and priorities can influence which modelling results scientists compare with observations and what counts as a good enough fit with those observations' (Ibid.). Parker also acknowledges that model construction and model evaluation are not neatly separable, suggesting that interests and preferences run right through models such as complex computer simulation models that are continually adjusted to align the model's outputs with observed empirical findings. Purposes and priorities set when a model is first designed may continue to exert an influence even years later once the model's purpose has moved on, and further processes may be represented in ways that fit the model's existing contents, even if this demands a less accurate representation overall. This matters because models such as climate models have social and ethical implications, directing policy and public discourse, identifying which kinds of data are considered relevant, and what the 'space of possible outcomes looks like' (Parker 2018: 134). Setting thresholds for probabilities of future conditions, deciding ranges of tolerance and levels of approximation are subjective practices that often recede into the workings of technical models, becoming invisible as a model is adopted by practitioners. As models are aggregated, such as in the process of integrating models of different parts or vectors in the energy system, it seems clear that these implicit assumptions, priorities and interests can become embedded in far-reaching policy-influential representations of the world that are known as 'models'.

Looking around the modelling offices, our first question concerned what it was that was being described as a model and what they were for. Each of the modellers gave a different perspective on what a model is, partly reflecting their different aims and partly the different kinds of models they were working on. Later, on a joint visit to a Scottish university, we met Sumati, a senior statistician of Indian origin, sitting at a desk in her large, neat academic office that looked out onto trees at the edge of the engineering campus behind her. Her name had been mentioned several times by a group of energy-demand modellers sharing a tiny office two floors down in the same building, who spent some time making calls and arranging for us to meet. We couldn't help noticing a hint of deference when they talked about her, making it clear that we would be lucky to get her time. It wasn't a simple question of seniority nor age or gender, but rather they seemed to have enormous respect for the complexity of the statistical work that she carried out and saw that she was in demand among other modellers who needed her to help them with statistical processes. Mathematicians appeared to be in demand by engineers at this university, and they often found themselves appealing to mathematicians to help develop a model they had outlined. Welcoming us quietly into her office, Sumati began by summarising the general categories of models commonly used in the kind of electricity-demand modelling that she worked on. She referred to physical models, statistical models, and she mentioned machine-learning models as an emerging category, these being developed by colleagues in another building at the same university.

> Physical models are based on the physical dynamics … what physical processes are going on. These require expertise, how to run those models – it takes time, to estimate energy consumption or how a building will perform in the future. They have certain limitations … like the variability of the process. Then there are statistical models, that we work on. In this process we try to capture the data or the information recorded over a certain period of time, then we try to see the relationship between these data and past events, how time series evolve.

We had understood by this stage that a physics model of what happens to a piece of metal under strain (mimicking a laboratory test) differs from an economic model of the lowest cost combination of different energy sources (mimicking external infrastructures), for example. While all of them associated their modelling practices with futures, this future took different forms, as Sumati had indicated, either being one of many potential worlds not currently in existence that may or may not come into being, or a predicted or likely future that should be addressed. Some models, while framed in relation to the future, modelled present objects in relation to diverse scenarios. As Sumati explained, her statistical models,

> … try to capture the statistical dynamics of the process and use it to simu-late the process of another realistically possible event which has not occurred

but could have the potential chance to occur maybe in the future or some other time. But these use only the observed data, so anything that has not yet occurred, your model won't be able to include that.

Physical models may similarly be defined by the boundaries of what was to be studied – e.g. the conditions inside a cylinder of an internal combustion engine. Such a model allows the modeller to try out indicators of possible future lab technologies that are not available through experimentation, avoiding the necessity to build the machine and test it materially. This model is described as offering a kind of virtual test-bed, simulating how techniques and protocols perform. In such situations, computer models make hypothesised technologies 'real' so that researchers can generate understandings of possible future technologies. These models may also allow modellers to find ways for processes to be optimised for cost, efficiency or other priorities – demonstrating, for example, how waste heat might be incorporated into steel industries, or how a site not yet built might perform under various conditions. Models that account for concepts like cost stray well into areas that are both complex and uncertain, requiring the modeller to make informed estimates of future price ratios, or market regulations.

Some models enable researchers to 'know' the behaviour of an energy system before it has actually been manufactured, when it is still a 'future system'. Calculating potential errors and performance through simulated modelling allows researchers to think about future technologies before they are able to experiment with them systematically. As new technologies emerge – they are described as popping up all the time – models allow researchers to 'play around' with them, making them 'real', and depicting futures where new technologies might be applied on a large scale in the real world, one that may also, in its turn, be modelled and played with. The Energy Systems Integration centre, CESI, aimed to bring together diverse kinds of model of the energy system to see how the different aspects work together. But this meant finding a way to link energy demand models that take an empirical, quite sociological approach to energy usage based on recorded patterns and practices, with transmission and distribution models that calculate equipment ratings under different conditions, and economic models that are used to plan infrastructural maintenance and development. Such models are developed for electricity, gas, heat, transport, storage and so on and may be reliant on different kinds of baseline models, according to the sector they apply to. Put crudely, this is a challenge of integrating apples and oranges of the modelling world and requires quite radical changes in approach, such as reducing models to inputs and outputs – or 'response surface' models (a kind of black box) – that can be fed into one integrative model. The aim was to generate a particular type of future, one in which the diverse aspects of the UK's energy system could be planned and managed as one system. In practice, the outcome was partly a realisation that this aim was unrealistic. Instead, a more modest set of aims emerged, to work towards a system whereby different kinds of models could communicate with one another.

To summarise so far, energy system models form a rather loose or fuzzy category, ranging from physical models of equipment performance to material processes, energy flows through equipment and infrastructures, economic models of demand and supply, or replicas of actual recorded performance of material entities such as buildings or machines. While some models may be explicitly designed to represent a hypothetical technology that does not (yet) exist, others replicate existing situations and see how they respond to diverse stimuli or conditions that may be envisioned as future possibilities. The modellers were more than well aware that all models simplify to some degree, and all attract questions about how closely they correlate with the actual world. Taking Parker's point about priorities and interests of modellers, we note that our interlocutors were generally sanguine about the assumptions and simplifications that they worked with, some very aware of the sociological implications of approximations, one referring to the model as a 'pantomime' that mimics reality, others barely interested in potential ramifications beyond the purely machinic.

If a model represents reality, it necessarily only represents a selection of that reality, and it simplifies. I asked Sumati if there were datasets, she did not have but would like to have. She laughed, saying 'oh yes, many!'. In detail, she explained,

> we don't have sufficient high resolution which has been measured for a long period of time and for diverse cases. So the three things, actually, if you want to combine all those characteristics, you hardly get any datasets which tick all three boxes. So that's where we have the limitations with the data.

Much of the complexity of creating statistical models, in particular, lies in accounting for 'gaps' in the data, or 'data quality', leaving the modellers to make educated judgements, use calculative techniques to estimate what the missing data might present, and/or evaluate how certain, or rather, how uncertain they might be about the estimated data they were using.

A model is not a Borgesian one-to-one replication, but a codification, and thus the process of developing a model entails a long series of choices and approximations. Which factors are important to include, which can be set aside, how accurately must each factor be reported: these questions are implicit in the design and development of models, such that the limits of a model remind us of the limits to defining an ethnographic field. Suffice it to say here that models are normally iterated, to meet levels of accuracy that are defined in relation to purpose. Validation of a model is an entire discipline in its own right, entailing various methods. The most straightforward method would compare modelled outputs with real-world data, but for many of these models, real-world data do not exist, so validation relies on projections or mimetic simulations. Sometimes, validation relies on what is known as 'expert elicitation' – i.e. asking people defined by the modellers as expert, whether technical expert or socially informed, to evaluate how effective the model is and whether it is good enough for the purpose envisioned. And just as Parker and others show, levels of accuracy can become embedded in models that are then incorporated into other models, solidifying the errors in one model into another. Alongside these limitations, boundaries and tolerances are a set of presumptions and assumptions about the future.

## Futures, projections and predictions

Models incorporate a range of future-oriented concepts and forms of future. Some models are replications of the present that can use measurements from sensors in the current world to generate predictive processes for future conditions. In a simple example, sensors that measure the energy consumption of metro trains, combined with models of solar radiance, can be used to predict energy consumption in alternative configurations of metro trains, or future consumption as weather or climate vary. Such futures can be conceptualised as a variance of the present, if we argue that all other contextual factors are assumed to remain constant. Similarly, models of train passenger demand may take current conditions and vary some factors to produce the future not as an input to the model but as an output – the model shows what may happen if certain factors vary. In other words, these models explore and test present assumptions, in what might be thought of as a future where such assumptions are already in place. Such futures have in common with other concepts of future that they project the present forward, allowing for some selected elements to change, but others to remain constant. The elements that remain constant tend to be the larger more socially oriented contextual factors such as the political structure. Energy use and production models may assume that flows of fuel may vary, but they rarely model for a revolutionary change in political structure, for example. And none of the models we encountered had considered the possibility of a national or international lockdown.

These futures should not be confused with future scenarios of the kind produced by National Grid (See National Grid 2017, 2018). These scenarios are elaborated around a two-by-two matrix whose axes are defined as, for example, 'speed of decarbonisation' and 'level of decentralisation' (National Grid 2018). Scenarios use so-called optimisation models such as UKTimes to project possible outcomes based on different rates of change along the axes promoted. These are clearly politicised and partially contextualised projections, feeding regulatory and political ambitions through a technical and economic modelling evaluation to outline investment priorities. For example, National Grid states in 2018 that 'We now have two scenarios that meet the 2050 carbon reduction target: Two Degrees, based on centralised and transmission connected technology; and Community Renewables, based on more decentralised technology' (2018: 14), while noting that 'the relationship between green ambition and prosperity has changed' (Ibid.) since their previous scenarios were published in 2017 using the axes, 'prosperity' and 'green ambition' (National Grid 2017: 10). The 2017 scenarios also attempted to take into account the consequences of the Brexit referendum.

According to Richard Loulou (et al 2016),

> Scenarios, unlike forecasts, do not pre-suppose knowledge of the main drivers of the energy system. Instead, a scenario consists of a set of coherent assumptions about the future trajectories of these drivers, leading to a coherent organization of the system under study. A scenario builder must therefore carefully test the scenario assumptions for internal coherence, via a credible storyline.

The use of terms such as storyline and scenario indicates just how difficult the combination of social and technical elements is in a socio-technical system such as the energy system, or parts of it. TIMES uses external data on population, GDP, households and so forth and is, as such, vulnerable to all the inadequacies and flaws in such data. It further insists that such data generate coherent output growth rates in different regions, again suggesting deeply problematic assumptions. Research on planning for housing demonstrated unequivocally that the only agreed understanding of UK population figures is that they are wrong, yet because they exist, they are used to guide housing development policy at national, regional and local levels (Bramley and Watkins 1996). In engineering terms, one might say that population figures are good enough – indeed engineers describe their own future projection activities in terms of being 'good quality' rather than 'accurate'. Clearly, a model cannot be validated against the future, since future observations are not available. Instead, as models appear to align with real data inputs and outputs – i.e. actual observations – the modeller can become more confident in the model's ability to make predictions. In this future, the modeller's own competence has also increased as the model has become closer to reality, so the direction of travel is one in which both the model and the modeller's abilities become more closely aligned to future observations and the model more and more accurately reflects the observed world. But, of course, the future is also continually receding, and therefore the modelling process remains ongoing. Models have to be updated to adapt to a changing reality in the present, and changing expectations of the future. For example, current energy system models have to take account of new developments in energy storage, radical changes in energy costs such as the recent drop in UK wind energy spot prices by nearly half, which changes the decision-making algorithms for future energy planning. Current debates about the emergence of electric vehicles, and consequently the changing demand for EV charging capacity, also loom very large for energy demand modellers, for example, and they think a great deal about such issues, wanting to know how they would affect the calculations in their models.

Models themselves therefore also have futures, and the future of a meticulously developed model may also be deeply uncertain. We have noted a striking institutional lack of learning from the models developed by doctoral students. Students themselves tell us that it is easier to start a new model than develop one that has already been written, since developing an existing model entails getting inside the head of the previous modeller, coming to terms with all the implicit assumptions they have included and all the choices they have made that may, or may not, be documented within the code. This degree of complexity makes model development potentially very slow, and for PhD students who need to complete and come out with something to show potential employers, being able to present their own model is the more effective option. Some reported that modellers can be possessive of their intellectual property, making collaborative work potentially difficult. Some of the PhD students we have talked with saw the lack of institutional learning as a problem and would have liked to generate more cumulative approaches, but at present modelling techniques themselves are not necessarily taught and learned institutionally. Instead, postgraduate modellers told us that they learn coding techniques and how to use existing standard models from YouTube.

Amongst the more senior modellers, there was ongoing discussion about the merits of proprietary models versus coding one's own models. Sumati spent some time discussing a range of existing models, including well-known systems such as MATLAB or a system known as 'Hidden Markov' models which use standard software packages. But Sumati preferred to use open source models, not least to avoid copyright issues. She could incorporate bits of open source code into her own modelling that she did mostly in R or C, or, like many colleagues in this field, a code called Python. Open source also offered resource, in terms of help between people who put work in open source repositories: 'If I'm doing something and I find that ok, this function can do this type of task, I can write a package and put it in the repository and share it among lots of people'. R and Python are both open source coding languages that tie into online communities through discussion forums. From her office, Sumati can be in touch with statistical modellers across the globe, some working in industry, some in financial roles, for example, all using open source software to develop statistical models in a wide variety of applications. Being part of this community, and being able to write her own code, was both satisfying and effective, since learning a new proprietary system would take significant time and would not give her control over valuable parts of the model.

Phil is a relatively young senior lecturer in building-demand modelling. He has his own teaching office on the ground floor of the same building but works with the team in the crowded office upstairs as well. We meet in his office with one of his postdoctoral research assistants and discuss the merits of proprietary versus open source coding systems, before the post-doctoral assistant has to rush away to collect his baby from nursery. This is clearly a discussion they have frequently, and one that Phil has thought about a lot in relation to deciding which programming packages to teach. Phil feels very clearly that writing your own code is 'proper research', whereas applying a finished models feels a bit too easy. Proprietary models are widely tested and have particular attention paid to the interface, to make them more intuitive to use. In order to make them stable and reliable, however the model is standardised and the range of inputs is restricted. As he pointed out, 'if you don't understand something of what goes on in that black box, then you can't really judge if that's an improper application or not'. In other words, without an expert modeller who understands the choices, inputs and equations used in the model itself, the model is not complete. This in turn raises questions about how a model can be defined – does it include the 'engine' (the equations in the programme) and the modeller? What about the data? What are the trade-offs between reliable but standardised models and precise but idiosyncratic models? For researchers, the additional question emerges around the returns from designing versus applying a model, and thinking about how the models might subsequently be used. Precisely because knowledge of the model is needed to evaluate the application, Phil explains that he tries to get involved with the application and policy impact of the models he developed, rather than 'locking myself into physics', as he put it, so that he can ensure that the application is appropriate for the uses that are required by, for example, government departments. All these questions provide the context for the specific modelling work going on in these offices.

## Foresight and hindsight

Back in the large PhD and postdoc modelling office in the English university mentioned above, the atmosphere feels dampened, in that communication is muted and students rarely appear to discuss their work with each other. Most communication between desks is low-level chit chat, small talk about the weather or sports, or perhaps news. Research groups have perhaps monthly progress meetings (which we have not been able to observe), so clearly some degree of shared learning is happening, but perhaps less than one might expect. We do not know but do not anticipate that all other modelling offices work along the same lines, but this is an area where we are actively seeking further observation opportunities. However, we note a strong sense of private ownership over particular models developed at the PhD stage, at least. And in our experience with integrated modelling so far, we note some difficulties for modelling groups in working out how to share their modelling approaches and models. Mostly, this revolves around questions of inter-intelligibility and compatibility between models that may be based on quite different types of both theory and practice. How to combine a real-time representation of electricity balancing with a simulation of gas consumption or the readings from sensors installed in an actual house, whether occupied or a test-site? And when energy system models are used to depict future scenarios decades ahead, in 30 years, for example, the degree of uncertainty in each area is very great. The idea of modelling so far ahead contains assumptions about perfect hindsight and foresight, even though all modellers are aware that the greatest historic changes have occurred from unforeseen changes, such as unexpected innovations or significant political or environmental changes.[4] The UK energy ministry foresaw in 2004 that the UK would be entirely free of gas by the 2020s, a prediction that failed to materialise. The longer term effects of optimistic policy include the lack of investment in gas management systems now, and the exclusion of gas from integrated control systems that have now been developed commercially. Within energy models, methods such as game theory are included to try to account for economic patterns, and to produce what they see as more 'realistic' depictions of how actors interact, rather than simply through price signals. Yet few, if any, models can really account for radical innovation or changes in circumstance. Modellers agree that scenarios for the future are inherently biased and are affected by vested interests. Rather like social scientists, they are aware to some extent of their own interested roles and attempt to make these explicit where they can – yet they less commonly have the sorts of social science techniques available to them to do this systematically, or to appreciate the depth of cultural assumption and positioned perspective that reflexive theories offer.

One further form of the future demonstrates the convolutions among present, hypothetical, predicted and possible futures and shows that time is perhaps not really the distinguishing feature of modelling process. As part of the central method of the Centre for Energy Systems Integration to produce an integrated energy model for the UK, researchers chose to start with a small demonstrator project, reasoning that if they could produce an integrated model of a small-scale community for whom they had detailed and reliable data, then the lessons learned could then be scaled up to a larger model. Rather than discuss the pros and cons of this approach, we point instead to a part of the method that struck us as curious. The community chosen as the 'role model' is a small ecovillage in Scotland that has solar power, wind turbines, battery storage, a variety of housing styles and workplaces, and well recorded data on household energy consumption. Two factors made this community a problem for the integrated model. First, that a significant amount of their heating is obtained by woodstoves, and wood is provided from the surrounding forestry plantations as offcuts, for free. Hence this wood is not measured and therefore distorts the thermal equations in the heat models. Second, the community is not on the gas network. To respond to these challenges, the engineers in the different teams, from different universities, agreed to ignore the firewood element of the heating data, and secondly to generate a model that included a gas network, as if it existed on the site. Clearly, neither of these decisions represents a future in this community, nor does it represent the present. Instead, the model represents a possible future model of integrated energy systems that could become the baseline for modelling the UK's regional and national energy worlds, on which decisions about future developments could be built.

## Talking models – and future-oriented methods

The discussion above circles around the models as elusive objects, partly material, partly digital, partly conceptual. More traditional ethnographers might ask 'where are the people', and this question allows us to address three key issues. First, the imbalance between social and material objects in anthropological research that featured heavily in the early discussions around Actor Network Theory, whose aim was to redress the division between social and material research practices (Latour 1993, Law and Hassard 1999). We simply state here that our interest is primarily in the social life of the models rather than the material life of the modellers. Second, the problem of approaching abstract and primarily imaginary practices, which has primarily been explored ethnographically using narrative and observation. How do imaginaries take place in the world, and how are they materialised or narrativized? In the observations we made of project meetings towards the integrated energy system model, our sense was that the desired but still imaginary integrated model was conjured up through these very discussions, and in the grappling with the abstract challenges of the modellers reworking their models back in their own workplaces. Much of the project was spent in trying to imagine this integrated model – what form would it take, what purpose would it serve, what was the route to producing it? These, in themselves, are not only intensely futuristic practices but also primarily imaginative. Although some of the models to be integrated were, in fact, material (equipment in labs), most were digital, appearing on the screens of the researchers and invisibly on the drives and computers behind them. So while, above, we have considered primarily the futurity of the models themselves, all of the modellers were working towards generating future models themselves. This is related to the promise of innovation that does not yet exist – as Lanzeni and Pink discuss (this volume) – while here being conceptual, still far from the possibility of commercialisation, even if this possibility lurks in the conversations. The models we refer to are at the research stage. Research itself consists of generating future findings, so that research activities can be thought of as means of achieving desired futures. Even while recollecting and reflecting on research findings, the process of writing a research article such as this is oriented towards publication that may be months, sometimes years away. We anticipate that you will read this and reflect on your own future orientations, both in your research practice and in the research objects that interest you. There are multiple futures here, wrapped into and around one another, imagining different temporal horizons (the five-year funded research centre, the work-package meeting calendar, journal publication timetables, the 2030 net-zero goal, the urgency of addressing climate change, and the institutional promotion round or the career trajectory).

Third, the project raises questions of how to pay attention to sociality in cosmopolitan contexts, and how to take seriously workplaces without the domestic ancillary picture of the workers' home lives. Malcolm Chapman reflected on the implications for method of studying business organisations, suggesting that long, unstructured and multiply repeated interviews were 'not exactly fieldwork' in the anthropological sense, but that they generated companionability, shared experience and reflection (2001:26). In our study on modelling, we did (and continue to) socialise with the interlocutors we refer to, but we did not follow them home. We are, however, aware that they also seldom follow one another home, so the focus of their interactions remains at work and work events. While predominantly male researchers, with qualifications in sciences, maths, engineering and economics, they came from different countries and different class backgrounds, were at different positions in terms of research career or institutional hierarchies and held different political and party-political views. The programme of research we are referring to was also a collaborative project between different research groups at and between different universities.

They were united in an ambition to respond to climate change, and to see infrastructure-engineering as a route to doing this. One might conceive of them as a community of practice, yet their practices were, in fact, also very diverse within the very broad umbrella category of modelling. The models and the inputs/ outputs could be completely different in type or scope for, say, modelling the heat generated in a cable, versus market behaviour. This was discussed numerous times in project management meetings as the project developed. In one such meeting, the lead researchers from engineering, physics, maths, computing and economics met in a smart glass-walled seminar room in a new university building in a large northern city. They took turns to scribble on a wall-length whiteboard, drinking coffee from a catering flask supplied by the university with paper cups and packets of biscuits. As well as being from different disciplinary departments, the meeting participants came from very different modelling backgrounds, including physical modellers, demand modellers, statisticians, economists, working on electricity, gas, heat, transport as well as conceptual matters such as 'uncertainty'. At this particular meeting, they wanted to take stock of progress and work out where to take the project next. While the project's overall goals were clear – to produce an integrated model of energy systems in the UK, what that meant in practice, and how to achieve it were still difficult to articulate, not least because it depended how this integrated model might later be used (chiming with Phil's concerns outlined above). But the problem of reconciling qualitative, quantitative, probabilistic, deterministic, data-driven and physics-driven models itself remained difficult and occupied a great deal of the conversation. This very diversity explained why 'it's so bloody hard' to present integrated models. Even attempting to develop a matrix of the different types of models proved problematic, since 'type of model' presupposed that a typology existed.

But tackling complex problems is a core engineering challenge, so it was not surprising that they tried to translate their concerns into the formal abstract language of equations, a language that they all shared. The project leader did this as follows by sketching on the whiteboard the following equation:

$$I/P + M (p) = O/P$$

This translates as: Inputs + models (with parameters) gives Outputs (with uncertainties).

Given this basic process, a computing researcher illustrated the challenge as:

$$M_1(P_1) + M_2(P_2) = M_3$$

Or: Model 1 (with its parameters) + model 2 (with its parameters) produces a new model 3.

This second equation enabled the researchers to reframe their problem as, 'how do you do that equation'? Having made the problem abstract, they had to then find a route to turning it back into a practice (*pace* Latour 1993). The equation helped them to clarify the problem but did not offer any solutions, generating instead interesting questions. Would the parameters of the models 1, 2 and 3 be similar, and could you 'ask the same questions' of each of the models, for example, or would they make sense over the desired timescales? Would they apply to system operation as well as investment decisions? Was it even realistic to model thirty years into the future if the detail was intractible and possibly spurious? Framing the problem in this light led to a discussion about what the models were for, how an integrated model would be used, and by whom: what should be the 'value proposition' of the integrated model? If the new model was to be delivered with a handbook on using it, what steps should the handbook include? Most importantly, under what conditions could models be integrated? Some models were already integrated, so was the aim instead a methodology for integration rather than a final integrated model? And so on. The language of equations thus had to become a language for our research as well, one that we take seriously as a meaningful mode of communication that is central to modelling practices. Within these equations and their attempts to formulate the aim of the project lies the struggle to formulate what kind of a future was to be anticipated, and what kind of response could be created. All the layers of the modelling process, up to and including the model's own purpose in the future, were uncertain, with multiple layers of uncertainty about futures with different scopes, and of different scales, temporal and geographical. The complexity of the models and the sophistication or simplicity of their mathematics were all attempts to address these radically uncertain futurities. The meeting broke up with an agreement to hold a modelling theory workshop next, on knitting together complex models, with a subsequent meeting to consider energy issues specifically, and the researchers wandered out, returning their security badges at the front desk before heading back to their respective universities. Future meetings offered a prospect of ongoing process that may, or possibly may not, lead them closer to finding ways to link together the various models that, at the time, appeared possibly incommensurable, while the walk to the station offered a moment for small talk and a little gossip about things said in the meeting, other ongoing projects or university politics. As we walked away down the hill to the station, we wondered who would wipe the whiteboard clean and whether we would see the equations again at our next meeting.

## Summary

When discussing emerging technology, it may be tempting to look at product design or laboratories, but we argue that infrastructural technologies in particular often emerge through stages that include modelling and simulation processes. While one might assume that models are future-oriented, what future-orientation means can incorporate many different kinds of future, and many different orientations. Some of these future orientations are possible futures, some are impossible and others are implausible. The evaluation of what is implausible or what is likely can be seen as a weak link in the modelling process, precisely at the point where the social and technical are most closely aligned, in the political, regulatory and real economic practices that people engage in. While the future behaviour or perform-ance of motors or cables may be relatively stable and accessible to simulation, their performances in the real world of climate change, geopolitical instability, changing household formation, and so on are immediately more challenging for modelling approaches. Attempts to integrate models of different sectors of the energy system carry with them dangers, not only of the potential failure of an integrated model, but also through the carrying through of errors and assumptions that may result in injustices in the longer term, in relation to infrastructure decisions, investment strategies or changes in relative energy costs between technologies, between regions or between social classes.

Looking through our notes from interviews with modellers, we find over 40 different ways of discussing the kind of future that models engage with. What is emerging is not only a technology but also a range of possible futures that open up and close down at least partly as a result of how they move through the modelling sequence. Some anticipate future demand and explore how infrastructures could meet it, others explore changing infrastructure and see what kinds of demands might emerge. Some are quick and dirty, others detailed and nuanced. And the models themselves have a temporal life that is affected by intellectual competition and col-laboration that varies between modelling communities. And through this complex field, we repeatedly meet modellers who are well aware of the limitations of their models and the concept of modelling, who realise how contradictory different mod-elling approaches are and how counter-intuitive is the notion of integrating different modelling types. Integration is on the political agenda, nationally and internation-ally, and significant amounts of research money are currently supporting work on integration activities. Primary among these activities is the modelling of integrated systems, while the modelling of integration itself relies on social scientists observing, interviewing, and to a limited degree, participating in the activities of modelling.

## Notes

1  https://www.ncl.ac.uk/cesi/
2

> The TIMES (The Integrated MARKAL-EFOM System) model generator was developed as part of the IEA-ETSAP (Energy Technology Systems Analysis Program), an international community which uses long term energy scenarios to conduct in-depth energy and environmental analyses (Loulou et al., 2004). The TIMES model generator combines two different, but complementary, sys-tematic approaches to modelling energy: a technical engineering approach and an economic approach. TIMES is a technology rich, bottom-up model generator, which uses linear-programming to produce a least-cost energy system, optimized according to a number of user constraints, over medium to long-term time horizons. In a nutshell, TIMES is used for, "the exploration of possible energy futures based on contrasted scenarios".
>
> *Loulou et al., 2005*

https://iea-etsap.org/index.php/etsap-tools/model-generators/times

3 All names are pseudonyms.
4 Our fieldwork pre-dated both the pandemic and the international energy crisis.

## References

Bramley, G. and C. Watkins. (1996). *Circular Projections*. London: Council for the Protection of Rural England.

Chapman, M. (2001). Social Anthropology and Business Studies: Some considerations of Method. In D. N. Gellner and E. Hirsch (Eds). *Inside Organizations: Anthropologists at Work*. Oxford: Berg.

Jeffrey, R. C. (1956). Valuation and acceptance of scientific hypotheses. Philosophy of Science, 23(3), 237–246.

Latour, B. (1993). *We Nave Never Been Modern*. Cambridge, MA: Harvard University Press.

Law, J. and J. Hassard. (Eds) (1999). *Actor Network Theory and After*. Oxford: Blackwell.

Loulou, R., G. Goldstein, and K. Noble. (2005). *Documentation for the MARKAL Family of Models*. ETSAP. https://www.iea-etsap.org/docs/Documentation_for_the_TIMES_Model-Part-I.pdf

Loulou, R., U. Remne, A. Kanudia, A. Lehtila, and G. Goldstein. (2016). Documentation for the TIMES Model – PART I 1–78. https://iea-etsap.org/docs/Documentation_for_the_TIMES_Model-Part-I_July-2016.pdf

National Grid. (2018). *Future Energy Scenarios (System Operator)*. http://fes.nationalgrid.com/media/1363/fes-interactive-version-final.pdf

National Grid. (2017). *Future Energy Scenarios*. http://fes.nationalgrid.com/media/1253/final-fes-2017-updated-interactive-pdf-44-amended.pdf

Parker, W. (2014). Values and uncertainties in climate prediction, revisited. Studies in History and Philosphy of Science, 46: 24–30.

Parker, W. and E. Winsberg. (2018). Values and evidence: How models make a difference. European Journal of Philosophy of Science, 8: 125–142.

Peterson, M. and S. D. Zwart. (2014). Introduction: Values and norms in modeling. Studies in History and Philosophy of Science, 46:1–2.

Rudner, R. (1953). The scientist qua scientist makes value judgments. Philosophy of Science, 20(1), 1–6.

# 3

# INNOVATION ROUTES AND MULTI-ENGINEERING IN ENTREPRENEURIAL SCIENCE AND THE ANTHROPOLOGY OF FUTURES

*Roxana Moroșanu Firth and Nathan Crilly*

## Introduction

The term 'innovation' is increasingly being employed as a signifier of good news. Together with its adjective pair, 'innovative', the term is often applied when referring to artefacts and techniques of social organisation that are expected to improve current and forecasted economic and environmental conditions (Fagerberg et al., 2006). This promise of improvement brings an extra layer of meaning to the term beyond its initial understanding as novelty proposed by Schumpeter (Hansen and Wakonen, 1997), to include normative connotations (Adolf et al., 2012; Suchman and Bishop, 2000). When an artefact or technique is being labelled as innovative, it is typically assumed to be positive or desirable.

While it may seem that innovation is everywhere, some of the most well-known, celebrated or controversial innovations are new technologies. The field of innovation studies itself was initially established to look at technological change, as argued by Godin (2015). Engineers, scientists and technologists are at the forefront of many recent innovation success stories, from smartphones to electric cars. They are also the beneficiaries of specialised innovation policies, for example those that encourage new forms of cooperation and knowledge exchange between academia and industry. Innovation models inspired by successful environments for 'entrepreneurial science' (Etzkowitz, 2002), such as that at the Massachusetts Institute of Technology (MIT), have been implemented worldwide (Pfotenhauer and Jasanoff, 2017). These models aim to make the transition from scientific discovery to commercial product faster and leaner. This acceleration has been facilitated by other changes in scientific culture: instead of having to choose a career in either domain, it is much more common for scientists and engineers today to move back and forth between industry and academia (Shapin, 2008) or operate within both domains at the same time (Schneiderman, 2016). New hybrid spaces of inquiry emerge at the

DOI: 10.4324/9781003084471-4

intersection of these domains, for example when academics set up spin-off companies with the purpose of commercialising their research.

This chapter discusses the findings of ethnographic research we conducted with award-winning innovators who work at the intersection of academia and industry. It focuses, specifically, on the creative processes that engineers undertake when designing new technologies in hybrid spaces of inquiry that combine engineering and business knowledge. After presenting our methodology, we describe in detail one ethnographic example – the invention of an anaerobic food waste digester. We then look at the ways in which engineering knowledge and entrepreneurship were combined in the development of this innovation. Two other ethnographic examples are discussed afterwards – a nano-engineering product and a microcomputer – with a focus on the innovators' opinions on the role of business knowledge in their work. We then introduce the concept of multi-engineering to describe a specific mode of knowledge production that our research participants employed when designing new technologies. This involves connecting multiple fields in a flat epistemology, where each engineering field provides the tools to solve one part of the problem that is being addressed. These fields are placed in a relationship of complementarity and they are given equal interpretative power. We argue that the engineers who took part in our research make sense of entrepreneurship by integrating the information they access on this topic within a multi-engineering approach. Finally, we ask what it would mean for the anthropology of futures to develop and employ a multi-engineering approach in interdisciplinary collaborations with engineers and technologists.

## Methodology

The empirical material discussed in this chapter emerged from ethnographic fieldwork conducted by the first author between October 2016 and June 2018 in the UK. The fieldwork involved four studies that employed the following methods: interviews and work-place visits with award-winning engineers and designers; interviews with independent inventors; participant observation with an engineering student society that was designing a water filtration device; interviews with an engineering student society that was developing a solar panel-powered race car. This range of studies led to a number of entry points into the work and ways of thinking involved in engineering design, as the first author moved from taking an active role in student engineering design projects (see Figure 3.1) to that of designing and conducting a study addressing cutting-edge innovations. The ethnographer benefited from additional interactions with engineers by spending three years as a member of staff in an engineering department. These interactions included taking part in research seminars; running sessions as part of a graduate reading group module; helping with specific queries of engineering design PhD students who were interested in qualitative research; as well as everyday forms of communication.

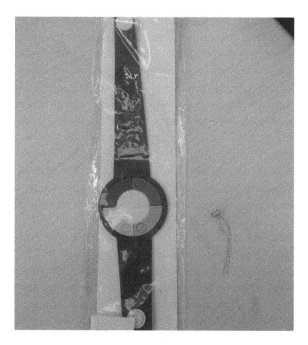

**FIGURE 3.1** A UV radiation bracelet and a UV sensor. The first author was given these devices in her fieldwork with a student society that was designing a water filtration technology. She had to test the bracelet by wearing it in various weather conditions and writing down the values that were generated

The material discussed in the empirical parts of this chapter emerged from the study on cutting-edge innovations, and it was co-produced in ethnographic interviews with award-winning engineers and designers. The participants were selected from the 2015–2017 winner cohorts of the annual innovation awards offered by the two largest professional associations of engineering based in the UK. A total of six innovations were analysed, three of which are discussed here. Our research followed the technique advocated by Deeb and Marcus (2011) of approaching the participants as epistemic partners and building interpretations together. In our case, we asked the participants about their own interpretations of their success stories, and we actively involved them in generating interview questions. First, we talked at length about the processes of envisioning and developing the innovative technologies that brought awards to our participants. As these processes were undertaken over many years, our conversations led to self-reflective retrospectives that are not usually part of the day to day work of technologists, who are often focused on solving more immediate problems. The participants found these retrospectives valuable, saying that they were learning from the conversations, and asking to receive a copy of the recording and transcript to consult later on for other projects. Second, we aimed to probe the participants' more personal understandings of creativity and their own thought processes and inspiration-seeking practices. After addressing our pre-prepared questions on this subject, we asked the participants to contribute their own questions to our inquiry. These contributions were related to two main topics: questions about creativity that we did not address but the participants thought we should; and questions that they would ask the engineers and inventors they admired if they had the chance to meet them face-to-face. These contributions to our inquiry helped us to revise our partial understandings and our interview scripts as the study progressed. The empirical examples in this chapter are drawn from the study described above. However, the concept of multi-engineering was developed by accessing the overall ethnographic knowledge that the first author accumulated while working for three years as part of an engineering department.

## The invention of a food waste digester

Before developing an anaerobic food waste digester, Adaeze had studied and worked in quite a few fields of engineering. She started by doing a degree in civil engineering, going against her parents' advice to study a more 'feminine' field, such as chemical engineering. She loved civil engineering because she found it very practical and it opened the way into other aspects to do with building structures, such as water and wastewater management, traffic and highways. Her first job was for a dredging company and that made her interested in understanding the environmental challenges that provided the context for many engineering projects. She then went back to university, to study for an MSc in environmental engineering. The project she worked on during her master's degree was about retrofitting wastewater treatment plants for energy efficiency. The site she was working with had an anaerobic digester that converted waste from water into energy. That required an engineer to be there all the time to monitor the process and readjust parameters as problems came up. This prompted Adaeze to think about how to make such systems more efficient, and potentially autonomous. She enrolled for a PhD looking at developing an artificial intelligence model that would predict how the microbial populace of such digesters is behaving, and how that behaviour changes with every cycle of waste digestion. She conducted multiple sets of experiments looking at the microbiology of treatment plants and created a predictive model that allowed for the automation of treatment processes.

At this point, Adaeze was interested purely in research and in developing a good model. This required advanced knowledge in a range of fields: bioengineering and chemical engineering to understand the microbial populace; electrical and mechanical engineering to put together sensor systems for monitoring the process of converting waste into energy; computer science and software engineering to develop an artificial intelligence system. Because Adaeze's research topic was linked to renewable energy production, her university supported her attendance at an energy start-up workshop. There she presented her research topic, as did every workshop participant. 'It was never my intention to be entrepreneurial', Adaeze says. After participating in the workshop, she went back to her research. A few months later, she received an email from the workshop organiser who was now preparing the launch of a competition for climate-focused innovation. He told her about this competition and asked her to apply with a business idea. When she first read the email, Adaeze thought, 'I'm not interested, I just want to finish my PhD and get on with my life'. However, the organiser persisted and sent her a more personalised email referring to her research and to the potential of developing an original business idea. Adaeze was half persuaded and she started to think about 'what on earth in my research am I going to put out there for the competition?' That was how she came up with the idea of developing an anaerobic digester for food waste. While the treatment of waste water requires large-scale reactors, food waste can be tackled on a smaller scale. Adaeze thought that restaurants and fast-food chains might be interested in installing a small digester in their kitchens to get rid of food waste autonomously, rather than having it transported to landfill sites. This would be an environmentally friendly approach for two reasons: reducing the amount of food waste in landfills; and producing energy from the process of waste digestion.

When Adaeze presented her business idea in the competition, she received unreserved positive feedback and even interest from some investors. She was amazed by this response. Following the event, a local incubator programme for low-carbon innovations invited her to join them, offering office space, training opportunities and a group of peers. In order to join the incubator and access the support they offered, Adaeze had to incorporate a company. This is how she became an entrepreneur. What followed was a set of training courses with mentors who taught her the steps of developing a business. Adaeze says that having that support from day one helped her move fast and acquire the necessary knowledge for running a business. As the mentors kept checking her progress, she was really disciplined and followed the suggested steps, applying for various types of start-up funding and completing the stages she was expected to progress through.

> They check you all the time to make sure you're doing the right things, so you never make mistakes. In fact, they will know even before you do it. That's been a massive support now for start-ups, especially in the low carbon sector.

Adaeze describes this approach as 'very strategic' and 'thorough'. The support she received for developing her business meant there was no room for doubt; the process she needed to follow was laid down for her. Adaeze's discipline in learning entrepreneurship brought immediate results in the form of funding, such as grants for completing the business model development and customer validation process, and for undertaking the preliminary design of the product.

At the time of the interview, having completed these stages, Adaeze was applying for funding to fully develop the product. In parallel, she had also finished her PhD. She was hopeful that the predictive model she developed for anaerobic digesters for waste water would provide a good starting point in her work on the new product. Her most recent achievement was that of receiving an award for engineering innovation. She went to the ceremony with her dad, who afterwards said he now better understood the field of civil engineering, the discipline which Adaeze had studied against her parent's preferences. She points out that engineering is a profession that allowed her to follow her passion by providing her with tools for making positive change in the world.

> Whatever you have a passion for, it's something you can achieve through engineering. As an engineer, you can make the environment better […] You can start to think, what is the problem with this system and how to improve it? I think the innovation in engineering comes when you reach a better understanding of what you're working on, then you can do something different from the way it's already structured to work.

## Engineering and entrepreneurship

This case shows an accurate example of entrepreneurial science in practice. The fact that access to information and support with setting up a company are available for PhD researchers leads to situations where scientists can become entrepreneurs. Moreover, such information and support are often facilitated by the academic organisations that researchers, such as Adaeze, are engaged with. Entrepreneurship is no longer an alternative to an academic career, but a complementary strand of work.[1]

For Adaeze, the turn from research to entrepreneurship was not anticipated. In fact, it is less of a turn than a continuation of one's research interests in a new administrative setting, that of a company. Adaeze follows and accepts this change of setting as she is encouraged by the favourable response and circumstances she suddenly finds herself in. To act as an incorporated company, rather than as an individual researcher, means to be able to access a wider range of grants, not only for research, but also to develop a business model and strategy. In this sense, entrepreneurship is not a change of direction, but a means for Adaeze to continue to explore her passion for engineering by focusing on new applications. Being able to choose the field of engineering she studied, the process and technology she specialised in and the system she wanted to change were important cornerstones in Adaeze's development of her professional trajectory. The resources she can access as an incorporated company would provide further support to her building an independent path.

Entrepreneurship can be made to serve what Adaeze is trying to achieve as an engineer, which is to change systems in relation to environmental concerns. This comes as a surprise, after Adaeze's initial attempts to decline the invitation of proposing a business idea. However, once she realises that by operating in the commercial world she can generate more impact for her research ideas, Adaeze embraces entrepreneurship with no reserves. She carefully follows the frameworks suggested by mentors in training courses, keen to learn fast and to make no mistakes. To develop a product for food waste digestion and to have it adopted in the restaurant sector is suddenly an opportunity for Adaeze to implement her research on a large scale. She has moved from conducting doctoral research to promoting an idea that could have a real impact on the world in reducing food waste and producing renewable energy.

With this sense of purpose and possibility in mind, Adaeze approaches the new information she encounters, on business management and commercialisation, as an unproblematic body of knowledge. She has no time to question, or to critically assess it; it is a means that can serve her passion and help her achieve her objective. If engineering provides concepts and frameworks for understanding, and acting upon, the natural world, business studies provide the tools for understanding the commercial world. Both disciplines are concerned with existing systems and the ways they operate.

For her PhD research, Adaeze brought together knowledge from a range of engineering fields. She employed bioengineering and chemical engineering to understand the behaviour of the microbial populace in an anaerobic digester; electrical engineering and mechanical engineering to develop the sensor systems that she used to monitor this behaviour; and computer science and software engineering to transform the knowledge she achieved from her experiments into an artificial intelligence-predictive model. From her previous experience working for a dredging company and studying for a master's in environmental engineering, she knew that in order to understand a system and to propose a change, she would need to have an advanced understanding of multiple engineering fields. She developed this understanding over many years of studying, working and researching.

Therefore, at this point, she was not intimidated by not knowing anything about entrepreneurship. Instead, she looked at this body of knowledge as yet another field she wanted to incorporate in her work, in order to take her ideas further. She learned and applied the essential information in this field in a disciplined and structured way, similarly to how she had learned about the fields of engineering she employed in her PhD.

## A spin-off and a start-up: bringing business knowledge into engineering

Adaeze's approach to entrepreneurship is reflected in how other research participants talked about the role they attributed to business knowledge in relation to their scientific research activities. Andy is a lecturer in electrical engineering and he is leading a research lab on nanotechnology. He is also the director of a spin-off company, which is focused on deriving commercial applications from his research. He says that he has always been interested in having an understanding of the technology market and of how the commercial sector works. During his PhD, he found out that he could take a course on the management of technology innovation in the business department of his university. He took the course, and the information he learned gave him the confidence to set up his spin-off company later on. He says that there is a lot of potential in nanotechnology research, but very few research ideas make it through to find commercial applications. This is because many research teams narrow down their focus to one particular research-led aspect and do not often look up at what the market is doing.

> I think the challenge is to have that wider understanding, and that wider network, and to be able to say, okay, you can really be focused on this particular esoteric idea, but really have a broader view of the market, how you'd get there, who you'd interact with to get it there. Sadly, I don't think an idea in itself is enough to get it through, regardless of how innovative it is.

For Andy, having an understanding of how the commercial sectors operate is as important as having an innovative research idea. Combined together, these two forms of knowledge can lead to an impactful outcome.

This mix of knowledge is what inspires Rowan as well. Rowan is the co-founder of a company that developed a microcomputer. He first learned how to programme a computer in his childhood and went on to study computer science. After completing a PhD in computer science, he went back to study for an MBA. He says that he is 'enjoying the intersection of technology and business'. Before embarking on the MBA program, Rowan already had a business idea, and with a small group of friends he had started working on developing the microcomputer. The product evolved while he was studying in parallel for his business degree. They had the first prototype ready in the year he finished his MBA. Only one year later, they launched the product. During that relatively short time, Rowan and his team faced a wide range of challenges, from technical issues to do with finding the right components that would keep a low price for the final product, to the challenge of finding the right business model. Rowan's company was registered as a not-for-profit company, which limited their options for attracting investors. Instead of having to find the funding that would allow them to manufacture the product themselves, Rowan had the idea to implement a licensing business model. This meant that they would select and offer the licence to manufacture the product to a number of external companies. Rowan refers to this idea as a 'eureka' moment.

> Thinking of the licence business, actually, was a 'eureka' moment. We were originally going to build them ourselves. It's not a technical eureka moment, but a business eureka moment, which is just as important. When we realised that we could do this licence, a) when we thought of doing licensing instead of manufacturing, and b) when we found that we could actually find the companies to be licensees.

In this case, figuring out the business model was as important as making the technology work. The two fields of knowledge, on computer science and business management, are interlinked in Rowan's account. He needs to select the right solutions from one field and connect them to the right solutions from the other field in order for his product to work.

## The concept of multi-engineering

When one studies, works or conducts research in engineering, one is always operating across a number of areas of knowledge. The discipline of engineering is divided into multiple branches, each dealing with specific processes, and parts of the natural world. For example, while optical engineering is concerned with light and lenses, mechanical engineering looks at forces and movement, and electrical engineering deals with waves and fields. Few technologies can be designed by following a single body of engineering knowledge. In the development of most of today's new and emerging technologies, these bodies of knowledge are combined. For example, to build a photo-voltaic (solar) panel, one needs to employ optical engineering, electrical engineering and materials science. Engineering students, academics and professionals are aware of this fact and learn to work across engineering fields early on.

In our research with innovators, we found out that individuals understood that they needed to have advanced knowledge in a number of engineering fields in order to develop an innovative technology. This was not simply the job of a multidisciplinary team that brought together experts from each domain. Instead, the lead innovator, who was often working alone, had to have that level of multifield knowledge. The creativity of the innovator was manifested in how she or he combined those areas of information. The solution to a problem could have come from any of the engineering fields that were employed. For example, in Adaeze's experiments on the behaviour of the microbial populace, a measurement that initially looked like an error could have been explained by further study into the bioengineering and chemical engineering fields to discover an abnormal behaviour that someone had already explained; or by looking at the sensor systems she developed and finding ways to improve them to make more accurate measurements. Because these multiple engineering fields are given equal weight in the development of a new technology, the innovator always has a number of pathways to follow when looking for a solution. Navigating these paths requires time, creativity and intuition. How far one would go on a certain path before trying the next is always an individual decision.

We use the concept of multi-engineering to refer to a way of making knowledge and developing technologies that connects multiple fields in a flat epistemology. This means that no single field has the power to offer an interpretation of what is happening in the different fields. In other words, when engineers are making knowledge and things, they draw upon an implicit understanding of the multiple engineering fields as complementing, rather than competing with, each other.

We argue that the innovators we refer to in this chapter apply this mode of knowledge production to make sense of entrepreneurship. If each engineering field can explain one part, or aspect, of the natural world, business studies can explain how the commercial sector operates. The commercial sector is just another part of the world that the engineer wants to understand. This newly acquired understanding is placed alongside the innovator's existing knowledge in engineering. In this way, a new field, that of entrepreneurship, is added to the innovator's multi-engineering approach.

## Multi-engineering and an anthropology of futures

Innovation stories, such as the ones we describe here, are always stories about innovators' imagining of the future. They are also stories about the work undertaken in trying to enact change, and therefore in efforts to change the future by converting existing or anticipated situations into preferred ones (Simon, 1969). Can the mode of knowledge production that we call multi-engineering provide any inspiration for the approaches of the anthropology of futures?

The Future Anthropologies Network manifesto states that anthropologists of futures aim to intervene in the challenges of contested futures. They engage in collaboration and are 'stubbornly transdisciplinary' (EASA, 2014). Such contested futures, as this book suggests, will be interlinked to the emergence of new technologies and the social and political changes they might trigger or respond to. In order to intervene in the design and production of new technologies, anthropologists of futures could try, indeed, to collaborate in a transdisciplinary fashion with the designers and makers of these technologies. We suggest that multi-engineering can inspire a novel model of collaboration between anthropologists and technologists.

First, multi-engineering is an ethnographic concept that emerged from long-term fieldwork on the design of innovative technologies. It reflects the ethnographer's attempts to take seriously the world views and the practices of the people who took part in the study and to communicate them to a wider audience, outside the engineering community. In a way, the concept represents an anthropologist's efforts to learn to think like an engineer. Therefore, it already incorporates a dialogue between engineering and anthropology. Multi-engineering is what one sees when looking at engineering from the perspective of anthropology. For engineers, the concept might make little sense, because the practices it defines are part of their trade. It is obvious that the natural world is divided into parts that can be individually understood by following a dedicated engineering field. When one is concerned with systems that combine a number of such parts, then one needs to study and combine those respective engineering fields. This combination takes the shape of a flat epistemology, where all fields are considered equal with regards to their interpretative power. A single field cannot provide an overall explanation of a system. Instead, all fields need to come together like the pieces in a jigsaw.

This brings us to the second point, which is that this mode of knowledge production is foreign to anthropology, and more generally to the social sciences. When producing work, such as a written piece, an anthropologist might often take a stand point with regards to the interpretative framework she or he is following. Multiple schools of thought compete in their views and interpretations of culture and society. Whether one is a critical realist, or a post-structuralist, might be declared or not at the outset, but it nevertheless becomes visible in the shape of the analysis that follows, including the concepts, theories and references that are employed. In a way, each school of thought proposes its own worldview, and it has its own group of followers, which are the scholars who support that particular interpretative framework (see Candea, 2018; Kuper, 1996). Traditionally, when producing a written piece, one had to make a choice between different styles of interpretation, rather than attempt to combine them. In this sense, it can be argued that knowledge-making in social sciences is based on an implicit understanding that the main interpretative paradigms available are in a relationship of competition, rather than of complementarity, with each other.

Our third point is that when the social scientific approach to making knowledge outlined above has been applied to represent and interpret the work of physical scientists and engineers, it has lead, in many situations, to weakening the trust that technologists might place in social analysis. One well-known controversy was referred to as the 'science wars' (Ross, 1996; Parsons, 2003). This controversy emerged in response to one of the early postmodernist waves that criticised truth claims in science. Some of the literature produced in this wave proposed to interpret the work of scientists and engineers in relation to specific concepts in social theory, such as social organisation and power, not paying attention to the actual content of this work but developing a critique of the wider structures that allowed scientists to make truth claims. This was possible because, unlike a multi-engineering approach where different fields can explain different parts of the physical world, social scientific paradigms often have the ambition to be all-encompassing. The literature that led to the science wars might have included the suggestion that the totality of a scientist's work can be interpreted solely through the use of social scientific concepts. However, in an ethnography, the vernacular categories employed by the research participants for making meaning must be taken seriously in order to produce a truly anthropological account. When the research participants are scientists and engineers, those categories are not likely to be 'social scientific' concepts. Not surprisingly, a number of scientists responded forcefully to that wave of literature, which they regarded as a politically motivated attack on science from the social sciences. They argued that this interpretation did not represent their practices and it showed that the social researchers did not take them seriously.

This brings us to our last point. Anthropologists of futures now have the tools to take engineers and their work seriously. These tools have emerged from debates on ethnographic representation that have been taking place over the last two decades (Rabinow and Marcus, 2008). One such tool, which we mentioned earlier, is that of approaching the research participants as epistemic partners (Deeb and Marcus, 2011), for example by inviting them to contribute to the inquiry. To employ multi-engineering in a situation where anthropologists and technologists collaborate involves giving equal weight to the two fields, and not trying to subsume the actions and ways of reasoning of the other party within one's interpretative framework. This means, for example, that a technologist would accept the fact that the anthropologist is the expert on the topic of how people would react to, and eventually use, the technology they are developing. They will not assume that a technology can determine human behaviour, but will solely be concerned with the technical aspects of the product they are developing, taking advice on the social aspects from the anthropologist they are collaborating with. On the other hand, the anthropologist would accept that an engineer's work involves specific theoretical and technical expertise and that it is rooted in an established knowledge tradition rather than in a desire to take over the world. They will not undermine this work simply because they do not understand it, or because they perceive technologists to have higher social status than anthropologists. A multi-engineering approach to collaboration would lead to partners finding more and more ways of complementing each other's work, rather than competing on the overall interpretation of this work. If such a collaboration will ever be possible, remains to be seen. We hope that the general principles we have traced here will inspire anthropologists of futures when they find themselves working together with technologists.

## Acknowledgements

This work was supported by the UK's Engineering and Physical Sciences Research Council (EP/K008196/1).

## Note

1 The reorganisation and rebranding of the UK's main funding body, Research Council UK, into UK Research and Innovation shows a clear discursive turn towards entrepreneurial science at national policy level.

## References

Adolf, M., Mast, J. and Stehr, N. (2012). The foundations of innovation in modern societies: The displacement of concepts and knowledgeability. *Mind & Society* 12(1): 11–22.

Candea, M. (ed.) (2018). *Schools and Styles of Anthropological Theory*. London: Routledge.

Deeb, H. and Marcus, G. (2011). In the green room: An experiment in ethnographic method at the WTO. *Political and Legal Anthropology Review* 34(1): 51–76.

EASA: European Association of Social Anthropologists. (2014). Future Anthropologies Network (FAN). https://www.easaonline.org/networks/fan.

Etzkowitz, H. (2002). *MIT and the Rise of Entrepreneurial Science*. New York: Routledge.

Fagerberg, J., Mowery, D.C. and Nelson, R.R. (2006). *The Oxford Handbook of Innovation*. Oxford: Oxford University Press.

Godin, B. (2015). *Innovation Contested: The Idea of Innovation over the Centuries*. London: Routledge.

Hansen, S. and Wakonen, J. (1997). Innovation, a winning solution? *International Journal of Technology Management* 13(4): 345–358.

Kuper, A. (1996). *Anthropology and Anthropologists: The Modern British School*. London: Routledge.

Parsons, K. (2003). *The Science Wars: Debating Scientific Knowledge and Technology*. Amherst, NY: Prometheus Books.

Pfotenhauer, S. and Jasanoff, S. (2017). Panacea or diagnosis? Imaginaries of innovation and the 'MIT model' in three political cultures. *Social Studies of Science* 47(6): 783–810.

Rabinow, P. and Marcus, G. (2008). *Designs for an Anthropology of the Contemporary.* Durham: Duke University Press.

Ross, A. (1996). *Science Wars.* Durham: Duke University Press.

Shapin, S. (2008). *The Scientific Life: A Moral History of a Late Modern Vocation.* Chicago, IL: The University of Chicago Press.

Shneiderman, B. (2016). *The New ABCs of Research: Achieving Breakthrough Collaborations.* Oxford: Oxford University Press.

Simon, H. (1969). *The Sciences of the Artificial.* Cambridge, MA: The MIT Press.

Suchman, L. and Bishop, L. (2000). Problematizing 'innovation' as a critical project. *Technology Analysis & Strategic Management,* 12(3): 327–333.

# 4

# DIGITAL ANTICIPATION

*Sarah Pink, Laura Kelly and Harry Ferguson*

## Introduction

In this chapter, we demonstrate a design anthropological approach to the anticipatory modes of everyday life with digital technologies and media.

We argue that to work towards a 'better' – ethical and responsible – digital future we need to prioritise the realities and benefits accrued by the digital lives through which everyday futures are made and imagined. To achieve this, the modes of intervention often advanced in academia need to be reframed. This entails combining academic and public scholarship, to critically but collaboratively intervene with – rather than against – key stakeholders.

To do this, we create a theoretical-empirical dialogue which draws on research into how the use of digital technologies, platforms and media shifted elements of child protection social work during the COVID-19 pandemic in the United Kingdom. This is a period for which some governmental and organisational digital and data practices have been understood as a 'second-order disaster', by increasing surveillance and exacerbating inequalities (Madinou 2020). Thus, it is clear that ethics and equity need to be at the core of any consideration of how new and emerging technologies and data are engaged in moments of crisis. The example of how digital technologies and media were engaged for child protection social work reveals new insights about the ethics entailed in taking forward improvisatory modes of digital technology and media use in a moment of heightened contingency. It shows how digital and data practices can emerge differently, when they come about through relations of care, within the sites of everyday life.

Everyday life with digital media and technologies is understood design anthropologically as playing out in an experiential and ongoingly emergent (Smith & Otto 2016) digital-material (Pink et al 2016) world where people continually improvise in contingent circumstances to create modes of practice that both take a

DOI: 10.4324/9781003084471-5

step forward into uncertainty (Akama et al 2018) and are sufficiently routine and familiar to offer them the sense of ontological security needed to feel comfortable as they move forward in life and the world (Pink et al 2018). A similar framework has more recently been advanced in media phenomenology, whereby 'the apprehension of contingency is rarely, if ever, revelatory, but rather a background hum that accompanies the improvisatory, provisional acts we engage in to sustain an at-handedness and at-homeness' (Markham 2020: 5). The emphasis on movement, contingency, improvisation and how life plays out in an ongoingly emergent world, which characterises media phenomenology and its philosophical underpinnings (Moores 2012, Markham 2020) more broadly coincide with design anthropological (Ingold 2007, Smith & Otto 2016) and future anthropology theory (Pink & Salazar 2020) as applied to digital technology and media (Pink et al 2016). These synergies provide a fertile and inspiring starting point. We advance an argument in which they cohere further and initiate a new focus towards anticipation and an interventional and applied agenda rooted in phenomenological design anthropology.

Below we take three steps to examine how our empirical research productively dialogues with and complicates the claims of theory, invokes new questions and creates new visions. We interrogate: the *contingency* of how experience, practice and everyday ethics emerge; the *anticipatory* modes and feelings of trust and anxiety through which everyday ethics are experienced; and the *improvisatory modes* of living with digital media and technology through which people approach the uncertainties of contingent moments and the anticipatory feelings that accompany them.

This approach both examines how ethics emerge within the everyday and reinvents the ethics of our work as scholars. We suggest we have an *ethical* responsibility to account for the anticipatory modes through which digital media and technologies are used in everyday life, and to make interventions that are appropriate to those very sites where futures are sensed and felt. Put differently, if (or in cases where) anticipation is so central to everyday practice, do we not have an ethical responsibility to attend to the ethics, politics and possibilities that it brings about? As Pink and Lanzeni have put it, the ethnographic method itself needs 'a revised approach to temporality that attends to the ethics of intervening and engaging with the uncertainty of what is as yet unknown rather than simply with an ethics of the past' (2018: 1).

## Child protection social work as a fieldwork site

Child protection social work is an area of professional practice where digital technologies had limited use before the pandemic, and where automation is not integrated with everyday social work practice. Recent debate concerning anticipatory and predictive digital technologies in social services has focused on big data, artificial intelligence (AI) and automation, to reflect on the growing use of algorithmic automation, designated apps and digital information (Henman 2019). The complexities of the relationship between digital technologies and media and social work have been emphasised, and researchers have called for further investigation (e.g. Megele & Buzzi 2020). However, in child protection social work in the United Kingdom at the start of our research in 2020, there had been limited use of such technologies. Moreover, where social work scholars had engaged with media theory they tended to turn to universalist sociological (Castells 2010, Bauman 2003) or culturalist (McLuhan 1964) theories of media, the internet and its relationship to social life. Where the use of digital technologies and media in everyday child protection social work was discussed (e.g. Cook & Zschomler 2020), they were connected little with theoretical and empirical scholarship in fields concerned with digital media and technology. Moreover, during the COVID-19 pandemic, a particular narrative and vision relating to the use of digital technologies was revealed within the UK government which defined the use of digital technologies and media in social work practice as 'virtual' and offered the guidance that it should only be used as a last resort when face-to-face social worker home visits are impossible (Department of Education 2021). In contrast, social scientists of technology and media have abandoned the concept of the virtual, defined as, 'no longer helpful' (Hine 2015) for understanding an internet that is entangled with the everyday. Elsewhere, we argue that a revised definition of the practices of using digital media and technologies in social work – as 'digital social work' – reveals its value to the profession and the families they work with (Pink et al 2020, 2022).

We draw on our qualitative longitudinal study of the experiences of 29 social workers, 10 social work managers and 9 family support workers, all involved in child protection, from four local authority areas in England, whom we interviewed approximately every month during the pandemic between April and December 2020. Forty-one participants were women and seven men. Seven participants identified as Black and Asian Minority Ethnicity (BAME). We undertook interviews remotely by video call using WhatsApp, FaceTime, Skype, Teams and Zoom, additionally a small number of social workers' online meetings with families were video recorded. Thus, we journeyed with social workers as they wrestled with how they sensed and felt their immediate futures – in person and on screens – in the contingent conditions of the pandemic. All interviews were audio-recorded, fully transcribed and have been thematically analysed using NVivo 12 Plus. Other outcomes from this project are written to address social work and applied anthropology readerships, and we highlight this since in addition to the theoretical and empirical contribution we wish to make to the study of digital media and technology here, we are committed to having impact and to disseminating the applied dimension to our endeavours across academic disciplines rather than debating just within one.

## Contingency

Phenomenological and design anthropological (Ingold 2013, Smith & Otto 2016) theories inform an approach to digital technologies and media that attends to the ongoingly emergent nature of everyday life and the inextricability of the digital from how life is experienced and constituted. Core to this approach is an acknowledgement of the processual and ongoingly emergent status of the worlds we inhabit (Smith and Otto 2016), rooted in Ingold's insistence that we should understand ourselves as of and inhabiting an ongoingly changing environment, rather than as separate from it. Recent work in media phenomenology concerning how we live with digital technologies and media (Moores 2012, Markham 2020) and digital ethics (Lagerkvist 2020, Markham 2020) also foregrounds the everyday as a generative site.

Media phenomenologist Tim Markham questions the stance of critical scholars who suggest a sequence by which the generation of public awareness would rupture dominant discourses, to constitute a new digital ethics. Markham outlines how such critical research defines the unconsciousness of the practices through which we live and improvise with digital technologies and media negatively. Yet he argues it is in fact these very practices that generate ethics. That is, he writes, ethics 'emerge through and not in spite of one's mundane navigation of digital environments that are as compromised as they are generative' (Markham 2020: 140). Furthermore, Markham suggests that 'although the contingency of what has become the digital normal matters, raising awareness of it is unlikely to lead to the kind of decisive shift that many scholars and campaigners would like to see' (Markham 2020: 141). Instead, he locates transformation within the activities we perform in practice. This leads him to suggest focussing what he calls peoples' 'digital ethical inhabitation' and subsequently designing and regulating digital environments to acknowledge these modes of inhabitation. The media phenomenologist Amanda Lagerkvist's notion of 'co-existers' similarly acknowledges how they are 'Contingent upon limits of both knowledge and self-awareness' and 'exist within the biosphere together with other humans, machines and more-than-humans' (Lagerkvist 2020: 25).

Similar points are made in design anthropology and sociology of technology, where empirical studies and theoretical arguments have shown that awareness does not change human behaviour (Fors et al 2019), and whereby people are understood as inhabiting environments, where digital data and biological organisms alike are part of the configurations that we co-constitute (Pink & Fors 2017). This is a crucial and underpinning element of the ethics of a digital design anthropology: in knowing their worlds sensorially and being inseparable from their environments, people cannot be understood as rational actors who respond according to the demands of the one-dimensional categories through which organisations or government define them as consumers, publics or users (even when well-meaningly). Rather, as the examples below illustrate people – in this case, social workers and families – ongoingly navigate contingent circumstances.

When the pandemic started to take hold, social workers and the families they worked with were flung into lockdown. They had to rapidly adapt in a situation where traditionally the principal ways of knowing and sensing that children were safe had been through home visits, or by seeing those children at their schools. While some social workers continued to visit the children deemed to be at the highest risk in their homes, or on their doorsteps, often wearing masks, some could not, since they were themselves in an at-risk group regarding the virus. One social worker described how, at the time of her first interview with us, she was surrounded by boxes of smartphones she was preparing to send out to families, another told us how she had rapidly had to adjust her own smartphone to conceal her personal number for an emergency WhatsApp video call to a young person she was concerned about. Social workers also emphasised digital exclusion and the unpreparedness of some families:

> A lot of families struggled with video calls because of their connections so I've got loads of families who just didn't really know how to use WhatsApp very well and they were like, "Oh, okay", and then you basically had videos that were to their ear or to – and I was like, "No, you can put it to your face". And it's not that they didn't know how to use the technology; they just were unfamiliar with a social worker using that sort of way to – because a lot of these families I work with have obviously had a lot of social care input for a lot of their childhood and their adult life as well.

Social workers (and families) were effectively leaping from a familiar known practice into an uncertain and unknown mode of living, working and connecting with each other.

Child protection social work conventionally depends on the home visit through which social workers establish close relationships with families. While such closeness cannot always be achieved in conventional in-person encounters, when successful it entails what Ferguson (2011) has called 'intimate child protection practice' involving for instance empathy, touch and movement, undertaken in respectful and ethical ways. Thrown into circumstances where this was impossible, social workers sometimes found it difficult to have confidence in both their own assessments and what they were seeing on video. We discuss this further below. However, we also learned of many instances in which modes of 'digital intimacy' (Andreassen et al 2017; Dobson et al 2018) were generated through WhatsApp video calls and the use of other digital platforms. This included engaging younger children in playful activities and getting up close to the camera when communicating with babies. In video recordings of the calls between social workers and mothers that we were sent, phones were often held close to research participants' faces, and conversations – in these cases with social workers and mothers who had already established a relationship of talking via video call. Their discussions tended to focus on mothers' feelings, with the empathetic but guiding frames offered by social workers as they structured and sensed their way through conversations which sought to, for instance, boost mothers' confidence. As a social worker described one such call:

> For me she is a parent who doubts herself quite a lot or feels a sense of guilt quite a lot. So those solution focused questions kind of empower her to say that she is doing the best that she can despite the difficulties that she has been

experiencing. … because often she will say "I know sometimes I am a crap mum", … it is about empowering her… yes to think about the positives not the negatives.

In these cases, the tactility of visual and digital technologies and images as screens (Pink et al 2016, Hjorth & Richardson 2017) and in the sense of the invocation of touch through vision (Marks 2000) was evident. This, coupled with the closeness of the smartphone camera to research participants' faces and subsequent possibilities for embodied modes of empathy and for moving with others with mobile media both align with Ferguson's (2011) notion of intimate child protection practice\the emphasis on touch and movement in media phenomenology (Moores 2012, Markham 2020) and in video ethnography (Pink 2015). Indeed, as social workers discussed the progression of cases over time, it became clear how the significance of digital intimacy developed. For instance, in one case a group siblings were sent to live with their father. As the pandemic progressed, digital social work practices evolved to reveal an implicit awareness of the intimacies of the video encounter. The father, who collaborated keenly with the social worker, used WhatsApp to send holiday pictures to the social worker and proposed sending video recordings of the children to the mother (since he felt video calls would be too challenging, for the children). Additionally, the support provided by the digital intimacy and presence offered by the social worker was significant, as the social worker commented, the father had told her that 'he's always felt quite secure with me'. She reflected that

> I suppose that long term relationship has given him that security to know that even though I'm not going to be physically present for them and-and for his children virtually or on the phone or whatever I will be present for them in some, in whatever form I can be.

The practices of talking and seeing established in video calls over periods of time, were seen by social workers as differing to face-to-face meetings in a number of ways. They entailed different: levels of control for the families, who could more easily determine what was seen; frequencies of access to support for families as new routines and rhythms for calls were established; and feelings of closeness and possibilities for empathy. Significantly by working through the uncertain and contingent circumstances that emerged in the COVID-19 pandemic, social workers and families created new and evolving digital practices.

When it is apprehended theoretically, contingency can be kept in the moment and suspended in a critical argument. Conversely, when contingency is found in life itself, or in the stories people tell us about what has happened in life, it is their very movement through it, and the state of being poised to jump into the as yet unknown that we must attend to. As the examples discussed in this section highlight a sense of intimacy, reflected in the concept of digital intimacy, enabled social workers to step forward with growing confidence. This brings us to the second concept we mobilise, since when contingency is experienced in everyday life it is inseparable from anticipation.

## Anticipation

Child protection social work practice is anticipatory in the sense that social workers need to evaluate children's situations in terms of safety and risk, which are concepts that belong to established anticipatory regimes of governance and regulation (e.g. Adey & Anderson 2011). Yet social work scholarship (Ferguson 2011) has demonstrated how, in practice, safety and risk are sensed and sensory as much as being rational or quantifiable. These feelings are therefore also implicated in how workers improvised with digital technologies and media, during COVID-19 and (as we attend to in the next section) in everyday ethics and values. As Lagerkvist has emphasised, anticipation happens not only at the level of the predictive analytics associated with AI but also in the lifeworlds of people, who she terms as 'coexisters'. For Lagerkvist, 'Coexisters are thrown into the contemporary digital limit situation; deeply entangled they still possess the capacity to act and chose and respond – and anticipate – yet within limits and never in isolation'. She therefore sees 'coexisters' as able to 'collaboratively chart a (media) future in carefully attending to the present' (Lagerkvist 2020: 25). In design anthropology, the concepts of trust and anxiety have been engaged to understand the modes and feelings of anticipation involved in such situations (Pink et al 2018, Pink 2021). A design anthropological definition of trust rallies against renderings of trust as a rational, interactional or transactional encounter whereby trust would be thought to come about 'as an epiphenomenon of social knowledge: what people's relationships look like after the fact of cognitive re-appraisals' (Corsin 2011: 178). Instead design anthropologically we interpret trust phenomenologically as a feeling concerned with our relationship to the immediate future (Pedersen and Liisberg 2015: 1). Thus, 'trust is experienced when things "feel right", a sensation often achieved through the accomplishment of mundane everyday routines'. Yet trust is never static but 'a feeling of knowing that is continually emergent'. Thus 'It can be thought of as the feeling between what we know and what we think we know. It is a way of imagining-in-the-body, or a sensuous mode of anticipation' (Pink 2021b).

The generation of digital intimacies described in the previous section enabled the generation of feelings of trust for social workers in our study. However, observing how digital intimacies came about has led us to a further insight into the anticipatory modes they generate: when social workers felt they could trust in the circumstances that had framed their use of digital technologies to communicate with families, they anticipated that the children they worked with would be safe. Nevertheless, this is not to say that such circumstances always arose. In contrast to trust, anxiety is often much harder to observe or account for empirically, in that it tends to surface in moments of breakdown, or crisis, where the familiar routines and ways of knowing that give us a sense of continuity, confidence and security are disrupted. Social workers often felt anxious that they could not know or sense enough about families' and children's situations to make assessments without visiting them in person. We address this next; however, first we note that in the cases where social workers felt confident (trusting) in the situation, it appeared that these feelings were also derived from the ways in which the improvisatory steps that they had taken to establish digital intimacies had become routine, reassuring and part of the ways in which a sense of ontological security was maintained. Indeed, at an institutional level, Local Authorities developed various ways of rating cases and formally routinising digital social work. For example, as a social worker described it:

> So, our rag [red, amber, green]-rating was if it was green you can do a video call once a month, and then if it was amber you had to do a face to face visit on a monthly basis but had to do a video call on a fortnightly basis, but on red you had to visit on a fortnightly basis and then do a video call on the other one.

The significance of routines in establishing a sense of trust resonates with earlier work (Pink, Lanzeni & Horst 2018) which found participants' everyday anxieties about if they would lose their data or not were usually obscured by 'routines and activities … used to repress the feelings of anxiety around data' (Pink, Lanzeni & Horst 2018).

It is equally significant to understand the implications of situations where such routines cannot be achieved. For example, over a period of months, one social worker discussed her experiences of a complex case involving a family with three children, two of whom were disabled, deemed clinically extremely vulnerable to coronavirus and initially living with their mother. To maintain contact with this family during the pandemic when she could not enter their home, the social worker devised a mode of working that would be safe for her and keep the children safe, in part by ensuring that certain everyday health routines required to meet the children's special needs, supported by digital social work routines, that had been agreed with the mother, were kept to. This involved a combination of socially distanced doorstep visits, daily video calls and a video diary sent to her by the mother, all practices the social worker had not used pre-pandemic. These practices and materials quelled some of the social workers' anxieties, but the ways in which they were performed alerted her to anticipate risks concerning the safety of the children which corresponded to a deterioration in their health. She was unable to build the digital intimacy needed to trust that the mother was following the health routines, or to establish the digital social work routines that would support her confidence in the process. The social worker described how

> within the last couple of weeks I have sort of upped my level of erm going to the family home instead of FaceTiming because I often wasn't getting a FaceTime back until 12 o'clock so it doesn't give me a clear picture of if the morning routine is being followed.

She also found it difficult to gain the sensory and intimate knowledge needed through socially distanced doorstop calls, since due to the COVID restrictions, she was trying not to go inside the house. Weaving between digital and in-person visits in this way enabled her to feel confident in her judgement and anticipation of risk to the children, and eventually it was determined that the children should live with their father.

These experiences of trust and anxiety are set in a world in movement in two senses: in the inevitable movement forward of life in an ongoingly emergent world (Massey 2005); and in that people are 'wayfarers' in the sense that the wayfarer literally "knows as he goes"' (Ingold 2000: 229–230) 'along a line of travel' (Ingold 2007: 89). Because wayfaring involves unplanned, unpredictable and uncertain circumstances, it offers an opportunity through which to conceptualise movement and to interrogate those moments where we experience being at the cusp of the immediate future, and how and where feelings of trust or anxiety emerge or shift. It focuses in on how the contingent circumstances of life as lived become visible and the improvisatory activities that people engage to re-establish the sense of ontological certainty that centres their being. Engaging the concept of digital wayfaring thus entails acknowledging the movement, contingency and improvisation that characterise how we live with digital technologies and media. While, to date, the idea of digital wayfaring has been engaged to understand movement as it happens or has happened already (Pink & Hjorth 2014, Markham 2020), it can also imply movement forward into the uncertainty of what might happen next. Indeed wayfaring is part of the process of what will happen next, that moment where we slip over from the present to the future, or where the present slips over to the past.

The example of how moving through digital and in-person encounters enabled social workers to gain a sense of confidence and trust provides insights into the anticipatory modes of digital wayfaring. Digital wayfaring – meandering through and learning in an in-person and digital world – enabled social workers to improvise as unexpected circumstances arose, to learn new ways of knowing and of assessing and anticipating risk and safety, and thus establish a new practice where the digital and in-person were interdependent. This practice was articulated by social workers as they discussed with us how they determined the routes their practice of 'digital social work' (Pink et al 2022) would take as they navigated the relationship between face-to-face and digital encounters with families. As the examples discussed above also show the ways they wove between video calls and in-person visits were also patterned by the concerns which lead to their involvement, which themselves were underpinned by their practice and ethics.

Social workers did not always feel that video calls enabled them to judge adequately if children were safe. However, they learned to sense when to feel confident as they anticipated the next move to be made and when an in-person meeting was needed. As one social worker described how this had evolved:

Actually, I arranged the other day to do a videocall. I needed to speak to a parent, and we couldn't co-ordinate a time … So we agreed a videocall then, which is something that I would never have done before, I would have just waited until they were available. Because just because it isn't something that I've ever thought of, and actually, if it's not a visit where I'm going to assess the home conditions, or I need to see interactions between people, and it's just where, on a one to one, I needed to speak to a parent, there's no reason why it can't be a videocall, if that works for everybody. So yeah, that's, I've become more confident in doing that.

As we elaborate next, the emergence of these new practices and ways of knowing also concern ethics. Ethics likewise concerns both moving forward in the world, and how we anticipate or imagine what might happen next.

## Ethics

Ethical approach to technology design must be grounded in ethnographic appreciation of the experiential worlds, uncertainty and ethics of the everyday (Pink 2021a; Akama et al 2018). This approach aligns with the media phenomenology approach to digital ethics as only 'meaningful to the extent that it originates from the mess of daily digital life' (Markham 2020: 7), since both locate ethics as produced and enacted in the everyday.

Social workers were concerned that they needed to be able to make reliable assessments relating to the safety of the children under their protection. That is, the professional values that underpinned their work, and that were indeed sedimented in the sensory embodied practice of social work, prevailed throughout the pandemic. These values constitute an everyday embodied ethics, which guided how digital social work practice was improvised, and how and when video calls became entangled with masked home visits, doorstop visits and other variations. The anticipatory concepts of trust and anxiety are helpful, because they stand for feelings that underpinned the ethics of social work practice; put simply when social workers trusted in a situation they felt confident that they could anticipate the safety of the children in their care.

The case of digital social work therefore effectively shows us how the ethics of digital technology in everyday life is inextricable from the circumstances of its use. Child protection social work is rooted in specific professional and personal ways of knowing, feeling and sensing, and values and ethics.

The ethics of keeping children safe underpinned when and how digital technologies were used, for instance, a number of social workers insisted that in-person visits were necessary when supporting parents in addressing unsafe or unhygienic home conditions, or when establishing if those were an issue. Using video calls and other forms of digital communication as an enhancement that allowed them to 'check-in' or provide therapeutic support around relationships, mental health issues or for children in secure placements, at least some of the time, did not present such concerns. For instance, one social worker felt confident in completing work through a video call because she had seen the home in person. As she described it:

> I have already seen the home and I have already spoken to the children at home so it is not a priority at this stage for me to go into the house again so we're going to do it by Zoom.

The examples cited in earlier sections similarly show how digital social work could be effective in both supporting families and ascertaining risk in the context of the pandemic. Video calls also raised questions about safety where the inability to establish digital routines alerted the social worker to issues that required further action. For instance, several months into the pandemic, one social worker determined that she needed to enter a home with a known infection risk wearing full personal protective equipment (PPE) because she felt that relying on video calls and partial reports from other services was not safe.

Thus, the case of digital social work demonstrates how the improvisatory and anticipatory digital practices that emerged during the COVID-19 pandemic constituted an on-the-ground ethics. First, the performance of digital social work involved embodied values which constituted an ethical practice, born out of improvisatory actions, which became routinised and familiar. The anticipatory modes through which social workers experienced and enacted digital social work were sensed, in ways different to their sensory experience of the home visit, and involved feelings of trust and anxiety, which can be seen as ways of knowing about the degrees of safety and risk they felt children were in. While these sensory and embodied practices represented professional ethics, they were enacted as the ethics of a community of practice of social workers, rather than simply as the transference of a set of institutional guidelines for social work practice. Different to the anticipatory regimes of neoliberal governance which seek solutions to problems and rational procedures of risk mitigation, everyday ethics evades a solutionist paradigm. It is creative and improvisatory rather than simply procedural.

This is why the everyday ethics of digital social work does not and cannot divide COVID-19 social work practice into separate spheres of in-person and virtual social work or home visits. It is an ethics that is rooted in everyday circumstances and constituted by the embodied digital wayfaring of social workers who improvise and learn as they go. From such a perspective, digital technologies cannot serve as technological solutions to the problems faced by social work during the pandemic. They also should not be seen as simply last resort, second best or less effective, ways to connect with vulnerable families. Rather they are part of the circumstances, and as long as they are used ethically, they stand to play a key role in enabling beneficial modes of practice which are equally and differently effective to in-person home visits. Therefore, the use of new digital or emerging technologies needs to put ethics first, and this involves putting everyday life and people first.

## Digital media phenomenology as intervention

We have called for and demonstrated the value of developing theoretical-empirical dialogues that reveal how the ethics of digital technologies and media emerge through improvisatory practice in contingent circumstances. We have suggested that such a focus offers new insights into the nature of the anticipatory modes of practice and how anticipation itself is implicated in the ways that the ethics of digital technologies and media are constituted and configured in the everyday.

We have engaged with the example of how child protection social workers used digital technologies and media during the COVID-19 pandemic. Critically (in both senses of the term), our findings suggest that the UK government's rejection of the 'virtual' as a last resort practice for social workers was naïve because it refered to a pre-digital ethics that cannot happen either theoretically or in practice. We argue that an ethical approach to futures is grounded in the relationship between people and environment, and as stressed above digital technologies and media are inseparable from this environment. It is only by considering this aspect that practical ways forward for social work or any other activity can be sensibly understood and formulated.

However, our focus on ethics on the ground does not imply there is any lesser need to attend critically to the digital ethics of corporations, public institutions and regulatory bodies. For instance: many social workers, endorsed by their organisations, adopted WhatsApp for digital visits with families, a platform which at the time of writing came under public scrutiny for its changed privacy agreement, leading to a mass exodus of its users; and concerns were raised about security and encryption in relation to Zoom, a platform often used for meetings between social workers, families and other organisations involved in their cases. Questions of digital surveillance, third party uses of data, security and privacy (Andrejevic 2020) and inequalities (Madianou 2020) are not dismissed by a focus on everyday ethics. Rather, we suggest that critical studies in this field should account for how these ethical questions become reframed by everyday engagement with these media and technologies: what new ethical issues are highlighted and which recede, and how might critical interventions account for this. This is a question to be explored with critical media scholars, rather than for us to develop alone.

However, such paths cannot be forged by simply developing critique from the ivory tower, but need to be collaboratively created with key stakeholders as we step into everyday futures, and to be reflexively and critically evaluated as they progress. To this effect, our project has an extensive public and applied dissemination programme, which engages directly with social workers, local authorities and other key organisations.

## Acknowledgments

The research this chapter is based on was funded by the Economic and Social Research Council, Grant Number ES/V003798/1, as part of the project: Child

Protection and social distancing: Improving the capacity of social workers to keep children safe during the COVID-19 pandemic. We are deeply grateful to the local authorities, managers, social workers, family support workers and families for their generosity in allowing us to observe and interview them for this study.

## References

Adey, P. & B. Anderson (2011). Event and anticipation: UK Civil Contingencies and the space-times of decision. *Environment and Planning A*, 43: 2878–2899.

Akama, Y., Pink, S. & Sumartojo, S. (2018). *Uncertainty and Possibility*. Bloomsbury: London.

Andreassen, R., Nebeling Petersen, M., Harrison, K., et al. (Eds) (2017). *Mediated Intimacies: Connectivities, Relationalities and Proximities*. United Kingdom: Taylor & Francis.

Andrejevic, M. (2020). *Automated Media*. New York: Routledge.

Bauman, Z. (2003). *Liquid Love: On the Frailty of Human Bonds*. Cambridge: Polity Press.

Castells, M. (2010). *The Rise of the Network Society*. Oxford: Wiley-Blackwell.

Cook L.L. & Zschomler, D. (2020). Virtual home visits during the COVID-19 pandemic: Social workers' perspectives. Practice 32(5): 401–408.

Corsin Jimenez, A. (2011). Trust in anthropology. *Anthropological Theory* 11(2): 177–196.

Department of Education. (2021). Coronavirus (COVID-19): guidance for children's social care services. www.gov.uk/government/publications/coronavirus-covid-19-guidance-for-childrens-social-care-services/coronavirus-covid-19-guidance-for-local-authorities-on-childrens-social-care#virtual-visits---local-authorities (accessed 8 January 2021).

Dobson, A.S., Carah, N. & Robards, B. (2018). Digital intimate publics and social media: Towards theorising public lives on private platforms. In: A.S. Dobson, B. Robards & N. Carah (Eds.) *Digital Intimate Publics and Social Media*. Cham: Palgrave Macmillan. 3–27.

Ferguson, H. (2011). *Child Protection Practice*. Basingstoke: Palgrave.

Fors, V., Pink, S., Berg, M. & O'Dell, T. (2019). *Imagining Personal Data*. Oxford: Routledge.

Henman, P. (2019). Of algorithms, Apps and advice: digital social policy and service delivery. *Journal of Asian Public Policy*, 12(1): 71–89.

Hine, C. (2015). *Ethnography for the Internet: Embedded, Embodied and Everyday*. London: Bloomsbury.

Hjorth, L. & Richardson, I. (2017). Pokémon GO: Mobile media play, place-making, and the digital wayfarer. *Mobile Media & Communication*, 5(1):3–14.

Ingold, T. (2000). *The Perception of the Environment*. London: Routledge.

Ingold, T. (2007). *Lines: A Brief History*. Oxford: Routledge.

Ingold, T. (2013). *Making*. Oxford: Routledge.

Lagerkvist, A. (2020). Digital Limit Situations: Anticipatory Media Beyond 'The New AI Era'. *Journal of Digital Social Research*, 2(3), 16–41. https://doi.org/10.33621/jdsr.v2i3.55.

Madianou, M. (2020). A second-order disaster? Digital technologies during the COVID-19 pandemic. *Social Media + Society*. July-September: 1–5.

Markham, T. (2020). *Digital Life*. Cambridge: Polity.

Marks, L. U. (2000). *The Skin of the Film*. Duke University Press.

Massey, D. (2005). *For Space*. London: Sage.

McLuhan, M. (1964). *Understanding Media: The Extensions of Man*. Cambridge, MA: MIT Press.

Megele, C. & Buzzi, P. (2020). *Social Media and Social Work: Implications and Opportunities for Practice*. Bristol: Bristol University Press, Policy Press.

Moores, S. (2012). *Media, Place & Mobility*. London: Palgrave MacMillan.

Pedersen, E. O. & Liisberg, S. (2015). Introduction: Trust and hope. In E.O. Pedersen & S. Liisberg (Eds.) *Anthropology and Philosophy: dialogues on trust and hope*. Oxford: Berghan. 1–20.

Pink, S. & Hjorth, L. (2014). The digital wayfarer: Reconceptualising camera phone practices in an age of locative media. In G. Goggin & L. Hjorth (Eds.) *Routledge Mobile Media Companion*. London: Routledge. 488–498.

Pink, S. (2015). *Doing Sensory Ethnography*, second edition, London Sage.

Pink, S. (2021a). *Doing Visual Ethnography*, fourth edition. London: Sage.

Pink, S. (2021b). Sensuous futures: Re-thinking the concept of trust in design anthropology. *Senses & Society*, 6(2): 193–202.

Pink, S., & Salazar, J. F. (2020). Anthropologies and futures: Setting the agenda. In Anthropologies and futures (pp. 3–22). Routledge, London New York.

Pink, S., Lanzeni, D. & Horst, H. (2018). Data anxieties: Finding trust and hope in digital mess. *Big Data and Society*, 5(1) https://doi.org/10.1177/2053951718756685.

Pink, S., Ferguson, H., & Kelly, L. (2020). Child Protection Social Work in COVID-19: reflections on home visits and digital intimacy. *Anthropology in Action*, 27 (3 – Winter): 27–30.

Pink, S., Ferguson, H., & Kelly, L. (2022) Digital social work: Conceptualising a hybrid anticipatory practice. *Qualitative Social Work*, 21(2): 413–430.

Pink, S. & Fors, V. (2017) Being in a mediated world: self-tracking and the mind-body-environment. *Cultural Geographies*, 24(3): 375–388.

Pink, S., Fors, V. & Glöss, M. (2018). The contingent futures of the mobile present: Beyond automation as innovation. *Mobilities*, 13(5): 615–631.

Pink, S., Sinanan, J., Hjorth, L. & Horst, H. (2016). Tactile digital ethnography: researching mobile media through the hand. *Mobile Media and Communication*, 4(2): 237–251.

Richardson, I. & Hjorth, L. (2017). Mobile media, domestic play and haptic ethnography. *New Media & Society*, 19: 1653–1667.

Smith, R.C. & Otto, T. (2016). Cultures of the future: Emergence and intervention in design anthropology. In R.C. Smith, K.T. Vangkilde, M.G. Kjærsgaard, T. Otto, J. Halse & T. Binder (Eds.) *Design Anthropological Futures*. London: Bloomsbury Academic. 19–36.

# 5

# ALGORITHMIC FUTURES AND THE UNSETTLED SENSE OF CARE

*Minna Ruckenstein and Sonja Trifuljesko*

## Introduction

In April 2018, the National Non-Discrimination and Equality Tribunal prohibited a financial company, Svea Ekonomi, the use of a discriminatory statistical model in credit scoring decisions. The company was found guilty of discrimination in an event that took place in Finland almost three years earlier, in July 2015. Svea Ekonomi did not grant a loan to a Finnish man, in connection of online purchases of building materials. Having received the loan rejection, the young man, in his 30s, requested the company to justify the negative decision. The company responded that their decision required no justification, and that it was based on a credit rating made by a scoring service that relied on statistical methods.

Since the protagonist of the credit scoring case preferred to remain anonymous, we can only imagine how he felt when the credit was denied. Perhaps he was surprised at first and then experienced a deep sense of injustice, knowing that he must have been credit-worthy. He might have been angry, going through the trouble of clicking to add all the building materials needed to the shopping cart, only to discover that he had wasted his time and could not get the purchases done and continue his building project as planned. Whatever the emotional range of feelings, they triggered in him a strong enough impulse to seek a correction to the harmful decision.

The man petitioned the Non-Discrimination Ombudsman that started to investigate the case and later brought it to the Tribunal. The Ombudsman's office discovered that the credit scoring service did not inspect the credit applicant's financial situation or income, and neither was this information required on the credit application. Instead, the scoring model evaluated the applicant based on factors, such as the place of residence, gender, age and mother tongue (National Non-Discrimination and Equality Tribunal of Finland 2018). With this information, the

DOI: 10.4324/9781003084471-6

system calculated, based on population information, the percentage of groups of people with poor credit history and awarded points proportionate to how common deficient credit records are in the group in question. As men had more payment failures than women, they were awarded fewer points in the scoring model and similarly, those with Finnish as their first language received fewer points than Swedish-speaking Finns. Had the applicant been a woman, or Swedish-speaking, he would have met the company criteria for the credit. As a Finnish-speaking male, residing in the countryside, however, he earned too few points and became profiled as unworthy of credit. As we cannot ask him why he decided to appeal to the Non-Discrimination Ombudsman, we can only speculate how he knew about the possibility to appeal in the first place. He had to have some prior knowledge of how judiciary bodies function, or perhaps he had a friend or a relative who consulted him, or wrote the appeal on his behalf. In any case, the process was successful. Svea Ekonomi was imposed a conditional fine of 100,000 euros to enforce the resolution to discontinue the discriminatory practice. The decision had also wider impact, as the financial services providers had to carefully assess what the decision meant in terms of the legitimacy of scoring mechanisms in service operations.

The credit scoring case, documented for the AlgorithmWatch report (Ruckenstein and Velkova 2019), illustrates beautifully the risks of using machine-generated models in automated decision-making (ADM). We had joined the European mapping exercise of the Berlin-based NGO, AlgorithmWatch, covering debates around ADM in 12 countries (Spielkamp 2019), in an effort to get an empirically grounded view of how ADM is implemented across Europe. The mapping included national artificial intelligence (AI) strategies and civil society organizations' perspectives, paying attention to regulatory proposals and oversight institutions and mechanisms in place.

According to the definition by AlgorithmWatch (n.d.), ADM consists of algorithmic operations used to analyze the chosen dataset, to interpret the results of data analysis based on a human-defined interpretation model and to make decisions, as determined in a human-defined decision-making model. Matthias Spielkamp, the founder of AlgorithmWatch, emphasizes the dual nature of algorithmic decision-making: it not only carries enormous dangers, but also enormous promise. In order to assess algorithmic processes, the human involvement needs to be carefully considered, from multiple perspectives, emphasizing the socio-technical complexity of ADM. As Nick Seaver (2018: 378) puts it: "if the idealized algorithm is supposed to be generic, stable, and rigid, the actual algorithmic system is particular, unstable, and malleable". It is thus not merely the algorithm, narrowly defined, that has sociocultural effects, but the overall system.

Participating in the work of AlgorithmWatch gave us the opportunity to be part of the interventionist public debate concerning the uses of ADM. We were aware that the collaboration was risky in terms of customary academic practice, as it positioned us as activists rather than researchers. In light of the anthropology of futures, however, this kind of blurring of positions is a necessary move in terms of committed knowledge formation. According to the Manifesto of EASA

Futures Anthropologies Network (2014), one should not fear academic contamination: in fact, the aim is to be political and interventionist, and take responsibility for interventions. As we will argue, ADM and its profiling powers are contemporary worldmaking activities that call for anthropological engagements with the uncertain, broken, emerging and as yet unknown worlds of present, possible and desired ADM futures (Pink & Salazar 2017).

Our earlier experience of moving between the insider and outsider positions when researching the technological imaginaries of data activism, while also feeding social scientific perspectives into the debate, had prepared us for the tensions around navigating different positions (Lehtiniemi & Ruckenstein 2019). We knew that the opportunity to test and develop what we had learned and were learning would complicate our research, as we would need to reassess our findings time and again. Yet, being part of a European network of researchers and investigative journalists promised to offer tremendous support in terms of considering the impacts of ADM on individuals, communities and societies. In an attempt to take a more interventional stance in working toward recognizing and "claiming back alternative futures" (Pink & Salazar 2017: 18), we discuss in the following how our participatory work has helped us in working toward present and emerging ADM futures.

## Profiles for everybody

When we started our work with AlgorithmWatch, both social scientists and data scientists in the United States had already provided ample evidence of the darker sides of ADM, for instance, how automatic processes reinforce biases by excluding some human aspects and amplifying others. Cathy O'Neil, a former Wall Street data analyst, demonstrates in *Weapons of Math Destruction* (2016) how ADM excludes and punishes underprivileged individuals and communities by identifying them as potential police targets, restricting their access to financial and health services, and reinforcing racial biases of the penal system. She describes current scoring mechanisms as a threat to democracy, if not implemented in a manner that carefully considers questions of justice. Virginia Eubanks (2018) provides an analysis of how ADM reinforces inequalities and intensifies the marginalization of the poor, who face automated scoring mechanisms when they try to access public services. In one of the examined cases, Eubanks shows how homeless people in Los Angeles speculate about the handling of information about their health and life, when they fail to get housing after years of waiting. Paradoxically, even a homeless person, living in a tent, can get a too low vulnerability score. In order to become classified in need of housing, one should also be *sufficiently* abused and suffer from mental health problems to qualify for the machinic classifications.

The Finnish credit scoring case is yet another example of harmful decision-making that underlines the fact that when assessing individual cases, we are talking about a larger trend, whereby automation processes are spreading from manufacturing products and services to making important decisions about people's lives. As the credit scoring case demonstrates, the assessments made, on the basis of a statistical model, can significantly differ from the characteristics of the individual credit applicant. ADM does not revolve around who people are, or what their data says about what matters to them, but on what can be inferred about how they are likely to behave. This process has been analyzed by a political geographer Louise Amoore (2011) in her study of border security practices. Amoore proposed the analytic of the "data derivative", to express that the algorithmic decisions are based on an amalgam of qualities disaggregated from lived social processes, correlated in a manner that is indifferent to their specificities and used to project onto futures.

The Finnish credit scoring case demonstrates the logic of data-driven processes in a manner that is particularly effective in terms of public debate. The discriminated individual is not a non-citizen, attempting to cross national borders, nor a member of a minority group. The credit applicant is not even a woman, more likely a target of discrimination, but what otherwise would be a credit-worthy man. As such, the credit scoring failure reminds us that *anybody* can be scored, profiled and grouped in a discriminatory manner.

The credit scoring model used by Svea Ekonomi is technically low level and its discriminatory powers are fairly easy to uncover. Yet, what it has in common with the more sophisticated ADM infrastructures is the goal of profiling people. These profiles claim to know us, even if they might contain factual errors, or they would argue against our values, or aims. The discrepancies between the machinic classification and everyday aims are often suffered in silence; the machine is merely seen to be out of sync. The credit scoring case, however, underlines that discordant machines can have discriminatory real-life outcomes that urge us to take the classificatory work conducted by machines seriously.

## Falling apart and repaired

In midst of grim assessments of how digital technologies are steadily becoming more invasive and discriminatory, the Finnish credit scoring ban is an exception, as it offers an inspiring counter example of how algorithmic decision-making powers can be challenged. The decision by the Finnish ombudsman's office was received with great interest among the European equality bodies, as it offered a reference case to potential future cases. The wrongly profiled young man that was "not seen right" by the machine became seen by the juridical system, to the degree that his involvement accentuated both citizens' and ombudsman's role in resourcefully using existing legal and political tools to combat automation biases.

The credit scoring case and its aftermaths speaks of the power of intervention and the need to get our hands dirty in order to discontinue discriminatory practices. The human confrontations and interventions in midst of technology developments emphasize that we should avoid techno-determinism at all costs. Even if technology developments appear to progress autonomously, in a stable and linear manner, algorithmic arrangements unfold multiple potential and actual futures, characterized by non-linear, recurring, unanticipated and unlikely human-machine associations.

Steven Jackson, an STS scholar, advances "broken world thinking" that promotes the aim of the anthropology of futures to absorb complexity and engage with differences and uncertainties (Jackson 2014: 221–222). Broken world thinking challenges normalized views about technology and innovation as linear and progressive and gestures toward the multisensory and material dimensions of co-habiting with technologies. Jackson argues for acknowledging efforts made to maintain stability: the constant work, repair, restoration, resilience and creativity that characterize technological developments. From this perspective, a world of conflicting aims emerges, an "always-almost-falling-apart world" that reminds us of the limits and fragility of the world, while recognizing ongoing activities through which stability is restored.

ADM is a product of a world of breakdowns and dissolutions, in a constant process of fixing and reinvention, reconfiguring and reassembling into new combinations. Many of the ADM cases documented for the AlgorithmWatch report have transformed over time, underlining how worldmaking by means of ADM is characterized by modifications and reconfigurations. The credit scoring controversy did not end the practice, but the scoring service could only become re-implemented after the statistical model was repaired.

The perspective of work and repair accentuate the importance of long-term documentation. A lengthier timeframe reveals the technological and conceptual fixing of ADM processes, their reinvention and discontinuation. A way for anthropologists of futures to further engage with the shifting ADM processes is offered by another STS scholar, María Puig de la Bellacasa (2011; 2017), who has outlined the concept of care as speculative ethics necessary for thinking and living in interdependent worlds of humans, algorithms and other species. Puig de la Bellacasa builds on Bruno Latour's (2004; 2005) "matters of concern" to de-objectify matters of fact by transforming them into gatherings around common concerns, which give them political voice and respectful position in the democratic assembly. She then contrasts matters of concern with "matters of care" to problematize the neglect of caring relationalities in the Latourian approach. With its focus on relationalities and neglected concerns, Puig de la Bellacasa's matters of care offer a fruitful approach to think about ADM in the always-almost falling apart-world. The commitment to neglected aspects of ADM in the current debate calls for recognizing socio-technical aspects of human-technology relations and engaging with their becoming, as they unfold.

Drawing on a rich feminist tradition, Puig de la Bellacasa (2011; 2017) rejects conceptualizations of care as a pleasant affection or a stable moralistic stance, but rather defines it as intrinsic to the fabric of the every day. Care consists of three dimensions, the practical, the ethico-political and the affective, which cover the concrete labors of the daily maintenance of life, the ethico-political commitment to concerns that are otherwise not seen, or attended to, and the inclusion of affective engagements in the representation of things. These three dimensions of care are not always equally present in relational situations, and occasionally challenge each other, exposing care's ambivalent character and its disruptive potential for knowledge-making. How to think with this unsettled sense of care becomes one of the central questions for Puig de la Bellacasa, which also frames our engagement with AlgorithmWatch and the Finnish ADM cases presented in the report.

## Toward not-knowing

The most controversial Finnish case in the AlgorithmWatch report features a company called Digital Minds, founded by two Finnish psychologists, aiming to develop "third-generation" assessment technology for employee recruitment. In this case, the ADM builds on the longer history of personality assessment technologies that have been used since the 1940s in job recruitment. At first, the prospective job candidates filled in paper-based evaluation sheets to have their personality traits assessed. Since the 1990s, such tests have become digital. With their new service, Digital Minds promised to make the personality assessment process faster and more reliable by analyzing the entire corpus of individuals' social media posts (Twitter and Facebook) and email correspondence (Gmail and Microsoft Office 365). By law, the company is required to ask the prospective job candidates for an informed consent to get access to their social media profiles and email accounts in order to perform the personality test. After that the candidate provides the company with access information.

The Digital Minds case raised controversy immediately after the report was published. The idea of sharing social media posts with the future employer was unsettling in many ways. Matthias Spielkamp and Nicolas Kayser-Bril (2019), a data journalist, wrote a continuation story for the Politico, underlining the need for critical reflection:

> A Finnish company has rolled out a new product that lets potential employers scan the private emails of job applicants to determine whether or not they would be a good fit for the organization. The company, Digital Minds, portrays its offering as something innocuous. If applicants give their consent, what's the harm? The truth is: We don't know the answer to that question. And that's what makes new, potentially intrusive and discriminatory technologies like this one so scary.

After the piece was published, we discussed its subject matter with Juho Toivola, one of the two founders of Digital Minds. With this move, the goal was to sustain the conversation by deploying a dialogical approach. It would have been easy to join the moral front, to conclude that Digital Minds was violating deeply held values of privacy and personal autonomy, and end the discussion. However, that would go against the effort to "think with care", which, as Puig de la Bellacasa (2017: 79) reminds us, cultivates "relatedness in diverseness". Seeking to maintain the conversation, while forming collective and accountable knowledge, suggests that one should not "negate dissent or the impurity of coalitions" (Puig de la Bellacasa 2017: 79). The lack of fear with regards to contamination of knowledge is in line with the ideal of the anthropology of futures to actively avoid moral and ethical comfort zones. Instead, fieldwork encounters are used as conversation openers and for sensitizing oneself to attunements – not merely following what is said, and done in the interactions, but also what the interactions evoke in one another. When studying ADM, it is particularly important to listen to the service developers and observe how they express themselves. The development of technologies tends to outpace academic research and in seeking more robust knowledge about the fundamental issues at the heart of the societal debate on algorithms and AI, company representatives offer important – even if anxiety-provoking – insights.

For Toivola, the piece in Politico was a "German take on the matter", reflecting a need to have a precedent in the fight against algorithmic powers. His suspicion got further confirmation when Nicolas Kayser-Bril reported Digital Minds to the Finnish data protection ombudsman to get an assessment of the harms of the personality assessment service and its legality in relation to the newly implemented European Union General Data Protection Regulation (GDPR), which came into force in May 2018. Toivola pointed out that in Europe, we operate inside "a GDPR bubble", while the rest of the world is busy developing psychometric services for work and recruitment contexts, with very few regulations in place. He did not see particular value in being more ethical than others, if it meant that European citizens merely end up using services developed in the non-GDPR zones of the world.

From Toivola's perspective, the critique of their service failed to appreciate the problem they were trying to solve: the goal was to make the employee assessment more convenient by enabling the utilization of existing data, rather than collecting all data separately with each recruitment. Developers of digital services, Toivola among them, tend to organize ADM futures as industrial horizons of efficiency and optimization. As the distinctive aim of automation is increased productivity, ADM upholds teleologies of modernity and capitalism. In the hiring context, the main aim is to offer support for the recruitment process, as promptly as possible. Toivola describes how personality profiles are typically made independently, each time a person applies for a job, with an online test lasting up to a half an hour. Digital Minds automates this process, based on data that is already out there, stored in clouds and on servers. The company did not develop their own technology, but the personality analysis was conducted with the aid of IBM's Watson, a widely used personality test across the globe. The analysis focuses, for instance, on how active people are online and how they react to posts or emails. Five different traits are analyzed about personality, such as agreeableness, or how extrovert or outward-looking a person is. When asked whether Toivola thought that IBM Watson offered a reliable personality assessment, he thought that the question was beside the point. He explained that employee assessments were not meant to be objective, but performative. Assessments offer support for making decisions that are not neutral in terms of the characteristics of the job applicant, but seek an optimal fit for the company.

With their aim of optimizing current infrastructures, digital service developers are confident about the aims and futures of ADM: their world is stabilized with products and services that align with the forward-looking goals of innovation and profit-making. The aim is to perform necessary tasks faster and add efficiency to infrastructural processes. In contrast, the work by AlgorithmWatch asks us to rehearse an anticipatory mode of inquiry and to let go of such confidence. Anticipatory orientation sees uncertainties ahead, since, as Spielkamp and Kayser-Bril point out, we do not know the possible harms of ADM uses.

The realm of uncertainties and not-knowing is where the anthropology of futures is comfortable operating. As Sarah Pink and Juan Salazar (2017: 16) describe: "The types of futures expertise that ethnographic not knowing can generate are distinctly anthropological". As experts of uncertain and unknown territories of ADM, anthropologists can ask what we miss, if we think that ADM is business as usual. In order to find out what is not known, we need to consciously remove ourselves from the expert position, listen to what others know, or do not know, and ask questions that nobody else dares to ask. We need to dwell in the always-almost-falling-apart world of breakages, failures and repair in order to engage in a speculative endeavor, that thinking with care assumes (Puig de la Bellacasa 2017: 16). The speculative approach is processual and open-ended, interested in how things, for instance cars and mobile phones (Pink et al 2018), do not remain separate and separable, but leak into each other and create circumstances of contingency. In the context of Digital Minds, the wider contextual aspects of everyday lives leak into job applicants' email conversations: the correspondence might reflect everyday care duties, relations with children, spouses or elderly parents, as much as the applicants' readiness to offer a good fit for the company. The speculative endeavor recognizes a digital presence that escapes straightforward notions of efficiency, or innovation, and seeks comfort in balancing everyday aims and duties.

## Fostering care

After the publication of the AlgorithmWatch report, we used the mapped cases of the report for exploring how ADM futures are imagined and experienced. In Spring 2019, together with a colleague, Linda Turunen, we arranged three workshops with journalists and students. Altogether, around 30 people participated in the workshops. Collaborative approaches, such as participatory workshops, foster a politics of listening, attend to questions people have and magine and articulate better futures. The move toward an engaged and collaborative approach aligned with our endeavor to think with care. Prior to our meeting, we asked the participants to choose one of the cases of the report, preferably one that raises most pressing ethical questions in terms of ADM futures. The goal was to start with a critical cut. Yet, critical cuts were not merely intended to raise concerns or trigger conflict, but were thought of as a starting point for more caring relations (Puig de la Bellacasa 2017: 62).

Some of the workshop participants were actively following developments around ADM. Others had less experience of thinking critically, or anticipating futures with digital technologies, and they had to shift their perspective. Relations between people and technologies tend to become naturalized: digital technologies are like household appliances, everyday necessities. ADM becomes activated with everyday doings, when people purchase goods and services online, take part in customer loyalty programs, use online search engines, click advertisements and track their steps with pedometers. These activations, however, remain out of sight. The goal of the workshops was to sensitize the participants to the idea of not letting technologies sink into the background. In order to explore the impacts they have on worldmaking, we need to think about the infrastructures and relationalities that digital technologies establish.

In light of broken world thinking, with an emphasis on care, working against the invisibility of technology-relations is the first step in the process of knowing and imagining alternative futures. The second step is to uncover the efforts of stability-maintenance in the always-almost-falling-apart world. In order to care about the work that machines do in the everyday, it is crucial to pay attention to how ADM "feels right." Affective suitability is an important stabilizing force of the digital world, normalizing forms of automation, as they become indistinguishable from the fabric of everyday life (Pink et al 2018). The affective suitability also emphasizes the importance of caring for its emotional opposites – when ADM feels wrong, or bad. The infrastructural misalignments and failures trigger confusion, irritation, and anger – negative reactions that stress the limitations of current technologies. Even if technologies promise convenience and relevance, we often get failures: dead batteries, frozen screens, sudden disconnects, and misinformation. In terms of ADM arrangements, failures involve missing and biased data, sloppy coding, badly thought out classifications, irrelevant recommendations, key words that are completely off target. A more comprehensive failure is an ADM service that nobody needs, or wants.

In all our workshops, Digital Minds raised the most negative reactions, as participants discussed privacy violations and access to intimate data. Yet, they also questioned how exactly ADM becomes a part of decision-making that has real-life effects (Table 5.1). The participants of the workshop were interested in who defines the criteria for the machine, and whether the algorithm favors extroverts rather than introverts. They cared about the consequences of ADM for their everyday lives and future interactions as citizens, and raised the question of human responsibility in relation to ADM: they asked whether a company that uses an automated personality assessment service as part of the hiring process outsources its responsibility over the recruitment process to the algorithm. In terms of thinking with care, this question was spot on. Similarly to other companies that offer hiring services, Digital Minds waives the decision-making responsibility by suggesting that they do not make actual hiring decisions, but they automate the process of assessment based on which decisions are made. By doing so, hiring services refuse to care about the relations that they assist in forming.

Finally, some workshop participants used the Digital Minds service as a probe through which to imagine a more caring arrangement: they suggested that the company could assist jobseekers rather than potential employers. Digital Minds

Does a company that uses artificial intelligence outsource its own responsibility over the recruitment process to the algorithm?

Does our history determine our future?

Digital Minds

Does the algorithm favor extroverts rather than introverts?

Who defines the criteria for the machine?

Can I see and govern my own data?

Can AI-driven analysis be trusted?

**FIGURE 5.1** Questions asked by the workshop participants

could teach jobseekers how current profiling services collect data, and are used for evaluating them. In the process, the job applicant would become empowered to take charge of the technical aids used in the process. The workshop was, thus, successful in promoting committed knowledge as a form of care, since it did not merely cause further concern about ADM futures, but brought to the fore how to foster more caring relations with the aid of ADM.

## Aftermath

After our workshops, in May 2019, the Finland's national public service broadcasting company (YLE) wrote a piece about the ongoing process of Digital Minds with the data protection ombudsman, suggesting that the company offers a service that is legally problematic. The ombudsman, Reijo Aarnio, commented to YLE that he suspected that the personality assessment by means of email correspondence violates the Labor Privacy Act that states that the information must be collected from the jobseeker. Aarnio questioned the validity of the jobseeker's consent when asked for permission to analyze emails. If the candidate is in a vulnerable position and needs the job, she might not be in a position to decline access to their data. Moreover, emails are covered by the letter secrecy.

Remarkably, however, the news piece revealed that less than ten jobseekers had participated in Digital Mind's analysis of their social media posts, and only one had agreed to participate in the analysis of the email correspondence. Not a single personality assessment had been conducted in a hiring context. The fact that the company had very few actual clients gave a new twist to the debate concerning Digital

Minds. Toivola explained that he was talking about "a proof of concept", rather than an actual service. Either intentionally or unintentionally, he had been collapsing contexts: founders of Digital Minds had experience of dozens of clients and they had been involved in thousands of assessments of job applicants. These assessments, however, had mostly been done by means of conventional analysis methods within the recruitment context. After the news piece, Toivola actively participated in social media discussions around their service, bringing to the fore their aims. Shortly after that, however, the service was discontinued. According to Toivola, Digital Minds was rethinking how to position their future offerings in an ethically more robust manner.

When an entrepreneur talks about a proof of concept, as if it were already an actual service out there, they operate in an anticipatory mode, trying to create actual worlds with imaginary projections. Anna Tsing (2000: 118) describes imaginaries of financial capitalism with the "economy of appearances" that necessitate that "the profit must be imagined before it can be extracted". Similarly to the ADM futures, financial futures are enmeshed with predicted sales. A proof of concept is a worldmaking device that gestures toward desired outcomes. When the goal of companies is to sell their services, they alter the details and exaggerate predicted results in support of marketing claims.

The details about ADM systems – which are often laborious to uncover – contain the most important information when it comes to successes or failures. This means that the work of an anthropologist can start to resemble that of a criminal investigator. All details need to be verified several times, as the company representatives might not only alter the details, but also hide them, or lie about them. Thinking with care in such circumstances, then, can take a form of petty fact checking. The tedious work pays off, however, when the details open further conversations and attunements. In order to create more robust knowledge about ADM futures, company representatives need to be part of the dialog. That dialog can only be nurtured in a culture that values openness: ideally, developers of ADM systems need to feel that they are not attacked, but participants in an ongoing societal debate. Pairing fact checking with careful listening requires various kinds of balancing acts, suggesting that anthropologists of futures need a reflexive approach to facts and fictions, truths and lies. This means, for instance, not getting stuck to lies, but exploring their productive powers in terms of projecting desired futures.

## Conclusions

In this chapter, we have offered broken world thinking, strengthened with the unsettled sense of care, as a move forward in the ADM debate that raises concerns about biases and discriminatory qualities of technologies. Social scientific research tends to focus on the negative and marginalizing forces associated with ADM. The more serious or troubling real-life consequences machinic classifications have in terms of biases and failures, the more they need societal uncovering and contesting. We do not deny the worrying qualities of ADM technologies, but we should still avoid generalizing ADM futures based on individual cases, or political developments. Discriminatory futures are not the only possible futures with ADM. In fact, as we have tried to show, we might not even know what ADM futures are.

In the course of our work, we have seen how civil servants are becoming active and energized in steering technology-related developments. In Finland, the non-discrimination ombudsman's office is an engaged participant in ongoing discussions concerning algorithmic systems, underlining in its communications that automation by itself is not a problem, but it needs to be implemented with an understanding of its limitations and consequences. Likewise, the workshops we held covered issues around ADM uses with the goal of helping to craft anticipatory futures that do not deny the value of digital technologies in future-making, but act imaginatively with and within them to develop conceptual framings and collaborations in order to better see and steer them.

We have argued that seeing alternative and other possible futures requires a clearly defined shift in perspective. ADM debate needs to let go of the techno-centricity that treats ADM as a stand-alone product, innovation, or a solution to existing infrastructural inefficiencies and gaps. Instead, ADM is a complex socio-technical system that develops over time and needs ongoing stabilization of human-technology relations. As such, ADM should be seen as a world-creating media that can support sustainable and habitable everyday conditions. We should nurture the qualities of ADM as technologies that can assist in planning and operating a better society, rather than using it for assessing and evaluating qualities of individual credit applicants or jobseekers. In order to move forward, we need to arm ourselves with thinking with care, commit to concerns that are currently neglected, bridge things that do not bridge. We need to keep talking to people, whose ideas and worldviews unsettle and do not align with ours. In order for the ADM debate to open possibilities for better and renewed infrastructures, technologies need to be repositioned as enablers, not as solutions. For this task, we need anthropology of futures.

As the two cases presented in this chapter show, broken world thinking with care is a speculative endeavor that "stays with the trouble", as the Harawayan trope goes (Haraway 2016). It challenges current views by highlighting the "invisible" dynamics, processes and power in our complex socio-technical systems by highlighting breakages, maintenance and repair. Our relations with technology are not only functional but also moral relations. ADM melds with other things. Ultimately, the organizational environment and the divisions on labor that socio-technically arrange ADM systems determine whether uses of automation are just and ethically robust. Machines fail to care about real-life consequences and ADM systems should take this into account.

## Acknowledgements

Research for this chapter has been conducted in the Algorithm culture project funded by the Kone Foundation.

## References

AlgorithmWatch (n.d.), 'What we do', AlgorithmWatch. Available online: https://algorithmwatch.org/en/what-we-do/ (accessed 23 October 2020).

Amoore, L. (2011), "Data derivatives: on the emergence of a security risk calculus for our times", *Theory, Culture & Society*, 28 (6): 24–43, doi: https://doi.org/10.1177/026327641 1417430

EASA Futures Anthropologies Network (2014), "Our manifesto". *Futures Anthropologies Network*, October 17. Available online: https://futureanthropologies.net/2014/10/17/our-manifesto/ (accessed 23 October 2020).

Eubanks, V. (2018), *Automating Inequality: How High-Tech Tools Profile, Police, and Punish the Poor*. New York: St. Martin's Press.

Haraway, D. J. (2016), *Staying with the Trouble: Making Kin in the Chthulucene*. Durham-London: Duke University Press.

Jackson, S. (2014), "Rethinking Repair", in T. Gillespie, P. J. Boczkowski and K. A. Foot (eds), *Media Technologies: Essays on Communication, Materiality, and Society*, 221–239, Cambridge-London: The MIT Press.

Latour, B. (2004), "Why has critique run out of steam? From matters of fact to matters of concern", *Critical Inquiry*, 30 (2): 225–248. doi: https://doi.org/10.1086/421123

Latour, B. (2005), *Reassembling the Social: An Introduction to Actor-Network Theory*. New York: Oxford University Press.

Lehtiniemi, T. and M. Ruckenstein (2019), "The social imaginaries of data activism", *Big Data & Society*, 6 (1): 1–12. doi: https://doi.org/10.1177/2053951718821146

National Non-Discrimination and Equality Tribunal of Finland (2018), "Assessment of creditworthiness, authority, direct multiple discrimination, gender, language, age, place of residence, financial reasons, conditional fine", National Non-Discrimination and Equality Tribunal of Finland, March 21. Available online: www.yvtltk.fi/material/attachments/ytaltk/tapausselosteet/45LI2c6dD/YVTltk-tapausseloste-_21.3.2018-luotto-moniperus teinen_syrjinta-S-en_2.pdf (accessed 23 October 2020).

O'Neil, C. (2016), *Weapons of Math Destruction: How Big Data Increases Inequality and Threatens Democracy*. New York: Broadway Books.

Pink, S. and J. F. Salazar (2017), "Anthropologies and Futures: Setting the Agenda", in J. F. Salazar et al. (eds), *Anthropologies and Futures: Researching Emerging and Uncertain Worlds*, 3–22, London: Bloomsbury Academic.

Pink, S., V. Fors, and M. Glöss (2018), "The contingent futures of the mobile present: automation as possibility". *Mobilities*, 13 (5): 615–631. doi: https://doi.org/10.1080/17450 101.2018.1436672

Puig de la Bellacasa, M. (2011), "Matters of care in technoscience: assembling neglected things", *Social Studies of Science*, 41 (1): 85–106. doi: https://doi.org/10.1177/030631271 0380301

Puig de la Bellacasa, M. (2017), *Matters of Care: Speculative Ethics in More Than Human Worlds*. Minneapolis-London: University of Minnesota Press.

Ruckenstein, M. and J. Velkova (2019), "Finland", in M. Spielkamp (ed), *Automating Society. Taking Stock of Automated Decision-Making in the* EU, 56–64, Berlin: AW AlgorithmWatch gGmbH.

Seaver, N. (2018), "What should an anthropology of algorithms do?" *Cultural Anthropology*, 33 (3): 375–385. doi: https://doi.org/10.14506/ca33.3.04

Spielkamp, M. (2019), *Automating Society. Taking Stock of Automated Decision-Making in the EU.* Berlin: AW AlgorithmWatch gGmbH.

Spielkamp, M. and N. Kayser-Bril (2019), "Resist the robot takeover", *Politico*, February 12. Available online: www.politico.eu/article/resist-robot-takeover-artificial-intelligence-digital-minds-email-tool/ (accessed 23 October 2020).

Tsing, A. (2000), "Inside the economy of appearances", *Public Culture*, 12 (1): 115–144. doi: https://doi.org/10.1215/08992363-12-1-115

# 6

# ORGANISING ARTIFICIAL INTELLIGENCE AND REPRESENTING WORK

*Bastian Jørgensen, Christopher Gad and Brit Ross Winthereik*

## Introduction

The allure of advanced techniques for data analytics pervades contemporary imaginaries. As such Artificial Intelligence (AI) has been recognised as a globally important topic in reports published by the European Commission and Organisation for Economic Co-operation and Development (OECD). According to these reports, AI already influences the daily affairs of European member states and their citizens, and they pose that the total global spending on AI will only increase in the years to come.

The Danish government has advocated that the country should aim to become a frontrunner in AI through an ethical and responsible perspective on algorithms (Danish Government 2019). This ambition shows how AI has become a site for contestation over how it is developed, implemented and used. Controversies around algorithms that have led to responses like the report by the Danish government are rooted in calls for recognising embedded authoritarian tendencies, and it has been argued that AI tends to obfuscate decision-making processes with dire consequences for people's lives (Danaher 2016; Pasquale 2015; Zuboff 2019). Both proponents and critics seem to agree that advanced techniques for data analytics are already pervasive in society and carry the potential to radically change organisations and societies. For both camps, the question is not whether or how AI works, but how to recognise the potentials/dangers of emerging technologies.

This is where anthropology can step in, because what if the problem is not about what kind of AI to develop (authoritarian or ethical)? What if the problem is something entirely different and concerns whether or how we invest in the people and the work practices that are to 'receive' AI?

In response to the growing advocacy for using advanced analytics, researchers have called for ethnographic studies of the use of algorithms and data (Iliadis and

DOI: 10.4324/9781003084471-7

Russo 2016; Kitchin 2017; Seaver 2017). Hitherto, much critical scholarship has namely focused on strategies and behind-the-scenes analyses of big tech companies such as Amazon, Google and Facebook (Pasquale 2015; Zuboff 2019), or on new forms of making business in organisations established 'after the internet' (Seaver 2018; Geiger 2017). Less attention has been paid to mundane practices around the development and use of AI, and even fewer studies focus on AI in the public sector (for a notable exception see Reutter and Spilker 2019).

This paper analyses a recent attempt to develop and implement advanced analytics in the Danish Tax and Customs Administration (Danish: 'SKAT'). The paper builds on scholarship within anthropological studies of technology (Suchman 1987, 1995, 2000, 2007; Seaver 2017, 2018; Forsythe 1993a, 1993b), Science and Technology Studies (STS) (Berg 1997; Star 1995; Star and Strauss 1999; Zuboff 2019) and work broadly conceived as critical data studies (Rieder and Simon 2016; Selbst and Barocas 2018; Iliadis and Russo 2016). It shows how the development of a new machine learning algorithm happened in conversation with already existing infrastructures and divisions of work (Karasti et. al. 2016: 7) and argues that while algorithms depend on existing forms of organisation, we should also make sure to attend to the arrival of new categories. One example of such a new category, which our analysis emphasises, is *data work*.

The empirical material on which the analysis rests is generated in The Risk Score Project in the Danish Tax and Customs Administration. The aim of this project was to develop a machine learning algorithm to assist the conduct of customs inspection. The hope was that the unit in charge of the project could use AI to develop a more efficient method for identifying packages imported to Denmark that might not have been taxed properly and then mark those packages for further inspection. In the chapter, we will draw attention to how the development of a machine learning algorithm is based on separating what we refer to as *data work* from the other forms of work that the algorithms are imagined to support. The aim of the chapter is twofold. On the one hand, it is to show what can happen when organisational contexts and their forms of contestation are disregarded in the development of digital technologies. On the other hand, we wish to question the widespread idea that advanced analytics constitute an unquestionable improvement of existing forms of work, even the forms of work classified as 'routine work' (Suchman 2000).

## Towards a data-driven tax administration

In recent years, the Danish Tax and Customs Administration has invested heavily in building its expertise and capacity for developing advanced analytics. In 2014, the tax administration established a new office which was referred to as the 'Centre of Excellence for Advanced Analytics and Machine Learning'. By 2018, the office had engaged 35 full-time employees including 27 data scientists. This development overlaps with the tax administration as a whole undergoing a significant reorganisation process. In 2018, the Danish Government split the tax administration into seven independent agencies and made those agencies responsible for managing different areas of expertise. One of the new agencies was named the IT and Development Agency. With HQs in the Copenhagen Capital Region and about 1000 employees across approximately 70 offices nationwide,[1] this agency became the 3rd largest of the 7 new agencies. This development reflects the current political and managerial belief in the importance of investing in and developing the *internal* IT capacities of the State, as expressed in a government report which introduced the newly organised tax administration: 'New organizing, more employees, and *IT that works*' (The Ministry of Taxation 2016, our emphasis).

The organisational changes were in line with technologically optimistic ideas expressed by the OECD's Forum on Tax Administration (FTA) (OECD 2019). In a series of reports called 'Tax Administrations of the Future Series' the OECD urges tax administrations to stimulate the development of 'a data-driven culture' (OECD 2016a; OECD 2016b; OECD 2016c). The report 'Technologies for Better Tax Administration' states:

> Bringing a data-driven culture into a tax administration implies developing a culture in which data and analysis drive all aspects of the organization. This is a journey, not a destination. It will continue as new technologies emerge; digital disruption creates even greater innovation and customer expectations change.
>
> *OECD 2016c: 58*

This statement combines technological determinism (data as the driver) with a processual outlook (an imagery of the future where the only stable element seems to be continuous emergence of new technologies). The vision is clear: Tax administrations must continually transform themselves in order to stay relevant in the 21st century. In the report 'Advanced Analytics for Better Tax Administration – Putting Data to Work', attention is directed towards how tax administration can 'extract value from data using advanced analytics' (OECD 2016a: 3). The report uses a cross-national survey to show that the primary use of advanced analytics is related to inform case selection, achieve tax compliance and manage taxpayers' debts (OECD 2016a: 27). As the report states, it 'makes no assessment of the relevant capability of administrations working in these areas; it seeks only to identify where work is being carried out' rather than discussing specific technologies, implementation strategies or challenges. The report animates a mapping of where work that could be supplemented or replaced by AI is happening; European tax administrations have many areas where AI could potentially play a role.

In what follows, we analyse some of the concrete outcomes of these imaginaries in the Danish Tax and Customs Administration.

## Fieldwork

In February 2017, shortly after the first author, Jørgensen commenced his fieldwork in the office for advanced analytics and machine learning, a manager introduced

The Risk Score Project. The goal of the project was to develop a new method for determining risk scores, which assist the customs department in detecting tax and VAT fraud for packages imported to Denmark. Jørgensen and the manager agreed that he would be allowed to follow the development of the new risk score model based on machine learning principles. Soon after, however, the future of the project became uncertain, when a newly appointed manager explained that he had been employed to close down the project. Jørgensen was advised to study 'something else'. He followed this advice but remained in contact with the participants in and around developing algorithms for risk scoring. This was possible because, even though The Risk Score Project was terminated, the data scientists kept working to deliver an algorithm, which could be tested on the custom officers' inspection of packages.

Empirically, the present chapter draws on observations, interviews, document studies and email conversations with the data scientists and their collaborators in developing and testing the algorithm for use in inspection. This empirical material was generated from February 2017 to July 2018.

## Theoretical-analytical resources for situating AI

The belief that AI has the potential to improve private and public organisations is not unprecedented. As M.C. Elish and danah boyd notes, a similar enthusiasm characterising discussions around AI in the 1980s and 1990s. In this period, a strong interest in AI, in the form of expert systems, spread from universities to commercial settings (Elish and Boyd 2018: 4). If we look back at some of the research that happened in the 1980s, we find computer scientists who were developing systems that intended to imitate human experts. Expert systems, as they were called, were widely imagined to be capable of replacing crucial elements of an expert's work, and the computer scientists were tasked with explicating the rules and facts that experts would supposedly follow in their daily work. 'Facts' were stored in databases often referred to as 'the knowledge base', whereas rules for how experts would apply facts were used as the foundations for an 'inference mechanism'. By embedding facts and rules in code, expert systems were imagined to, for example, be able to provide relevant information to help doctors diagnosing patients.

Assisting doctors in diagnosing patients was one of the most popular cases for research and development of expert systems. An important assumption at stake was that automating certain parts of the doctors' work would relieve them of time-consuming routine tasks and 'rationalize' their work by eliminating personal idiosyncrasies in doctors' work practices (Berg 1997).

Since experts carry out many tasks that cannot be reduced to rules or formulae without a significant loss of meaning, it was soon discovered that expert systems would never be able to replace absolutely crucial parts of expert work. And so, expert systems never really made it into the thick of clinical work practices. One of the reasons that was pointed out was the problem of idealisation of work and the necessity of disregarding social and organisational contexts (Collins 1987; see also Collins 2018).

As an anthropologist working in the tech industry of 'the Valley', Lucy Suchman proposed instead to focus on how facts and rules would emerge as part of situated action (Suchman 1987). Through a landmark study of some of the world's brightest computer scientists failing to operate a 'smart' photo copier, her PhD dissertation argues that not only is intelligent action an emergent phenomenon, but expertise must also be understood in relation to the material and social circumstances, in which experts act (ibid.: 70). Intelligence depends on contextual resources available, but as such resources cannot be easily formalised, they remain invisible (see also Star and Strauss 1999). Suchman ultimately warned against operating with a narrow view of intelligence as symbol manipulation, and not to assume similarity between humans' activity and machine operations when developing automated systems (Suchman 2007: 37, see also Broussard 2018).

Fast forward to today where AI seems to have shifted from being concerned with expert systems to being concerned with machine learning. Research describes this as a shift from a *rule-based logic* to a *machine learning-based logic* (de Vries 2013); from a *top-down approach* to a *bottom-up approach* (Dourish 2016: 7); and from *symbolic representation of human knowledge and procedural logic* to the *crunching of vast amounts of data, detecting patterns and producing probabilistic results* (Elish and Boyd 2018). The shift is very important for understanding the role of work and expertise in AI projects today.

More specifically, constructing a 'knowledge base' for explication of 'facts' has been replaced by methods to create facts by means of data in a database. The assumption now is that knowledge is already present in the data; it just needs cleaning, sorting and analysis. Rather than computer scientists explicitly constructing and defining the rules for the 'inference engine', machine learning is based on the idea that the algorithm will itself infer rules by identifying statistical patterns in historical data. Data scientists will then develop models for presentation of those patterns, with some of those referred to as 'dashboards'.

This embedding of expert knowledge may be one of the reasons why current public debates of AI tend to focus on the opaqueness of machine learning algorithms (see also Burrell 2016; Castelvecchi 2016). Still, despite attempts to develop 'ethical AI', what happens 'on the ground' is that machine learning algorithms are developed that embed the idea that there is no need to explicate the work and knowledge of experts, because the knowledge is already present in the data. This has organisational and societal implications. In the following section, we dive into specific ramifications of such developments in the Danish Tax and Customs Administration. We follow a suggestion put forward by Elish and Boyd to situate the magic of AI, writing that 'In the face of an increasingly widespread blind faith in data-driven technologies, we argue for grounding machine learning-based practices and untethering them from hype and fear cycles' (Elish and Boyd 2018). We also follow Ziewitz, who asks: What do we mean when we talk about algorithms? (2016). Our aim is not to 'disenchant'

AI but to scrutinise relations between AI and existing practices and infrastructures in a public sector organisation.

## Work in the customs inspection

The process of selecting packages for customs inspection is already highly reliant on IT systems and algorithms. The current risk system is managed by system monitors and assesses packages using three different methods: *Risk profiles, risk scores* and *random selection.* As indicated by the name of The Risk Score Project, the algorithm to be developed was meant to replace just one of the existing ways of calculating risk (*risk scores*), which marks packages for inspection based on variables such as weight, price, country of origin and the package type (The National Audit Office of Denmark, 2017: 22). In the future, if a risk score for a package exceeds a certain threshold the risk system will flag the package for human inspection. The idea of replacing the existing rule-based risk score with a machine learning-based risk score can be compared to the shift from expert systems to machine learning as outlined above.

At the time when the project commenced, replacing the existing risk score calculation with a machine learning-based risk score seemed like an obvious choice. This was first of all the case, because the current risk score had not been in use since 2014, as reported by The National Audit Office of Denmark:

> The Danish Tax and Customs Administration has given up on this part of the risk system and is now developing a new function instead. This new risk score will be created automatically based on historical data and the results from previous inspections. It will provide the tax administration with the opportunity to find abnormal patterns, which can cause an inspection. The tax administration does not know yet when the new risk score can be taken into use.
>
> *The National Audit Office of Denmark, 2017: 23*

Replacement was also in line with the OECD report mentioned above which recommends using advanced analytics for 'case selection' in order to *put data to work* (OECD 2016a).

During a workshop in the system monitors unit, the first author observed some of the discussions around implementing machine learning algorithms. About ten employees from the Danish Tax and Customs Administration were present.

> A large table divides the employees into two groups: Four system monitors are seated at one of the sides and three data scientists on the other. At the end of the table, a project manager stands next to a whiteboard and guides a brainstorm. Within an hour, the project manager has attached thirty post-it notes to the whiteboard. On the post-its, I read sentences like: *'More data'*,

*'A better understanding of data', 'Different types of algorithms'* (Except from fieldnotes, Jørgensen).

The conversations at the workshop concerned questions around what data would be available for the algorithm and what algorithm to deploy. A data scientist said that he had spent 90% of his time in the risks score project 'preparing data' and 'establishing an environment' for analysis, and only 5% of his time on 'actually writing code'. The workshop illustrated some of the work that goes into implementing an algorithm: Bringing different professional groups into the same room, facilitation of a discussion, as well as sense making around whether the current conditions in the organisation allows for the technology. First, author was puzzled that no customs officers were present as participants. When he asked a data scientist about the absence of the customs officers at the workshop, the data scientist told him that the system monitors were 'the customers' of the project. The logic was that system monitors were the ones who managed the current risk score, and they were the ones who were knowledgeable about IT systems and data, not the customs officers. The attention of the data scientist was thus directed towards understanding IT systems and databases rather than understanding the work practices of the customs officers.

Is this a case of bad user involvement? Maybe, but something else may also be at play: What is at stake is a representation of work in the tax administration that favours *data work* over practical, situated work that the algorithm is supposed to support. In the remaining part of this section, we further explore the enacted distance between data work and other kinds of work.

While customs officers were not present in the workshop, one question at the workshop directed everyone's attention towards their work. Just before the end of the brainstorm, one of the system monitors raised his hand and said: 'I just thought about an additional need. It would be beneficial if the customs officers could get an explanation of why the algorithm selects a specific package for inspection'. After a moment of silence, one of the data scientists replied:

> The problem with some of these algorithms is that they are a bit black-boxed. That means that they are difficult, if not impossible, to explain. But we are testing another algorithm called LIME, which can provide explanations of machine learning algorithms.

The system monitors raised a concern about how the data work happening at the workshop would align with the practical work of customs officers. But rather than making further inquiry into what kinds of explanation the customs officers might need and why – questions that would direct attention further towards the practical work of the customs officers – the response by the data scientists immediately redirected attention back to data and to the development and implementation of explanation algorithms.

Later, when asked about the importance of getting an explanation, a system monitor tapped his nose with his finger and said: 'The question is how we make sure that the nose of the customs officers become part of the system'. He elaborated that for customs officers to perform an efficient inspection, they would have to know both *why* and *how* to inspect a given package. The new risk score seemed prone to embed its own risks simply because it would be difficult and time-consuming for customs officers to figure out how to inspect packages without an explanation of why the package had been scored as suspicious in the first place.

In the article 'How to Talk About the Body', Bruno Latour (2004) argues that bodies learn to be affected by material surroundings and conventions (Latour 2004: 205). He provides an example of how specialists, 'noses' are trained in the perfume industry. The training of noses happens through the use of an odour kit, which teaches the noses to discriminate subtle differences in smells and to tell different smells apart from one another. If we compare to what was said in the workshop, for the system monitor, the nose of the customs officers could be an important addition to the algorithm. Yet, the trouble was that the customs officers' 'noses' had already been through a deskilling process due to years of systematic attention and funding of digitalisation and data work.

> **Customs officer:** [In the past] we would get a large flight manifest with information about what kind of goods there was on board of aeroplanes. Who is the sender, who is the recipient, and what is the package declaration? Then we could see 'ahh a plastic bunny for Mr. Jensen; there is always something shady about that'. How do we get the system to think like that? [Today] we can ask for them [the flight manifests], but they always arrive at night, and we do not have night shifts anymore, so most of the time, we do not look at them. If we went through the manifests again, it would require that we were allowed to have night shifts.

The customs officer's reflections on how to use his nose in this interview does not focus on knowing why packages are selected for inspections in advance. Instead, the customs officer focused on the use of materials, such as flight manifests, and former ways of organising work, such as night shifts. In this way, the customs officer situated *the nose* as part of the material learning practices and organisation of work. The customs officer insinuated that the nose had already been lost due to earlier organisational changes which introduced the division of labour into the selection of packages and inspection. This had removed customs officers from doing an essential part of customs inspection – which allowed their nose to be trained (cf. Latour 2004). In this light, the new machine learning algorithm would only seem to reproduce and fortify this situation. According to another customs officer, the turning point was the formation of the monitoring unit in 2014. When asked if system monitors were able to represent their work in The Risk Score Project, a customs officer stated:

**Customs officer:** The system monitors do not have their 'hands in the dirt'. They don't look at the result of inspections. That was exactly what was so great back in the days where we decided which packages to inspect by looking at the flight manifests. It was my job to determine which packages to inspect and to perform the actual inspection; in that way, I became smarter and smarter. I learned that a company was like this and that, and that we should not inspect packages from that company. We became smarter and smarter from our inspections. We still inspect, but where does our knowledge go?

From this perspective, the nose of the customs officer is not just an expression of a specific type of human intelligence or tacit knowledge, which customs officers possess, and which can be trained over time. Rather it is expertise that is contextual and situated, and maintained through interaction and relations to materials (flight schedules), ways of organising (routines, relations to other processes). A strict separation of work processes into the tasks of selecting and inspecting packages seems to put the contextual knowledge in danger and possibly create new kinds of risk, because it is only the IT-system, not the human worker that will learn from experience.

## Discussion

As public sector organisations direct attention towards AI, and in particular the application of machine learning algorithms, they risk losing sight of the practical work they are imagined to support. Above we have shown how machine learning algorithms work on the basis of historical data, rather than on input from human experts. The algorithm moreover requires a work situation where data, in one way or the other, is already present or that data from outside of the organisation can be procured. The risk score project exemplifies how processes that human experts consider part of the work practice are divided up. Thus, the development of a machine learning algorithm creates distances in the formal organisation of work. The distance is exacerbated when system monitors, who manages the existing IT systems, and customs officers, who inspects packages, are not brought into dialogue as part of the development process.

Because the development of machine learning algorithms in the public sector involves organisational units that are not already collaborating, it may not be straightforward for management, who should actually be part of the development of a technology which potentially impacts the organisation across several units. Viewed as a tool for organisations to make more accurate and efficient decisions, machine learning algorithms direct anthropological attention towards the relation between emerging technologies and the wider situation of work.

In The Risk Score Project, the machine learning algorithm was imagined to assist the overall customs inspection by being one among several methods for selecting packages to be inspected. Following Suchman (2000, 2007), we can describe this as directing attention to the *knowledge work* of an organisation at risk of becoming cast in terms of *routine work*. Representing work cast as routine work in terms of knowledge work requires ethnographic insight into the day-to-day organisation and discussions in a project, as well as to how 'the project' is itself an organising frame that directs resources to some activities and not others.

When organisations invest in improving knowledge work, they may then assume that current organisational inefficiencies are caused by a lack of knowledge. Studying work in the Danish Tax and Customs Administration made it clear that sometimes inefficiencies and risks are distributed and enacted in new ways through the automation of a small part of a complex process. In this way, it seemed as if a more accurate logic for selecting packages would, at best, only be able to make minor improvements to the overall customs inspection. One may ponder – given the difficulties demonstrated here – how public sector institutions assess the potential risks when implementing AI in work practices that are themselves emergent like in the social services, for example.

## Conclusion

We have argued that the development of machine learning algorithms is connected to changes in what counts as human intelligence and expertise. We have brought forth the concept of the custom officer's nose as a way of highlighting how human intelligence in a machine learning project was framed as 'additional knowledge' that could be embedded in the algorithm. One reason for why anthropologists should be concerned with emerging technologies is that an emerging technology like a machine learning algorithm forms a window into human-machine relations where human labour is represented and configured in particular ways, which makes certain kinds of expertise obsolete. The introduction of machine learning in the Danish tax administration not only illustrates that expertise is varied, but also that some forms of expertise are harder to represent than others. Since the customs officers were not the customers of The Risk Score Project, but 'just' users, we may ask if the orientation towards user-involvement in technology development that anthropologists have successfully inserted themselves into has transitioned into a new phase. If so, anthropologists must equip themselves to be partners in and analysts of user-driven tech development without users.

## Note

1 Accentuating the fact that understanding IT systems, code and algorithms in general require expert knowledge, machine learning principles have been conceptualised as complete black boxes. Legal scholars have discussed the implication of use of black-boxed algorithms for citizens, and for the conduct of law, and suggested that special legislation is required (Goodman and Flaxman 2017; Selbst and Barocas 2018). This has also led to the development of a subfield in computer science on so-called explanation

algorithms – algorithms able to provide 'explanations' of those algorithms considered black boxes (Ribeiro et. al. 2016; Adadi and Berrada 2018). An anthropological response to this is forming at University of Copenhagen (SODAS), where Morten Axel Pedersen calls for a 'machine anthropology'.

## References

Adadi, A., and M. Berrada (2018). 'Peeking inside the black-box: A survey on Explainable Artificial Intelligence (XAI)', *IEEE Access*, 6: 52138–52160.

Berg, M. (1997). *Rationalizing Medical Work: Decision-Support Techniques and Medical Practices*. Cambridge, MA: MIT press.

Broussard, M. (2018). *Artificial Unintelligence: How Computers Misunderstand the World*. Cambridge, MA: MIT Press.

Burrell, J. (2016). 'How the machine "thinks": Understanding opacity in machine learning algorithms', *Big Data & Society*. https://doi.org/10.1177/2053951715622512

Castelvecchi, D. (2016). 'Can we open the black box of AI?' *Nature News*, 538(7623): 20.

Collins, H. M. (1987) "Expert systems and the science of knowledge." In *The Social Construction of Technological Systems: New Directions in the Sociology and History of Technology*, W. E. Bijker, T. P. Hughes, and T. J. Pinch (eds.), 329–348. London: MIT Press.

Collins, H. M. (2018). *Artifictional Intelligence: Against Humanity's Surrender to Computers*. Cambridge, MA: MIT Press.

Danaher, J. (2016). 'The threat of algocracy: Reality, resistance and accommodation', *Philosophy & Technology*, 29(3): 245–268.

Danish Government. (2019). *National strategi for kunstig intelligens*. Accessed February 3, 2020. www.regeringen.dk/media/6537/ai-strategi_web.pdf

de Vries, K. (2013). 'Privacy, due process and the computational turn: A parable and a first analysis.' In *Privacy, Due Process and the Computational Turn*, M. Hildebrndt, and K. de Vries (eds.), New York: Routledge.

Dourish, P. (2016). 'Algorithms and their others: Algorithmic culture in context', *Big Data & Society*. https://doi.org/10.1177/2053951716665128

Elish, M. C., and D. Boyd. (2018). 'Situating methods in the magic of Big Data and AI', *Communication Monographs*, 85(1): 57–80.

Forsythe, D. E. (1993a). 'Engineering knowledge: The construction of knowledge in artificial intelligence', *Social Studies of Science*, 23(3): 445–477.

Forsythe, D. E. (1993b). 'The construction of work in artificial intelligence', *Science, Technology, & Human Values*, 18(4): 460–479.

Geiger, R. S. (2017). 'Beyond opening up the black box: Investigating the role of algorithmic systems in Wikipedian organizational culture', *Big Data & Society*, 4(2). https://doi.org/10.1177/2053951717730735

Goodman, B., and S. Flaxman. (2017). 'European Union regulations on algorithmic decision-making and a "right to explanation"', *AI Magazine*, 38(3): 50–57.

Iliadis, A., and F. Russo. (2016). 'Critical data studies: An introduction', *Big Data & Society*, 3(2). https://doi.org/10.1177/2053951716674238

Karasti, H., F. Millerand, C. M. Hine, and G. C. Bowker. (2016). 'Special issue: Knowledge infrastructures: Part I', *Science & Technology Studies*.

Kitchin, R. (2017). 'Thinking critically about and researching algorithms', *Information, Communication & Society*, 20(1): 14–29.

Latour, B. (2004). 'How to talk about the body? The normative dimension of science studies', *Body & Society*, 10(2–3): 205–229.

Ministry of Taxation. (2016). *Et nyt skattevæsen – Ny organisering, flere medarbejdere og velfungerende IT*. Accessed February 3, 2020. www.skm.dk/media/1371591/Et-nyt-skatt evaesen.pdf

National Audit Office of Denmark. (2017). *Rigsrevisionens beretning om SKATs kontrol og vejledning på toldområdet*. Accessed February 3, 2020. www.rigsrevisionen.dk/media/2104 734/sr0717.pdf

OECD. (2016a). *Advanced Analytics for Better Tax Administration: Putting Data to Work*. Paris: OECD Publishing. http://dx.doi.org/10.1787/9789264256453-en

OECD. (2016b). *Rethinking Tax Services: The Changing Role of Tax Service Providers in SME Tax Compliance*. Paris: OECD Publishing. http://dx.doi.org/10.1787/9789264256200-en

OECD. (2016c). *Technologies for Better Tax Administration: A Practical Guide for Revenue Bodies*. Paris: OECD Publishing. http://dx.doi.org/10.1787/9789264256439-en

OECD. (2019). 'Forum on Tax Administration.' Accessed February 3, 2020. www.oecd.org/tax/forum-on-tax-administration/

Pasquale, F. (2015). *The Black Box Society*. Cambridge, MA: Harvard University Press.

Reutter, L. M., and H. S. Spilker. (2019). 'The quest for workable data – building machine learning Algorithms from public sector archives.' In *The Democratization of Artificial Intelligence – Net Politics in the Era of Learning Algorithms*, A. Sudmann (ed.), Bielefeld: Transcript Verlag.

Ribeiro, M. T., S. Singh, and C. Guestrin. (2016). 'Why should I trust you? Explaining the predictions of any classifier.' In Proceedings of the 22nd ACM SIGKDD international conference on knowledge discovery and data mining, ACM: 1135–1144.

Rieder, G., and J. Simon. (2016). 'Datatrust: Or, the political quest for numerical evidence and the epistemologies of Big Data', *Big Data & Society,* 3(1). https://doi.org/10.1177/2053951716649398

Seaver, N. (2017). 'Algorithms as culture: Some tactics for the ethnography of algorithmic systems', *Big Data & Society,* 4(2). https://doi.org/10.1177/2053951717738104.

Seaver, N. (2018). 'What should an anthropology of algorithms do?' *Cultural Anthropology,* 33(3): 375–385.

Selbst, A. D., and S. Barocas. (2018). 'The intuitive appeal of explainable machines', *Fordham Law Review,* 87: 1085.

Star, S. L., (ed.) (1995). 'The politics of formal representations: Wizards, gurus, and organizational complexity.' In *Ecologies of Knowledge: Work and Politics in Science and Technology,* 88–118. Albany: State University of New York Press.

Star, S. L., and A. Strauss. (1999). 'Layers of silence, arenas of voice: The ecology of visible and invisible work', *Computer Supported Cooperative Work (CSCW)* 8(1–2): 9–30.

Suchman, L. (1987). *Plans and Situated Actions: The Problem of Human-Machine Communication*. Cambridge: Cambridge University Press.

Suchman, L. (1995). 'Making work visible', *Communications of the ACM,* 38(9): 56–64.

Suchman, L. (2000). 'Making a case: 'Knowledge' and 'routine' work in document production.' In *Workplace Studies: Recovering Work Practice and Informing System Design*, C. Heath, J. Hindmarsch, and P. Luff (eds.), pp. 29–45. Cambridge: Cambridge University Press.

Suchman, L. (2007). *Human-Machine Reconfigurations: Plans and Situated Actions*. Cambridge: Cambridge University Press.

Ziewitz, M. (2016). 'Governing Algorithms: Myth, Mess, and Methods', *Science, Technology, & Human Values,* 41(1): 3–16. https://doi.org/10.1177/0162243915608948

Zuboff, S. (2019). *The Age of Surveillance Capitalism: The Fight for a Human Future at the New Frontier of Power*. London: Profile Books.

# 7

# MAKING SENSE OF SENSORS

*Ajda Pretnar Žagar and Dan Podjed*

## Introduction

This chapter presents human relations with a smart building, the purpose of which is to detect events or changes in the built environment and provide feedback to people about indoor and outdoor conditions. The building, located in Slovenia, is one of the largest infrastructural investments of the University of Ljubljana in recent years. It was designed as an automated building, with approximately 20,000 input and output signals coming from sensors into the SCADA[1] monitoring system every second. The sensors are used for managing the state of cooling and heating systems, air ventilation, lighting, room occupancy, window opening and water supply. These signals are processed to regulate the environment for the people working and studying in the building. The aim of the sensors and automation systems is to provide a healthy and productive indoor climate, reduce energy consumption and assist the maintenance staff with their work.

In our study, we show that the state-of-the-art building, equipped with technological solutions, does not necessarily guarantee the well-being and satisfaction of its occupants. On the contrary, "smartness" of the building has often proven to be a source of discontent and disappointment, especially when it tries to appropriate agency from the people and make independent choices regarding their needs and wants. In such cases, people tend to find innovative solutions for outsmarting the building and taking back control. In this chapter, we identify such examples and explain why it is necessary to highlight the needs, analyse the expectations, and study the habits and practices of people *before* we start designing smart buildings. In this way, we can truly make sense of thousands of sensors and the data collected by them.

DOI: 10.4324/9781003084471-8

## Smart building: control or care?

Before we enter our case study building and present the findings, we should briefly explain what a "smart building" is. According to a recent definition, such building accounts for "intelligence, enterprise, control /.../ with adaptability, not reactivity, at its core, in order to meet the drivers for building progression: energy and efficiency, longevity, and comfort and satisfaction" (Buckman et al 2014: 104). However, the experts explain it is not the same as an "intelligent building", which is sustainable in terms of energy and water consumption and responsive to the requirements of occupants, organisations and society (Clements-Croome 1997). In other words, a smart building is based on the Internet of Things (IoT), collecting the data, enabling remote control and home automation, while intelligent building leverages gathered data and uses predictive models to provide the optimum environment for the occupants. In addition, the increased amount of information available from a range of sources, including the built-in sensors, allows these systems to become adaptable and enable a building to prepare itself for context and change over time (Buckman, Mayfield and Beck 2014: 106).

A desired feature of this kind of automated building – either a smart or intelligent one – is to support the lives of the people and other beings in an unobtrusive way. Albrechtslund and Ryberg (2011: 35) explain that its purpose is to make the technology less visible as they become an integrated part of the surroundings rather than being objects that need instructions. However, for being unobtrusive and "caring", it needs to monitor everything that goes on within the walls of the house. For being able to carry out constant monitoring, the building needs sensors, i.e. devices that respond to inputs from the environment. These inputs can be light, heat, pressure or any other measurable input, including, of course, human activities: motion, presence in a room, interaction with the building by opening windows and doors, etc.

The idea of a smart building encapsulates the ultimate ideals of any kind of smart solutions: "efficiency, security and utilitarian control in a technologically mediated and enabled environment" (Strengers 2013). In this sense, the "smartness" of the building reflects the classical concept of the panopticon, showcased by a philosopher and social theorist Jeremy Bentham, who proposed in the 18th century a circular building design which allows prisoners of the institution to be observed by a single guardian (Bentham 1995). Two centuries later, Bentham's idea, which has not been realised in its original form, was criticised by Michel Foucault (1977), who claimed that the panopticon as a disciplinary institution creates "docile bodies", i.e. people who obey commands and try to improve their habits since they are being controlled and supervised. In the 21st century, the panopticon got a new shape: its "all-seeing gaze" is supported by digital technologies and enabled by sensors. The single gaze of a guardian has turned into a dispersed and multilateral type of surveillance, called the "surveillant assemblage" (Haggerty and Ericson 2000), which is an enabling platform for "lateral surveillance" (Andrejevic 2005) and a fundament of the "surveillance society" (Lyon 2001). In addition, it has become more difficult to distinguish between different effects of surveillance and control which are often intertwined with support and care.

Since we believe care and control in the context of a smart building should not blur into a single concept, we propose to make a clear distinction between surveillance and monitoring. Surveillance, which reflects Bentham's ideas about the building that can control habits and improve behaviours, implies guiding actions of the surveilled subjects, while monitoring proposes a more passive stance of observing behaviour (see Marx 2016) and is more related to actual care. We should also mention that the present study was not designed to guide behaviour and control people, but to observe and understand them.[2] Hence, it is more focused on monitoring than on surveillance. And even if we considered these sensors surveillance-like, Marx proposes "a broad comparative measure of surveillance slack which considers the extent to which a technology is applied, rather than the absolute amount of surveillance" (Marx 2002: 23), meaning that surveillance is harmful proportionately to the power it has over the surveilled subject. As sensors in a smart building monitor predominantly neutral human behaviour, they, in our opinion, deserve some surveillance slack.

## Thousands of sensors under one roof

How does the building in the focus of our study reflect the concepts of care and control? The building is a part of a new university complex hosting the Faculty of Chemistry and Chemical Technology (FCCT) and the Faculty of Computer and Information Science (FCIS). The complex, located in the swampy outskirts of Ljubljana, was finished in 2014, after two years of construction. It is one of the largest investments in the history of the University of Ljubljana and the largest infrastructure project at the time, co-financed by the European Union, which cost €81.6 million. The structure consists of three connected volumes, with the total area of 44,268 m². Each university's faculty[3] has its own building and the two of them are connected with a common, general-purpose building with a cafeteria, a library and two large lecture rooms (Figure 7.1).

One of the main features of the university complex is the synchronisation of the maintenance system and the control of fittings and fixtures. Built-in sensors enable energy management, automatic control of the building and detailed analytics, all of which are processed in SCADA. The system is shared between the two faculty buildings and it is managed by a common maintenance staff, which is in charge of ventilation in the rooms, supply of hot and cold water, filtering of laboratory fumes at FCCT, electrical installations, functioning of outside shades and other tasks. The "smartness" of the smart building means not only a large amount of sensors for monitoring the state of the environment, but also automated control of certain parts of the building. One such part, for example, are semi-automatic shades that turn with respect to the sun's position in order to keep the sun from overheating the rooms and also to block intense light from coming in. The shades are large installations covering three quarters of the perimeter of the building. They were

**FIGURE 7.1** The smart building, equipped with thousands of sensors, which should assure the optimal indoor climate, reduce energy consumption and improve the well-being of people (Ljubljana, 10 August 2018, photo: Dan Podjed)

intended as an aesthetic and functional addition to the building, aiming to, at least partially, automate the management of the incoming light.

A part of the research, carried out for purposes of this chapter, focused on the FCIS alone. This particular building has an area of 13,000 m², consisting of a large auditorium, 8 lecture rooms, 13 computer classrooms, 23 research laboratories and offices for teaching and research staff. The reason we chose this particular building was that one of us (Ajda Pretnar Žagar) is employed at FCIS and has a close relationship with the building and its inhabitants. The fact that Ajda was staying in the building for eight hours a day, five days a week, was a great advantage for the research and enabled not only "traditional" ethnographic fieldwork but also autoethnography and constant data analysis of measurements from the sensors.

## Thickening the big data

In our study, we decided to investigate how the sensors, in all their numerousness, and other available technologies help people control their working space, how effective they are in decreasing energy consumption and whether they indeed provide the optimal environment for the building occupants. Our research was connected to the activities of two international projects. The first was the EU Horizon 2020 MOBISTYLE project, which aimed at raising awareness and motivating behavioural change by providing personalised IT services on energy use, air quality, health and well-being. The project enabled us to carry out comparative analysis of the Slovenian case with other similar buildings in the Netherlands, Denmark, Poland and Italy. The second was the EU Erasmus+ PEOPLE project whose aim was to integrate people-centred development (PCD) approaches into research, teaching and learning practices in four countries: Slovenia, the Netherlands, the United Kingdom and Czech Republic. In both projects, MOBISTYLE and PEOPLE, the smart building of the University of Ljubljana was a research platform for studying and a demonstration case for improving human-technology interactions. Since we were part of the research team working in the building and visiting it for meetings and other reasons, we were constantly exposed to "engaged learning" (Carrithers 2005) about the building and its functionalities and were able to see it on a daily basis how people interact with the built-in technologies, what kind of problems they encounter and how they proceed to address them.

An important part of our exploration was quite unusual for anthropologists (cf. Knox and Nafus 2018): we looked into quantitative data the sensors were recording and used findings from surveys, carried out in spring 2018 as a part of the PEOPLE project. The unexpected findings regarding dissatisfaction with room temperature revealed some weaknesses of the smart building and were used to address the most relevant topics in our ethnographic research. In addition to the survey, we selected 14 rooms, among which there were 7 offices (cabinets), 4 laboratories (common offices) and 3 administrative offices. Then, we observed the rooms' occupancy, window opening, temperature settings, energy consumption and air quality in a longitudinal study spanning from 2016 to 2019. We used statistics, interactive visualisations and data mining to establish how people live and work in the building.

At the same time, we conducted a three-year ethnographic fieldwork in the building, lasting from 2016 to 2019. We interviewed the inhabitants, shared their offices with them, browsed through institutional fora and performed focus studies for designing monitoring apps. These methods expanded our perception of the behaviours, values, practices, habits and hacks people used in the building and "thickened" our "big data" (Wang 2013). Going back and forth, from quantitative to qualitative and *vice versa* (see Anderson et al. 2009; Blok and Pedersen 2014; Cury et al. 2019), enabled us to establish a research problem as suggested by the data, gauge new perspectives on the known problems and account for outliers and patterns in the data. The circular research design enhanced the quality of information, which did not derive solely from a quantitative or qualitative approach. By combining the two, we assured a research loop that provided an additional perspective in both sets of data – quantitative data was verified with ethnography in the field, while ethnographic data became supported with statistically relevant patterns (Pretnar and Podjed 2019).

## SENSORS: SENSORY MACHINES OR EXTENSIONS OF SENSES?

**Dan:** Don't you think we should add a reference to sensory ethnography to the chapter?

**Ajda:** Well …. I understand sensory anthropology as being focused on anthropology of human senses and sensations, not so much on sensors as technological products.

**Dan:** This is exactly the point! Phenomenologically speaking, sensors are senses of the building and at the same time extensions of human sensations. If sensors are available, we can detect what would stay unnoticed, e.g. increased $CO_2$ level in the room.

**Ajda:** I still have a hard time equating sensors with senses. In my opinion, senses and sensors register two different things. In addition, the word "sensory" means focusing on senses, subconscious reactions of the body, associations, evocation of memories. Sensors, on the other hand, are devices that measure situations in a physical environment, without reactions and a complex spectrum of experience, evoked by sensory interaction.

**Dan:** I am still not entirely convinced by your argument. After all, sensors can detect identical events in the environment as humans with their senses. Afterwards, devices process the signals in their own way, and people respond to information. A sensor in a "smart device" is therefore an extension of our agency and gives us a "push" when necessary, for example to open a window. The device therefore *is* an extension of our senses, it augments, enhances and upgrades them. It is yet another proof we have become cyborgs with "super-senses".

**Ajda:** Senses, on the other hand, don't record data, they cannot really tell you it is 25 degrees outside, they just tell you it is warm. And you feel good about it, because, for example, you like being warm. If another person *sees* measurement of the temperature on the screen, this is the same information for you and for him. But if he *feels* 25 degrees, the experience is entirely his own. The levels of experience are different. In my opinion, experience is what defines the difference. Apparently, we have different views of what sensors are: either sensory machines or extensions of senses.

**Dan:** You know what, let's continue the debate outside, it's sunny and warm. And by the way, look at the sensor light: it's almost completely red. Let's get out of here!

## "It's too cold!"

Among the first tasks of our research was establishing how people perceive the building, how they feel in it, what their preferences are and how they adjust (to)

| | Sample size | Feedback | Feedback rate (%) |
|---|---|---|---|
| **FCCE students** | 1413 | 429 | 30.4 |
| **FCCE employees** | 180 | 89 | 49.4 |
| **FCSI employees** | 150 | 62 | 41.2 |

**FIGURE 7.2** Feedback rate of the survey on satisfaction at work and on human-technology interactions in the building

the environment. We conducted a survey in both faculty buildings, Faculty of Chemistry and Chemical Engineering (FCCE) and Faculty of Computer Science and Informatics (FCSI), and included the teaching staff, administrative staff and the students. In the end, we got 584 responses (33.5%) from 1,743 addressed participants (Figure 7.2). A part of the survey included multiple- and single-choice questions and questions with a Likert scale. Another part, which was more interesting from an anthropological perspective, was the free text sections, where people could comment on a specific issue, such as temperature, lighting, air quality and the general design of the building. In total, 234 (40%) decided to fill at least one free text question.

With respect to the lighting, the occupants complained about the colour of lights and their position in the building. One respondent, apparently familiar with technical terminology, complained about the hue with particular emphasis on its effect on the health of the inhabitants: "*Industrial lights are unacceptable. 2700 kelvins is proven to be detrimental for eyes, circadian rhythm and general well-being. But mushrooms would grow well!*". However, most complaints focused on the incomprehensible set-up for turning off the lights and how they often – apparently randomly – turned off.[4] This was the first indicator that the smart building is making the lives of people more complicated than if they simply had to turn the light on and off themselves.

Another important concern was the air quality. Even though the building is designed to ventilate lecture rooms, the air that is coming in is not perceived as "fresh". As one person put it: "*You can only get fresh air by opening windows, which is a necessary, regular morning routine*". Opening windows in the smart building is, a bit paradoxically, one of the few activities that are not automated. There are several hatches at the top of the building that can be opened remotely, especially in a case of fire to draw out the smoke, but this is not the case in lecture rooms and offices. Some offices and all lecture rooms have ventilation, but people in most cases prefer windows. Windows still require human intervention and people are often happy to intervene but unable to in some rooms that have windows installed very high or don't have windows that can be opened at all. It is a striking finding that people are very sensitive to air freshness and that only the air coming in from the outside is considered fresh. If the air is coming in from the ventilation system, people perceive it as stale and unpleasant. Air freshness is, as it was exposed in the survey, highly related to health and productivity. "*There is often not enough fresh air in the lecture rooms*", a respondent explained, "*so I find it hard to concentrate and I feel nauseous*".

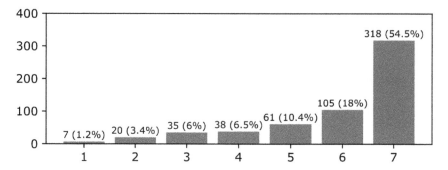

**FIGURE 7.3** In the survey on energy, well-being and health in the smart building, a significant share of participants expressed that it bothers them if they are exposed to the flow of cold air in a lecture room or office. (The survey carried out in spring 2018, n = 584.)

In addition to air freshness, room temperature was an important concern among the survey participants. Overall, 54.5% of respondents expressed that it bothers them if they are exposed to the flow of cold air in a lecture room or an office (Figure 7.3). The main reason for dissatisfaction is apparently the ventilation system that is designed to rapidly blow in "fresh" air to accommodate a room for 200 students, but the air is often quite cold and blows at a high speed. The stream of cold air makes people perceive the room as colder than it actually is. Thermal comfort is, no doubt, to a certain degree a matter of perception and personal preference, but it does highly contribute to productivity. "*In the library I am unable to focus*", one person explained, "*because it is always too cold*". To accommodate for cold, people mostly brought additional layers of clothing with them: "*It is too cold at the faculty, so we wear jackets at lectures*". How relevant the topic is for the people is apparent also from the writing style of respondents (Figure 7.4). One person, for example, expressed discontent regarding the room temperature by "screaming" for help in capital letters: "*It is way TOO COLD in the lecture rooms!!!!!! PLEASE, INCREASE THE TEMPERATURE FOR AT LEAST 3 DEGREES!!!! THE STUDENTS SOMETIMES WEAR WINTER JACKETS AT LECTURES BECAUSE OF THE COLD!!!!!!!*"

Results of the survey hinted we are getting into a relevant research topic for in-depth ethnographic research. First of all, the answers people provided by the questionnaire helped us redirect our research focus to an important topic: health and well-being in the smart building. In addition, we used data from the sensors to get additional information on how people interact with the building and what could be the sources of their discontent.

## What sensors reveal

Alongside survey analysis, we gathered sensor data from the SCADA system. We focused on analysing 14 rooms of different types, 4 laboratories, 3 administrative

It bothers me if the **cold air blows directly into my feet or onto my head** in the lecture rooms. Because of a badly designed ventilation system, I caught cold several times, both in the winter and summer.

It is very uncomfortable, when the **cold air blows into your feet** in lecture rooms. Ventilation doesn't seem as efficient to me as opening the good old windows.

I am not feeling good at FCCE because I am **ALWAYS cold**!!!

It is **cold in the lecture rooms**. 22 degrees is not enough when you are sitting still for 90 minutes.

The room temperature in the summer is too low. Actually, you have to come dressed in long trousers, closed shoes, and a sweater, otherwise **you will be cold**.

It is not comfortable if you are **cold in the lecture room** and you don't have a jacket.

We all want fresh air in the lecture rooms, but it just isn't there. Either you **can't open the windows,** or they don't even exist.

Ventilation is installed under the seats in large lecture rooms, and the **air blows directly into the students' feet** (badly designed system)!

**It is very cold** at the faculty in the winter, which does not positively affect my health. In the lecture rooms **the air from the vents blows directly into the feet**, which is very uncomfortable and interferes with lectures. Even in the summertime, the temperature is not appropriate.

**FIGURE 7.4** Selected opinions about room temperature in the smart building. The opinions were collected by the online survey, emphases made by the authors of this chapter

offices and 7 cabinets, with a mixture of men and women working in the rooms to account for differences in thermal comfort (Parsons 2019). We measured room occupancy, window opening, temperature, interactions with the thermostat and for some rooms also $CO_2$ levels (Gall et al. 2016) and energy consumption. In total, we collected over half a million measurements, making our data too big for any kind of manual analysis.

Quantitative data, acquired with sensors, helped us identify behaviour patterns for each room individually and for the building as a whole. One such "typical" pattern that emerged was that people mostly open windows between late spring and early autumn (Figure 7.5). There were very few instances where people would open the windows in the winter, even though almost all of them said in the interviews that the first thing that they do upon coming to work was open the window. One respondent was explicit: "*The first thing I do is open the window. Because it is always a bit stuffy inside. So we have to let the air in*".

This was not the case, as sensors showed. Most occupants forgot to mention that they open the window exclusively when it is sufficiently warm outside. There was only one room where both interviewees explicitly said that they don't open the windows in the winter. Moreover, people grossly overestimated their habits of opening windows. This is a typical case of "attitudinal fallacy" (Jerolmack and Khan 2014), where people either intentionally misrepresent their behaviour to make them look like they're adhering to the desired behaviour or their actions are simply too subconscious to report them accurately.

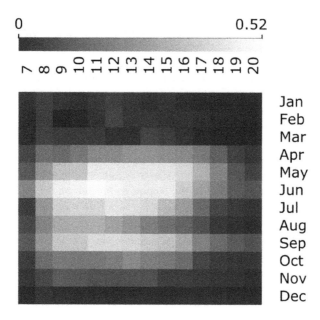

**FIGURE 7.5** A heat map of window opening frequency for six rooms in 2018. The colour reflects the share of time the window was open at that particular hour. Light gray represents a high and dark gray a low frequency

Another behaviour we noticed by sensor data analysis was that people frequently open windows when they come into their office (normally around 8 am or 9 am), but rarely in the afternoon, even though the air gets quite bad by the end of the day. In one room, for example, they opened the windows regularly in the morning, despite the sensor showing low to mid-low $CO_2$ levels. In the afternoon, however, they rarely opened the windows, even though the sensor recorded mid-high to high values of $CO_2$. There was a slight increase in opening windows at 1 pm, because a lot of the occupants returned from lunch and noticed the bad air. This changed significantly when the sensor started showing $CO_2$ levels with a coloured light (green representing good and red representing bad air quality). Once the light was activated, the frequency of window opening in the afternoon increased.

### The game of death[5]

"*Open the windows else we're going to die!*" The person entering the room made this remark in a joking manner, based on the little red light of the sensor measuring air quality in the room. It has become a standard game for the room's inhabitants, joking about how close to death we are and then frantically trying to bring in some fresh air to pacify the "angry" sensor for measuring air quality, which was installed for purposes of the MOBISTYLE project research.

The air quality sensor had, for a little while, become our "boss", telling us when to open windows and when to close them. It made us feel guilty, with the orange, or even worse, red light letting us know how poorly we care about our $CO_2$ levels. So we instantly obeyed it and made the necessary adjustments to make the sensor happy. We cared little about prevention and only acted when the sensor was already at a critical state. Just like a lazy worker, we did little outside of the strict instructions from a supervisor.

Sensor measurements were treated as a joke, a kind of game we played in the office. The one who first noticed the sensor made a little joke (usually it was a visitor to the office) and we opened the windows. The bossing around didn't last for long, though. Sensor's constant requests for attention faded in the background, because it was just too needy. We were busy doing actual work. We didn't want to have extra duties on top of that.

The position of the sensor was the key to how much people noticed it. It was placed next to the door to the neighbouring room, near copy machines. Most of the desks were far away from the sensor and a line of plants additionally obstructed the view. There's a saying "Out of sight, out of mind" and the same can be said for our sensor: if you don't notice it, it's like it doesn't exist. So even when the sensor turned red, it took us a while to realise it. The minimum requirement was for someone to get up and walk past it or to have a visitor who would notice it upon entering the room.

It was the same with the other laboratory who got the sensor. When the sensor got red, the recurring joking question was: "*Who farted?*". As a response to the red light, only two people regularly got up and opened the windows. The rest said they like the idea of data gathering and suggestions about air quality, but they just "*don't have the time to be bothered*". It is interesting that people, in principle, like the fact that they can *observe* themselves and figure out clever solutions about living healthier, happier and better. However, when it comes to the practicalities of actually *doing* something about it, the sensor soon becomes yet another annoyance.

### Making the sensor happy

During our research, the sensor acted like a needy and demanding person: it wanted to be seen, respected and obeyed. When we were busy actually working, we didn't pay all that much attention to the sensor. When we finally noticed it was telling us to open the window, someone had to get up from her desk and open the window. This was a hassle we wanted to avoid as much as possible. We were in a sense lazy or, as we liked to say, "*busy working*".

Just after we got the sensor, we wanted to please it as much as possible. It had to be green at all costs. So we kept opening the windows, making the air flow, enduring the cold breeze, the frozen hands, the chill on our skin. We tried everything to make the sensor happy. But alas, the sensor was still red! We could not figure out why it was "angry" with us, even though we were sitting in the cold next to an open window.

It was time to do some research and see what influences the colour of the sensor. We realised it was not just the fresh air, but also the temperature. So when we were ventilating the room in the chillier months, the score did not improve as much as we wanted to, because air temperature decreased the score. Moreover, the sensor was placed far from the windows, so it took a long time for the fresh air to reach it. Another obstacle was the poor conditions for ventilating – both windows in the room are positioned on the same wall, making it difficult for the air to circulate. Two years after we got the sensor, we found a hack to ventilate the room properly – we blocked the self-closing doors with a stick to keep them open for a while and opened both windows. This made the air circulate faster, which means we could have a short ventilating session and avoid the occupants being cold.

### Trick, no treat

Most of the time, people responded to the sensor. If it was red, they opened the window. Opening the window was essentially the only thing one could do to change the sensor's colour. That is, change it the "right way". But the right way is not the only way. Upon a complaint from a colleague that the sensor is not turning greener, another colleague replied: "*The light is red, also when it is cold*". And then he added: "*But you boil the water in the kettle and put it under the sensor. The steam from the kettle makes it green again*". So one can also change the sensor in the "wrong way", that is without addressing the cause, just alleviating the symptoms. Another trick the room occupants found was if you blow into the sensor for a few seconds, it will also turn greener, likely from the decreased level of volatile organic compounds (VOC). Tricking the sensor into turning green was not really that uncommon, but in the end it defeated the purpose of measuring air quality.

However, the occupants of this room were not the only ones "hacking" the system. Above, we wrote about people complaining of cold and overzealous cooling systems. In the lecture rooms, this was a significant problem, where there was always a spot under the air nozzle where nobody would want to sit, because you got cold in an instant. Some lecturers were aware of that and they rearranged the students so that no one would sit under the nozzle if possible. Another trick, which they figured out, was that the cooling stops working when the window is open (not to waste energy, of course). Concurrently, lecturers started opening the windows frequently, so that the students wouldn't get cold.

While opening the windows to turn off the cooling was an easy and obvious fix, we noticed some cunning hacks as well. Next to each room, there is a console that lights up green when the person is in the room and orange when the room is empty. This is a clear sign to students and co-workers if the person is present or absent. When professors, especially those with individual office rooms, wanted some peace and quiet, they locked the room, so that the console would show orange and stayed in the room to work. In this way, people wouldn't bother to knock and enter as they assumed the room was empty and the professor was able to work without distractions. The fact that some people "tricked" the console also meant that some of the sensor data was actually incorrect. The data showed that the room was not occupied and only through ethnography we were able to identify people who used this trick and account for it in our analysis.

As the building is full of engineers, there was no lack of straightforward, engineering solutions. Lecture rooms have a strange lighting set-up – there are four switches, which would turn on a line of lights, but the line would be perpendicular not parallel to the lecturer. Therefore, the lecturer could either illuminate the left or right side of the room (or both), but not the back and front side of the room separately. This is particularly important because when projecting a slideshow on the whiteboard, the front lights had to be turned off so that the projection is visible and the back lights had to be turned on for the students to be able to make notes. Therefore, when the lecturer wanted to write on the blackboard at the same time, the lighting chaos reached its peak. To solve the illumination problem, a professor ordered an affordable portable reflector online and used it during his lectures. In this way, the students could see both the projection and his writing on the blackboard.

As we can see from these examples, when the built environment is designed contrary to peoples' needs, many of them will not hesitate to hack and appropriate it. In doing so, they can be very innovative, especially if they are engineers and computer scientists, who feel the "urge" to understand technologies and make them their own.

## Taking back control

During our study, rarely anyone forgot to mention the "mysterious" outside shades. The shades are semi-automatic, programmed to turn with respect to the light exposure of three rooftop sensors. This means that when the sun is shining onto one side of the building, the shades on that side would automatically turn and prevent the sun from overheating the rooms and causing discomfort to the room's inhabitants. When the sun was gone, the shades would open and let the light in. At least that was the idea.

Many occupants mentioned they have no idea how the shades actually function. It was bothering them, they couldn't figure out the system, especially considering the fact that most of the occupants were engineers. Most said there must be a bug in the system. In fact, there was. On the east side of the building, the motors that were turning the shades were installed upside down. This means that the shades would open when they should close and *vice versa*. Sometimes, they even stopped working; as a consequence, some people were destined to sit in the dark all day. Solution? Maintenance staff turned off automatic control for some rooms and the inhabitants were able to manually move the shades. And we literally mean "manually" – they opened the window and turned the shades by hand. In one room, there was a shade motor hanging from the ceiling and the user was able to control it with a push of a few buttons.

This example is yet another proof that people want to control their environment and technologies installed around them. They want to know how things function.

Alternatively, they wish to not notice how they function by the pure virtue of them functioning perfectly. If the system is broken, people notice right away. They also want to be able to adjust the settings as they wish. Quite often people felt alienated and powerless in opposition to the smart building and how it was managing the environment.

In a smart city, as Griffiths (2016) argues: "smart norms, protocols, procedures and considerations could develop which limit access or deny urban participation to stakeholders, if they are developed conceptually, democratically and empirically unexamined, without priority attention being paid to investigating project 'failures'". It goes the same for a smart home or building: if norms and procedures are implemented with a top-down, expert-minded approach, people might not like them, especially if they have a feeling that they are being controlled or supervised.

## Conclusion

As we tried to highlight in this chapter, people's attitude towards sensors is changing based on various contexts: social, temporal, personal, etc. They treat the presence of sensors as a joke or a nuisance, and often also as something to outsmart or ignore. Either way, when it comes to human relationship with technological devices, people want a feeling of being in control. It is frustrating, when the sensor instructs you to take action, but you simply cannot. For example, the sensor reminds you to open the windows, but windows cannot be opened, since they are installed too high or there are simply no windows in the room. Or perhaps the sensor tells you that the air quality is bad, but you don't know what to do about it. In such cases, people get frustrated and start to ignore the sensor since they have a feeling that nothing they do is right. Sensors, when giving feedback to the people, have to be understandable and related to an action people can very easily do.

Giving the agency back to people is therefore essential in designing buildings, be they smart, intelligent or just a regular type. Even with automation processes (or especially then), people want an option to regulate their environment, to adjust it to their needs, values, practices and habits. Therefore, smart buildings shouldn't do everything for their inhabitants; instead, they should participate in creating the perfect conditions for them. A key component to designing (more or less smart) buildings that take people into account is a PCD, which emphasises people should be involved in the making or improving products and services (Podjed, Arko and Bajuk Senčar 2019). By following the four steps of the PCD (1. identification, 2. analysis, 3. interpretation, 4. testing), we can develop technologies that serve the people instead of developing technological solutions that are served by the people (for more detailed recommendations for developers, see Tisov et al. 2017).

In conclusion, we should emphasise once more the distinction between a "smart building" and an "intelligent building". When people included in our research heard the new university building is going to be "smart", they actually imagined an "intelligent" building, where artificial intelligence would provide custom, data-based models of interventions. The building would be learning, adapting to people's needs and improving its activities. Instead, the building is "just" smart, which, if we consider the definition in the introduction, means sensors measure the state of the environment and enable remote maintenance and control. Any kind of decisions are hard-coded in the system, namely temperature changes and shade turning, and the system is never updated with respect to human behaviour. This is not bad in itself, since having a "smart building" is the first step towards maintaining a comfortable and healthy environment and at the same time lowering energy consumption. However, the decisions that get hard-coded in the system cannot be accepted by the decision-makers out of the blue but have to be based on actual human practices, habits, preferences and values. In this respect, anthropology is unbeatable, providing deep insights into the behaviours of people and co-creating meaningful technological solutions *with* the people. Had the system been designed with people in mind and according to their actual habits and practices, there would be significantly less friction and collision with the technologies and less need for hacks and impromptu solutions. As a result, the sensors would be actually able to provide a healthier, more productive and comfortable environment. Most importantly: they would allow symbiosis of a building and people living in it.

## Acknowledgements

The authors acknowledge the financial support of the European Union enabled by projects PEOPLE (Erasmus+) and MOBISTYLE (Horizon 2020). In addition, the support was provided by the Slovenian Research Agency core funding programmes P6-0088 and P2-0209.

## Notes

1 SCADA is an acronym for Supervisory Control and Data Acquisition, a computer system for gathering and analysing real-time data, usually used in the industry.
2 During the research, we also worked on the MOBISTYLE project, which aimed at guiding behaviour by encouraging healthy habits and decreasing energy consumption. In this sense, the guiding of the project was more suggestive than prescriptive.
3 In Slovenia, the word "faculty" is used to describe a university school or a group of university departments that specialise in a particular subject or scientific discipline. It does not describe a person who teaches at a university.
4 Control of lights is in fact based on time and movement of people. However, the occupants are often not familiar with the time schedule and tracking of movements.
5 The following three sub-chapters move from pure ethnography to something akin to autoethnography. They describe behaviours for a room where one of us (Ajda) is working; hence, even though the findings are supported by quantitative data, there are a lot of intimate reflections intertwined with the analysis. Hence, we shift in parts of the section to the first-person narrative.

## References

Albrechtslund, A. and T. Ryberg (2011). 'Participatory Surveillance in the Intelligent Building', *Design Issues*, 27 (3): 35–46.

Anderson, K., D. Nafus, T. Rattenbury, and R. Aipperspach (2009). 'Numbers Have Qualities Too: Experiences with Ethno-Mining', *EPIC Proceedings*, 2009 (1): 123–140.

Andrejevic, M. (2005). 'The Work of Watching One Another: Lateral Surveillance, Risk, and Governance', *Surveillance and Society*, 2 (4): 479–497.

Bentham, J. (1995 [1787]). *The Panopticon Writings*, London: Verso.

Blok, A. and M. A. Pedersen (2014). 'Complementary Social Science? Quali-quantitative Experiments in a Big Data World', *Big Data and Society*, 1 (2): 1–6.

Buckman, A. H., M. Mayfield, and S. B. M. Beck (2014). 'What is a Smart Building?', *Built Environment*, 3 (2): 92–109.

Carrithers, M. (2005). 'Anthropology as a Moral Science of Possibilities', *Current Anthropology*, 46 (3): 433–456.

Cury, M., E. Whitworth, S. Barfort, S. Bochereau, J. Browder, T. R. Jonker, K. S. Kim, M. Krenchel, M. Ramsey-Elliot, F. Schüür, D. Zax, and J. Zhang (2019). 'Hybrid Methodology: Combining Ethnography, Cognitive Science, and Machine Learning to Inform the Development of Context-Aware Personal Computing and Assistive Technology', *EPIC Proceedings*, 2019: 254–281.

Clements-Croome, D. (1997). 'What do we mean by intelligent buildings? *Automation in Construction*, 6 (5–6): 395–400.

Foucault, M. (1977 [1975]). *Discipline and Punish: The Birth of the Prison*, New York: Pantheon Books.

Gall, E. T., T. Cheung, I. Luhung, S. Schiavon, and W. W. Nazaroff (2016). 'Real-time Monitoring of Personal Exposure to Carbon Dioxide', *Building and Environment*, 104: 59–67.

Griffiths, M. (2016). '"Imagine If Our Cities Talked to Us": Questions about the Making of "Responsive" Places and Urban Publics', in Mary Griffiths and Kim Barbour, eds, *Making Publics, Making Places*, 27–48, Adelaide: University of Adelaide Press.

Haggerty, K. D. and R. V. Ericson (2000). 'The Surveillant Assemblage', *British Journal of Sociology*, 51 (4): 605–622.

Jerolmack, C. and S. Khan (2014). 'Ethnography and the Attitudinal Fallacy', *Sociological Methods and Research*, 43 (2): 178–209.

Knox, H. and D. Nafus, (eds). (2018). *Ethnography for a Data-Saturated World*, Manchester: Manchester University Press.

Lyon, D. (2001). *Surveillance Society: Monitoring Everyday Life*, Maidenhead: Open University Press.

Marx, G. T. (2002). 'What's New About the "New Surveillance"? Classifying for Change and Continuity', *Surveillance and Society*, 1 (1): 9–29.

Marx, G. T. (2016). *Windows into the Soul: Surveillance and Society in the Age of High Technology*, Chicago: The University of Chicago Press.

Parsons, K. (2019). *Human Thermal Comfort*, Boca Raton: CRC Press.

Podjed, D. S. Arko and T. Bajuk Senčar (2019). *Four Steps for the People: People-Centred Development Toolkit*, Ljubljana: PEOPLE Project. Available online: http://people-project. net/wp-content/uploads/2019/12/M2.4_Toolkit.pdf

Pretnar, A. and D. Podjed (2019). 'Data Mining Workspace Sensors: A New Approach to Anthropology', *Contributions to Contemporary History*, 59 (1): 179–197.

Strengers, Y. (2013). *Smart Energy Technologies in Everyday Life: Smart Utopia?* Houndmills: Palgrave Macmillan.

Tisov, A. D. Podjed, S. D'Oca, J. Vetršek, E. Willems, and P. Op't Veld (2017). 'People-Centred Approach for ICT Tools Supporting Energy Efficient and Healthy Behaviour in Buildings', in Zia Lennard, ed, *Proceedings of the 5th Annual Sustainable Places International Conference*, 1 (7): 675, Middlesbrough: MDPI. Available online: www.mdpi.com/2504-3900/1/7/675

Wang, T. (2013). 'Why Big Data Needs Thick Data', *Ethnography Matters*, May 13. Available online: http://ethnographymatters.net/blog/2013/05/13/big-data-needs-thick-data/

# 8

# FLYING DRONES AS A GENDERED MATTER OF CONCERN

*Karen Waltorp and Maja Hojer Bruun*

## Introduction

The environments we inhabit change rapidly as digital technologies and infrastructures become ubiquitous. This involves major changes in the ways states regulate, corporations profit, and how people consume, produce, and (re)circulate digital media content. Drones, 'unmanned aerial vehicles' (UAVs), offer an apt illustration of this changing environment, which institutions and people are adapting to, modifying, and legislating as it emerges. In this chapter, we show how people immediately connect the flying drone to a camera filming and those images as potentially shared on the Internet in the same instant. The technologies of the drone, the camera, and the Internet – hardware, software, and material infrastructure – form a socio-technical assemblage in people's minds. Our empirical material points to how this drone-camera assemblage ties into existing norms and well-known notions of female modesty and the male gaze. Our research shows that women have more at stake than men in being surveilled, exposed, and circulated in images captured by the drone in private spaces or in public places with little clothes on, i.e. the swimming pool or beach. Furthermore, we found that the 'drone gaze' is constituted as a male gaze, and the drone pilot likewise as a male figure by participants in focus groups and a subsequent experimental phase of the study.

The drone-assemblage emerges as a gendered matter of concern around privacy and a fear of being surveilled and shared in intimate situations in a *flow of images* (Waltorp 2020, 2021), entwined and enabled by digital infrastructure. We propose that drones can provoke a fundamental shift in the public's understanding of privacy concerns in relation to modern technology, in line with Ryan Calo's proposal a decade ago (2011), that drones might function as privacy catalysts in the sense of publics emerging around matters of concern as these concerns become very visible and felt (see also Latour 2004, Marres 2005, Marres and Lezaun 2011).

DOI: 10.4324/9781003084471-9

> Drones and other robots … represent the cold, technological embodiment of observation. Unlike, say, NSA network surveillance or commercial data brokerage, government or industry surveillance of the populace with drones would be visible and highly salient. People would *feel* observed, regardless of how or whether the information was actually used. The resulting backlash could force us to reexamine not merely the use of drones to observe, but the doctrines that today permit this use.
>
> *Calo 2011:33*

Our analysis of the gendered reactions to civilian drones builds on findings from a research project on the Danish public's responses to drones, carried out in collaboration with the Danish Transport, Construction, and Housing Authority (Bajde et al 2017), from hereon 'The Transport Authority'.

The Transport Authority contacted the University of Southern Denmark and Aalborg University to help them shed light on the Danish public's attitude to drones, as they were working on new legislative proposals with a stated vision of "opening up another layer of airspace" for civilian use of drones. They lacked knowledge of ordinary people's reactions and attitudes to drones, and existing privacy concerns related to drones were the explicit focus in the research project. The drone-camera-Internet associations, which we show in this chapter that people instantly formed, connect the drone to an increasingly 'too smart' environment (Sadowski 2020). We are aware, as Adam Fish points out, that there are many 'species' of drones that span a diverse range of costs, abilities, sophistication, and not least purpose, and we should not "neglect this reality, conflating military and consumer drones…(and) ignore the many ways these technologies come into being in relationship to diverse environments and applications" (Fish 2019). We focused in this study on reactions to civilian drones exclusively, and within Danish law – yet people's imaginaries are limited neither to the borders of a nation, nor to the official uses of the drone. Participants draw from both fiction and media imagery, right away connecting drones and warfare, sci-fi movies etc. A gender perspective was not a part of this initial focus or problematization, but emerged as significant, and was included in the 2017 report (Bajde et al 2017). While privacy in relation to drones has been discussed (see Luppicini and So 2016 for a review of the literature), gendered reactions to drones have not. In hindsight, we wish our "politics of inviting" (Lindström & Ståhl 2018) had been sensitive to gender non-binary ways of identifying in the recruitment phase of the project, which was outsourced to a recruiting company. The politics of inviting is pivotal in every project, and opening up to understanding how feeling vulnerable and exposed has gendered connotations would have been very interesting to be able to discuss across a variety of gender identities. We can speculate that minority groups in relation to gender identities would align with the women's response and fear of being exposed but unfortunately have no empirical material to inform us.

The insights we discuss in this chapter relate to bringing matters of concern (Latour 2004, Marres 2005) into the public, democratic conversation around emerging technologies. As the Manifesto of the Future Anthropologies Network of the European Association of Social Anthropologists reads:

> We are critical ethnographers engaged with confronting and intervening in the challenges of contested and controversial futures … embracing larger ecologies and technological entanglements ….We get our hands dirty. We are ethical, political and interventionist, and take responsibility for interventions.
>
> *FAN manifesto in Salazar et al. 2017:1–2*

This chapter is a call for the participation of anthropologists around emerging technologies in processes of policymaking and legislation that bring overlooked perspectives, aspects, and positions into the room, daring to research what is not yet here (Halse 2013). Anthropologists find themselves in varying positions of power to define any given situation in such collaborations: Through ethnographic fieldwork, and anthropological problematization, we are able to point to blind spots often-times existing in the development of emerging technologies – and related policies responding to and shaping these. What products and services are developed and which ones proliferate depends on the social structure underlying the development. Working alongside and providing insight to policymakers, legislators, and other stakeholders therefore goes hand in hand with taking these issues into the public space, where it can be debated in democratic ways how new technologies (should) impact and shape our future – even as this may be an ambivalent position. The kind of debate which we hope to contribute to via such collaborative work entails rejecting technological determinism and notions of inevitability of a specific kind of technological progress. This constitutes small steps towards alternative techno-logical futures, insisting on looking at who is benefiting – or suffering – and which structures are uncritically built into specific technologies that needn't be, and both critique and help work towards alternatives. Below we present our methodology before discussing privacy, proxemics, and gendered fears.

## Methodology: bringing insights to policymakers and matters of concern to the public

The research was carried out in 2017 in Denmark as a jointly funded collab-oration with the Danish Transport Authority, University of Southern Denmark, and University of Aalborg. As anthropologists interested in how people and tech-nologies participate in constituting futures that cannot be predicted or necessarily imagined, we were keen to participate in this collaboration with the Transport Authority. It posed interesting methodological challenges in terms of how to elicit responses to a future situation which is not yet actualized. Our methodology was a combination of focus groups, repeat interviews with individuals in residential areas, including drone overflights of private homes, as well as drone overflights in public spaces, such as parks. Six focus group interviews were conducted, with 58 participants in total, across three of the larger cities in Denmark, Copenhagen,

Odense, and Aalborg, with people imagining and speculating together about drones (Bajde et al 2017). The second phase included home interviews with 16 participants and interviews in group settings with 72 participants. In all instances there were approximately the same number of (persons who identified as) men and women among the participants.

In light of an increase in the sale of civilian drones, a cityscape with higher numbers of drones is a very likely future scenario. We were to provide Danish people's responses to this imagined, probable future scenario to inform the Transport Authority in developing regulatory frameworks that considered and respected the public's concerns, while allowing private companies, public organizations, and drone hobbyists to "enjoy the benefits of drone technology", as the Transport Authority framed it (Bajde et al 2017). To elicit such responses, the two types of experiments with drone flyovers were carried out. The interviews and flyover experiments in residential settings were conducted in two stages. First, participants were interviewed about their general attitude towards drones with the research questions zooming in on how people responded to the presence of drones in public areas as well as nearby/overflying private homes; and how these responses were impacted by the altitude at which the drone was flying and other factors, such as noise and the nature of its use. The aim was to obtain a base understanding of their level of knowledge about drones, their attitudes towards drones, and their personal views on privacy – to understand whether the drone provoked privacy concerns and in which ways. Participants were then subsequently interviewed in their homes as a drone would be overflying unannounced and elicit immediate reactions in a directly experienced rather than a speculative situation. To understand reactions to different altitudes, a category 1B drone conducted a fly-by at 75, 50, and 25 metres. After and during this experiment, the second interview conducted focused on people's reactions to the drones, and reflections on the presence of drones in the vicinity of their homes.

In the project design and subsequent analysis, we were inspired by classic studies of human-machine interaction (Suchman 1987), and experimental methodologies at the intersection of technology, our everyday environment, and publics (Bowker & Star 1999, Marres 2005, Marres and Lezaun 2011, Marres and Stark 2020), including collaborative studies with public and private stakeholder, using simulation methods (Lindgren et al 2020, Pink et al this volume). Although the latter studies concern semi-autonomous driving cars on the ground, and we look at flying drones, several parallels exist in people's reactions to entities that seem to have agency and intentionality and move in the vicinity of us. Increasingly, the emerging technologies of (perceived) autonomous material objects such as self-driving cars and drones are moving in close proximity to our physical bodies. We follow scholars preoccupied with "political participation and citizenship (who) have increasingly turned their attention to the socio-material conditions of public engagement – to the devices, objects, substances and material settings in and through which publics are mobilized" (Marres and Lezaun 2011:490). When we point to flying drones as a 'matter of concern', this builds on a long tradition to make things public, stretching back to John Dewey (1946 /1927). Dewey's meditation on the public and its problems are concerned with the future of democracy in an age of mass communication, governmental bureaucracy, social complexity, and pluralism. This tradition is continued most recently by scholars within the fields of (techno)-anthropology, science and technology studies, media-, and critical data studies who oppose matters of fact with 'matters of concern': assemblages or gatherings of ideas, forces, players, and arenas in which 'things' and issues come to be and to persist, because they are supported, cared for, worried over. This approach in turn refigures (normative) understandings and theorizations of 'the public' (Birkbak et al. 2018, Latour 2004, Marres 2005, Møller Hartley et al. 2021).

Below we discuss privacy and proxemics in the focus groups and experimental research, before turning to the flying drones as gendered matters of concern. With emerging technologies introducing us to entities that move above and around us, and share the space with us, new theories of space and proxemics in human-machine interaction are overdue. These should consider the assemblage of related technologies that afford the spread and closeness of things – intimate and far apart – via digital technologies. Below we go into some of the reactions in the focus group exercises and discussions, and the experiments with drone overflights.

## Sensing privacy and distance in a new digital-material environment?

Spatial privacy refers to being protected from uninvited intrusions into one's physical and/or psychological sphere, in a manner that disrupts a person's right to be left alone (Solove 2004). We found that the disturbance of people's spatial privacy became particularly acute when the drone was being flown at the lowest tested altitude of 25 metres. Virtually everything that people are and do is associated with space (Hall 1966, Hall et al 1968), as one's sense of space is a synthesis of many sensory inputs: visual, auditory, kinaesthetic, olfactory, and thermal. In Edward T. Hall's work on proxemics, there are parallels to that of ecological psychologist James J. Gibson, whom Hall also quotes. Gibson (2014/1979) places the human in her environment and conceptualizes visual perception as both ambient and ambulatory: The perceptual system is developed as it is because we turn our heads and we walk up to, and around, entities in our environment to discern what they are, and what their *affordances* are in relation to us (ibid, see also Waltorp 2020). Flying drones are a new kind of entity, moving and acting in ways that we do not have any cultural scripts in place to understand properly, and neither do we have the opportunity to investigate the drone and ascertain its intent. This greatly frustrated many participants in our study, both when imagining this as a future scenario in focus groups and increasingly so when encountering a drone, which came closer, in the experimental phase of the study. Current policies stating that a drone hobbyist[1] must stay 50 metres away from other people do not

**FIGURE 8.1** Illustration of the height of the drone at 20 metres, 50 metres, and 75 metres relative to the height of trees and people on the ground. Reprinted with permission from Domen Bajde, *Public reactions to drone use in residential and public areas.* University of Southern Denmark (Bajde et al. 2017:5)

obviate the problem, that people have difficulty in perceiving and determining vertical distance.

In the individual flyovers at people's homes, the participants reacted negatively to the drone's presence and noise. Interestingly, some participants' attitudes to drones changed, provoked by the questions posed in the first interview. A change of mind regarding drones in the days in-between the first and the second interview occurred for some participants, even *before* the actual experience of the drone overflight in the follow-up interview. In accordance with the literature review, participants in this first round of interviews were generally open towards the possibility of having drones carry out different tasks. The Danish media review carried out in connection with the report (Bajde et al 2017) showed that drone technology is generally framed sympathetically, with a focus on professional use in contexts such as 'search and rescue', 'transport', 'inspection', and various forms of 'visual production' like photography. Some days after these initial interviews as the participants were revisited to conduct a drone test in their private gardens, this changed towards greater scepticism: While some participants began to express annoyance with the drone's presence at the 50-metre altitude, allowed currently, all participants without exception expressed concerns when the drone descended to 25 metres.

In addition to the mere presence of the drone, the fact that current regulations and designs of drones make it difficult for people to assess the purpose and legitimacy of the drones causes uncertainty. The inability to obtain information, such as information about who is operating a drone and for what purpose it is being flown over their house, significantly diminishes people's sense of privacy in both public and private residential settings in line with theories of visual perception and proximity mentioned above (Gibson 2014, Hall 1966, Hall et al. 1968). One of the participants, Freja, a woman of 28 years, used an apt metaphor for understanding proxemics in relation to drones: a personal *bubble* which the drone was transgressing. When the drone lowered to the altitude of 25 metres above Freja's house and garden she stated firmly: "*Now I think it's getting way too close, and it's making more noise. So, now it's starting to become disturbing … It's entering into my personal bubble*".

Another participant, Anton, a man aged 55, said in a similar vein as Freja above that he would not tolerate a drone hanging outside his window or entering his property without his consent, even at very high altitudes. It would feel *like having a camera attached to his shoulder,* he said. In this he instantly relates, and even conflates, the drone with a camera. Anton had a hard time determining the altitude of the drone during the interview with the introduction of a drone overflying, thinking it was higher up than it actually was. This surprised Anton, as he is used to estimating distances when he goes hunting. This difficulty of assessing distance in vertical space was also evident in the focus group interviews. In the below excerpt from a focus group, the participants discuss the related and pertinent question of 'who owns the airspace':

Vivi, a woman of 35 years: "But how close to a house should it fly then? I guess we are talking one, maybe a couple of metres from the house? It's difficult to say…"

Christian, a man of 48 years: "Well, I could ask you a question about that, because how far does your property extend upwards?"

Lilly, a woman of 52 years: "All the way up to the sky. Ha. No…"

Christian: "So that's what I'm a little doubtful about. How far up do you own the air?"

Lilly: "Way up. I don't know."

Eva, a woman of 47 years: "That's a really good question."

Lilly: "There's something to it, I mean, aeroplanes are also overflying."

Dennis, a man of 59 years: "So, that's what I'm trying to say, some places you don't own at all. If you live near an airport, you don't own it at all."

Christian: "Right, then you don't own it."

Minh, a man of 37 years, also ponders who owns the space above him. He thinks there should be a *minimum* altitude which drones must stay above, either way, in order to minimize the opportunity for surveillance − or perhaps just to minimize the *feeling* of being surveilled. He underscores that the idea of a constant presence of drones would make him feel surveilled, namely because he would not be able to tell the purpose of the drone: "*You cannot tell whether it is recording, or if it's the police …*". He is concerned that the many benefits of drones will lead to the sky becoming "overcrowded" with drones, like a "*cloud covering the sky*". Minh notes that the constant noise from drones would constitute a violation of his privacy because he would not feel in control of his environment …"*it's as if your free will has been taken away from you"*. Minh conceives of his privacy as the *freedom* to do whatever he wants without people knowing what he is doing:

> I can do what I feel like. If I feel like picking my nose, then that's what I'll do. Because it's inside my house. Other people should not be able to access that knowledge....

This inability to determine the purpose was a privacy-disturbing experience for Minh as for most participants. A drone hovering over one's dwelling or garden for a longer period provokes high levels of concern and has made people feel like they are being 'targeted', not least since this also enables the drone to better film and take pictures. This again underscores the expectation of a drone-assemblage with camera and Internet among the participants in the study. The emergence of the flying drone reconfigures the social and political worlds we inhabit – and not least our intimate sense of ourselves and our bodies in terms of privacy, optics, and proxemics. Technologies such as drones thus reopen questions of boundaries and privacy as related to technology, as in the quote by Ryan Calo at the beginning of this chapter. Prior to the presence of the drone, the research participants had rarely considered what separates their private space from the collectively owned airspace. Across focus group participants and participants in the experimental phase of the study, all underscored the need to have a system of *knowing* the drone – knowing its purpose. Apps were suggested to this end, as well as inbuilt chips, colour coding etc.

A theme that occurred several times during the various focus groups was related to Google Earth and to Big Brother scenarios: the fact that you are potentially being surveilled and recorded without your knowledge (Zuboff 2019, Solove

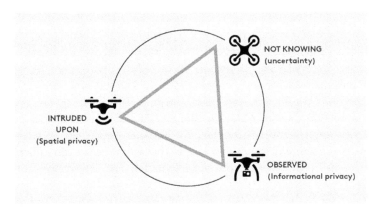

**FIGURE 8.2** Illustration of people's expressions of feeling observed by the drone, intruded upon, and not knowing the purpose of the drone; the relation and reinforcement between informational privacy, spatial privacy, and uncertainty that emerged. Reprinted with permission from Domen Bajde, *Public reactions to drone use in residential and public areas*. University of Southern Denmark (Bajde et al. 2017:6)

2004, Sadowski 2020). Informational privacy has been one of the most enduring social issues associated with digital electronic information technologies, and a fixture in public discourse since the 1960s, when the dominant concern was massive databases of government and other large institutions housed in large stand-alone computers. Since then, concerns have multiplied in type and extent as radical transformations of the technology have yielded the remarkable range of present-day systems, including distributed networking; the World Wide Web; mobile devices; video, audio, and biometric surveillance; global positioning; ubiquitous computing; social networks; databases of compiled information; data mining; and more. Associated with each of these developments is a set of worries about privacy (Nissenbaum 2010:1): "What people care most about is not simply restricting the flow of information but ensuring that it flows appropriately…" (ibid:2), something which scholars have connected to the emergence of drones (Fish 2019), and smart technologies (Sadowski 2020, Zuboff 2019).

As Daniel Orlove points out in his book 'The Digital Person: Technology and Privacy in the Information Age' (2004), privacy violations have traditionally been understood in a particular manner that does not account for key aspects of the unique problems the digital age has introduced, and our ways of understanding privacy must be rethought in order to fully comprehend the problems with 'digital dossiers' and Orwellian Big Brother scenarios (2004:7, 30). The Big Brother of Orwell's *1984* spying on people in their homes envisions a centralized authoritarian power that aims for absolute control, but the digital data harvested by businesses are not controlled by a central power, and their goal is not to oppress people (but might be to get us to buy new products and services). The (Danish) government is a far cry from Big Brother, and government officials do not act out of malicious intent or a desire for domination. Yet, 'informational privacy' is the valid concern that the drone will capture unauthorized personal information. The *most* common concern expressed is again related to the camera: being photographed or filmed in one's own house or garden – or the beach: this points to a gendering where the drone gaze is a male gaze (see Berger 1976 for a classic theory on the male gaze in arts, media, and everyday life). In the specific case of the drone-assemblage, this fear of loss of informational privacy is coupled with 'the invasion conception of privacy' (Solove 2004). It becomes an ontological question: What is this entity moving in my proximity; can 'it' see me? Does 'it' film me? And not least – what is the entity of 'it'? One cannot necessarily see the pilot of the drone (i.e. the person steering the drone remotely), and one cannot know what infrastructure the camera of the drone is coupled with. This occludes an adequate response and emerges as a matter of concern.

As the above discussion alludes to, our environment is changing, and we (will) increasingly relate to semi-autonomous machines moving in our vicinity, horizontally and vertically. This includes a digital infrastructure enabling a flow of images which people are aware of instinctively (Waltorp 2020, 2021), yet which can hardly be known or understood in its entirety. While both men and women experience the closeness of the flying drone as unsettling and disturbing for these sets of reasons, it is problematized by women in specific ways. These specificities relate to existing normative frameworks of female modesty and fears of being lurked upon, filmed, and exposed. Below we hone in on the gendered concerns around loss of privacy, surveillance, and exposure which surfaced in the focus group discussion and experimental phase of the study.

## Female modesty and the male gaze – drones as a gendered matter of concern

> I think I would have a hard time if they [drones] fly in front of the windows. I have my boundaries… I also think that people should have privacy in their house and likewise in their own gardens, so that you can wear a bikini without being photographed from above.
>
> *Tine, woman, 27 years*

The gendered aspects of a set of concerns related to the presence of drones emerged in several focus group discussions and solo-interviews, with women as well as men, and point to emerging technology's relation to existing gender norms. Privacy concerns are heightened in special conditions of vulnerability, such as being nude, changing clothes etc. In our report (Bajde et al 2017:10), we concluded that there is increased concern among women regarding the potential loss of privacy, or private space, and of not being secure from the gaze of others (via drones): Be it over the hedge from an overflying drone, or in one's apartment with a drone peaking in the window or in a public place, e.g. a beach. Men and women alike are concerned about *women's* nudity, as reflected in the phrase: 'if your wife or girlfriend was lying topless…'. Thus, drones and the flow of images – courtesy of Internet-enabled technology and existing digital infrastructure – are a highly gendered concern. Entangled in this is the simultaneously local and global question *to whom is this a matter of concern?* Who is taking part in negotiating and understanding how this technology should or should not be allowed in Denmark?:

> It turns into a bit of a surveillance society, doesn't it? You can just send one up and you can just… Well, lying in the backyard without clothes, that's going to slowly die out.
>
> *Andrea, woman, 40 years*

> But, what if your wife or girlfriend happens to be lying topless in your garden, and a drone takes photographs from above?
>
> *Vivi, woman, 35 years*

> "And then it won't be long before it's all online… We see that a lot these days…"
>
> *Eva, woman, 47 years*

Several times, male focus groups participants would refer to a woman lying naked in a private garden, but in the quote below the interviewee Anton mentions both people in general and that he himself would be uncomfortable with drones flying over beaches, feeling that this would be an invasion of his privacy:

> I believe it would be intimidating for many – because on the beach you lie to relax…I would feel offended (krænket)…spied on or lurked on
>
> *Anton, man, 55 years*

> Freja, a woman of 28 years whom we met above, says: "It can have a camera – but if it's to make a video in my garden, around my house – if it's for research or whatever – then that's ok, but I'd like to know so that we do not run around naked out here!"

Purpose and state of undress is of the essence to people. A drone with a camera attached can hover outside your window or in the backyard, and the knowledge that the communication technology affords the spread of images across the World Wide Web in a split second is something participants are instinctively aware of. Tine, a woman of 27 years, is one of the participants who changed her mind about drones in-between the two interviews in the experimental phase of the study. When she saw the drone half-way through the second interview, the change towards scepticism was augmented. She was very tolerant and trusting initially; full of confidence that drones would fly very high and not infringe on her privacy. This was before she had time or occasion to really reflect on drones, and before she encountered a drone hovering, as she did in the experimental flyover. 'Trespassing' and 'stepping over a boundary' (*grænseoverskridende* in Danish) were terms and phrases she used repeatedly to describe the experience with the drone. Another keyword in the interview with Tine is again the question of purpose, and that knowing this purpose is crucial for accepting the proximity of drones near her home. At 25 metres, she thinks the drone is very close and it becomes even more pressing to know why the drone is there, and why/whether she is being filmed. She has no way of knowing, though, her perceptual apparatus cannot decipher any signals from the drone indicating the intentions (from its pilots).

> I find it would be stepping over my personal boundary not to know why I was being filmed, by whom, for what purpose – on my private property. When somebody films you in the street, you see who it is and you can go and ask questions. But not when it is a drone. Then one can only leave the garden and go into the house. ….
>
> *Tine, 27*

Tine is disturbed, not only by the noise but in relation to her privacy, as is Lilly, 52:

> I don't want to be watched in my garden if I run around naked. It happens, right…? That's something you might want to think twice about. And you

might be doing other stuff than running around naked, if you feel like it. And
then it's suddenly public and you're exposed. So, I want my private space. In
public, they're free to watch me, for all I care.

*Lilly, 52*

The drone and the perception of it are emerging in – and being shaped by – existing
norms related to gender, nudity, and visuality, in a world increasingly mediated
and 'smart'. Technologies are not designed with a full range of bodies in mind as
pointed out by Lucy Suchman early on in studies of human-machine interaction
(1987). Torin Monahan (2009) points to this, writing that:

> … technologies privilege certain bodies – usually male, young, White, and
> able ones – over others… To varying degrees, many technologies, if not most,
> are like these: They are products designed better for use by men than by
> women; or, within their social contexts, they tend to empower men and dis-
> empower women. This is, in large part, a product of the frame of reference of
> technology designers, software developers, and engineers, most of whom are
> men designing with themselves in mind.
>
> *Monahan 2009:288*

Ruha Benjamin (2019) likewise takes a closer look at the racialized bias embedded
in technologies, which has been seen in connection with drone use in the U.S. context. We have here limited ourselves to a focus on the gendered aspects of civilian
drone use in Denmark but perceive these studies and concerns as intricately related.

How images flow in digital infrastructures is at stake here; how we understand
space, who controls it, and whom/what we share it with are at stake too. Building
on the focus group and experimental material, we point to a situation of hyper-
visuality, omnipresent cameras, and a lack of control over who gets access to the
flow of images. The socio-technical assemblage of drones, cameras, human bodies,
and the Internet tie into and reframe well-known notions of privacy, female nudity,
modesty, and the male gaze (Berger 1972, Biemann 2008). The drone, which can fly
close by, hover, film etc., is introduced into a context in which women's nudity and
modesty are historically and still today perceived differently than men's, and more
closely guarded (Berger 1972, Monahan 2009, Mulvey 1999).

Situating this in the Danish (digital) context, The Danish Foreign Ministry (the
department for gender equality) ordered a report on young people in Denmark
between 16 and 20 years old and their attitudes to sex, sexting and social media
(Dahl et al. 2018). The results clearly show that Danish young men are celebrated
for sexual activity, whereas young women must be careful not to be seen as 'cheap'
when engaging in erotic and sexual relations with young men, whether on- or
offline. Implications of images circulating of young girls naked or wearing little
clothes differ from young men, and constitute a matter of concern for the young
women interviewed, as their reputation suffers differently than young men's (Dahl
et al. 2018). This ties into a new digital-material environment, where a gaze can

be extended courtesy of the drone – and the images of women's naked bodies can be shared courtesy of the existing infrastructure. In the focus groups people expected in most cases that the drone pilot would be a man; research participants used 'he' (or 'kids') about the person flying the drone, and the drones were referred to by a participant as 'toys for boys' and another as 'play toys for grown up boys' (*drengerøve*). The drone pilots in the experimental material were actually male too, as it were. Initiatives exist aimed at inviting women into the drone industry, but in the understanding of the participants in this study, a drone was instantly coupled with a man.

Coupling technology and men is common. The imagined smart human, as Yolande Strengers argues (2013), echoing Monahan above, is cast in the male-dominated industries of engineering, economics, and computer science, and this technologically enabled and rational consumer she dubs 'resource man': He is imagined as highly functional and in masculine ways. The group targeted by the Transport Authority in their communication was (hobby) *drone pilots* and male, as it was assumed to be this group, for whom it would be relevant. Many of the people working at the Transport Authority were former pilots, and we discussed this tendency with them over lunch at a meeting in Copenhagen: Their perspective on drones was from the viewpoint of aviation. They related to and conceived of the drone as a 'small flying vehicle' where the pilot could be on the ground, and that could fly much lower than the height that planes are allowed to. We suggest that the anthropological empirical approach and collaborative problematization can serve to make apparent the discrepancies between people developing technology, those making policies and legislation to regulate the emerging world, and differently situated people whose perspective ought to make up part of these phases. The understanding from the Transport Authority departs radically from the perception of drones among research participants, who did not perceive drones as 'small aeroplanes' but instinctively reacted to the larger drone-assemblage. The pilots had technical insight on how large a drone would need to be for it to carry camera equipment, and how close it would need to be to then film and take photographs. Participants did not have this insight, and generally felt ambivalent towards drones. Situational factors played an important role. A system of 'knowing' the drone and its purpose was a wish from participants, and top of the list was knowing whether or not the drone had a camera attached (Bajde et al 2017:8). This instant relating made the drone emerge as a specific gendered matter of concern.

## Conclusion: thoughts on the future of drones and sharing our environment with them

In this chapter, we have sought to 'make public' the assemblage of drones, cameras, human bodies, and the Internet, and we have demonstrated how drones appear as a gendered matter of concern.

The drone today emerges at a time where there is a technological infrastructure in place that allows a merging of what the drones 'sees', what the pilot can see, and what s/he can share instantaneously – with a global reach. The drone as a socio-technical assemblage is thus a phenomenon, where the drone with camera and Internet access *becomes* an airborne digital information technology, courtesy of the larger socio-technical systems in place. The public should evidently play a vital role in shaping the future of the drone sector and the sector's fate is tied to the capacity to serve the public and convince it that drones *can* benefit society, and be used in a safe and considerate manner, continually addressing public concerns such as safety and privacy and securing these. The first step in this regard is understanding the nature of these concerns and how they are part of existing cultural norms, classed, racialized, and gendered.

In this chapter, we have shown how women have more at stake in being surveilled, exposed, and circulated in images captured by the drone in private spaces or in situations with little clothes on – and how the 'drone gaze' is (unconsciously) constituted as a male gaze. In this way, existing structures around female modesty and the male gaze are rehearsed in this emerging smart environment, and the drone as a flying entity augments fears around privacy; spatial and in terms of proximity, as well as informational and in terms of an unwanted flow of images beyond the individual's control or knowledge. When confronted with a drone, people may feel threatened and observed – regardless of whether that is actually the case – the actual and perceived are sometimes in tension here.

The 'smart' is today embedded with digital technology for data collection, network connectivity, and enhanced control "with data-collecting, internet-connected machines" (Sadowski 2020:3). Our empirical material shows how people are aware of this as they encounter, imagine, and react to the drone-assemblage. Discussions around what kinds of technologies we wish for – including drones – and how we imagine living with them in future should be democratized. If anthropologists sit at the table(s) where decisions around policies are made, and legislation is informed; in the labs where design is undertaken, and research at the sites where emerging technologies are tested, we can participate by making visible matters of concern related to emerging technologies and a future human-machine environment. Through knowledge dissemination, public debates, and collaborations, we can help push towards policies and legislation being democratically debated and informed, and not least, open to what is desirable and not just probable.

## Acknowledgements

The research leading to this publication received funding from The Danish Transport, Construction, and Housing Authority (Principle Investigator: Domen Bajde, University of Southern Denmark (SDU)). The authors would like to thank the participants, Domen Bajde, Jannek Sommer, Rune Hagel Skaarup Jensen, and all others from the research team at SDU for their collaboration and inspiration. We also thank Sarah Pink, Débora Lanzeni, Shanti Sumartojo, Jathan Sadowski, Melisa Duque, and Kari Dahlgren at the Emergent Technologies Lab, Monash University where Waltorp was visiting scholar in 2020, for engaging and thought-provoking discussions about technologies and the digital environment, which has informed the analysis.

## Note

1 It is quite easy and free of cost to obtain a drone certificate. A drone hobbyist flying a drone over 250 kilograms requires a drone certificate, a so-called *Drone Awareness Accreditation*. This can be obtained for free on the website droneregler.dk, by answering a theoretical test of 12 questions. This certificate allows you to fly the drone outside of urban areas; however, you must stay *50 metres* away from other people – unless these are part of an audience to the drone flight.

## References

Bajde, D., Hojer Bruun, M. H., Sommer, J. K., and Waltorp, K. (2017). *General Public's Privacy Concerns Regarding Drone Use in Residential and Public Areas*. Odense: University of Southern Denmark.

Benjamin, R. (2019). *Race after Technology: Abolitionist Tools for the New Jim Code*. Cambridge and Boston: Polity Press.

Berger, J. (1972). *Ways of Seeing*. London: Penguin.

Biemann, U. (2008). M*ission Reports. Artistic Practice in the Field – Ursula Biemann Video Works 1998–2008*. Umea and Bristol: Bildmuseet Umea/Arnolfini Bristol.

Birkbak, A., Petersen, M. K., and Jørgensen, T. B. (2018). Designing with Publics that Are Already Busy: A Case from Denmark. *Design Issues*, Vol. 34 (4): 8–20.

Bowker, G. C., & Star, S. L. (1999). S*orting Things Out: Classification and Its Consequences*. Cambridge, MA: MIT Press.

Calo, M. R. (2011). The Drone as a Privacy Catalyst. *Stanford Law Review*. Online, vol 64 (29).

Dahl, K. M., Henze-Pedersen, S., Vernstrøm Østergaard, S., and Østergaard, J. (2018). Rapport: Unges opfattelser af køn, krop og seksualitet. København: VIVE. e-ISBN: 978-87-7119-485-2.

Dewey, J. (1946/27). *The Public and its Problems*. Ohio: Swallow Press.

Fish, A. (2019). Drones at the Edge of Naturecultures. *Media Fields Journal: Critical Explorations in Media and Space*, Vol 14: 1–8.

Gibson, J. J. (2014). *The Ecological Approach to Visual Perception*. London: Routledge.

Hall, E. T. (1966). *The Hidden Dimension*. Garden City, NY: Doubleday.

Hall, E. T., Birdwhistell, R. L., Bock, B., Bohannan, P., Diebold, A. R., Durbin, M., Edmonson, M. S., Fischer, J. L., Hymes, D., Kimball, S. T., La Barre, W., F. Lynch, S. J., McClellan, J. E., Marshall, D. S., Milner, G. B., Sarles, H. B., Trager, G. L., and Vayda, A. P. (1968). Proxemics (and Comments and Replies). *Current Anthropology*, Vol. 9 (2/3): 83–108.

Halse, J. (2013). Ethnographies of the Possible. In W. Gunn, T. Otto, & R.C. Smith, (eds.), *Design Anthropology: Theory and Practice*, pp. 180–196. London: Bloomsbury.

Latour, B. (2004). Why Has Critique Run Out of Steam? From Matters of Fact to Matters of Concern. *Critical Inquiry*, Vol. 30 (2): 225–248.

Lindgren, T., Fors, V., Pink, S., and Osz, K. (2020). Anticipatory Experience in Everyday Autonomous Driving. *Personal and Ubiquitous Computing*, Vol. 24 (6): 747–762.

Lindström, K., & Ståhl, Å. (2016). Politics of Inviting: Co-Articulations of Issues in Designerly Public Engagement. In R.C. Smith, K.T.Vangkilde, M.G. Kjærsgaard, T. Otto, J. Halse & T. Binder (eds.), *Design Anthropological Futures*, pp. 183–198. London: Bloomsbury Academic.

Marres, N. (2005). Issues spark a public into being: A key but often forgotten point of the Lippmann-Dewey debate. In B. Latour & P. Weibel (eds.), *Making Things Public*, pp. 208–217. Massachusetts: MIT Press.

Marres, N., and Lezaun, J. (2011). Materials and Devices of the Public: An Introduction. *Economy and Society*, Vol. 4 (4): 489–509.

Marres, N., and Stark, D. (2020). Put to the Test: For a New Sociology of Testing. *The British Journal of Sociology*, Vol. 71 (3), 423–443.

Møller Hartley, J., Bengtsson, M., Schjøtt Hansen, A., Sivertsen, M. F. (2021). Researching Publics in Datafied Societies: Insights from Four Approaches to the Concept of 'publics' and a (Hybrid) Research Agenda. *New Media & Society*, 1–19. https://doi.org/10.1177/14614448211021045

Monahan T. (2009). Dreams of Control at a Distance: Gender, Surveillance, and Social Control. *Cultural Studies ↔ Critical Methodologies*, Vol. 9 (2): 286–305.

Mulvey, L. (1999). Visual pleasure and narrative cinema. In L. Braudy and M. Cohen (eds.). *Film Theory and Criticism: Introductory Readings*, pp. 833–844. New York: Oxford University Press.

Nissenbaum, H. (2010). *Privacy in Context: Technology, Policy, and the Integrity of Social Life*. Stanford: Stanford University Press.

Sadowski, J. (2020). *Too Smart: How Digital Capitalism Is Extracting Data, Controlling Our Lives, and Taking Over the World*. Cambridge, MA: The MIT Press.

Salazar, J. F., Pink, S., Irving, A., and Sjöberg, J. (2017). *Anthropologies and Futures. Researching Emerging and Uncertain Worlds*. London: Bloomsbury.

Solove, D. J. (2004). *The Digital Person: Technology and Privacy in the Information Age*. New York: NYU Press.

Strengers, Y. (2013). *Smart Energy Technologies in Everyday Life: Smart Utopia?* Houndmills, UK: Palgrave Macmillan.

Suchman, L. (1987). *Plans and Situated Actions: The Problem of Human-Machine Communication*. Cambridge: Cambridge University Press.

Waltorp, K. (2020). *Why Muslim Women and Smartphones: Mirror Images*. London and New York: Routledge.

Waltorp, K. (2021). Multimodal sorting: The flow of images across social media and anthropological analysis. In A. Ballestero & B. Winthereik (eds.), *Experimenting with Ethnography: A Companion to Analysis*. Durham: Duke University Press. (Experimental Futures Series).

Zuboff, S. (2019). *The Age of Surveillance Capitalism*. London. Profile Books.

# 9

# FUTURE MOBILITY SOLUTIONS?

*Sarah Pink, Vaike Fors, Katalin Osz, Peter Lutz and Rachel C. Smith*

## Introduction

The societal narratives, advanced by media, government and industry, that frame and explain emerging technologies have commonly presented autonomous driving (AD) cars as either utopian problem-solving devices or heralds of a dystopian future (Pink 2022). More recently, they have begun to suggest how AD cars might be integrated elements of new visions of technologically driven mobility solutions, including platform-based Mobility as a Service (MaaS) systems. Simultaneously, there is a growing consensus across a scholarly community of social science and humanity disciplines that such technologically determinist understandings of AD futures are unrealistic and bound up in a self-sustaining innovation narrative that serves to support the conservative and often competing agendas of industry and policy stakeholders, with little attention to the future people in whose lives they might be implicated (Cohen et al 2020). Collectively such work advocates a shift away from approaches to technology design, rollout and policy agendas that support what have been called a solutionist paradigm (Morozov 2013), a technologically determinist approach which assumes that technologically driven societal change will solve social and individual problems. There are many ways that solutionist arguments can and have been contested by science and technology studies (STS) scholars (Marres 2018, Stilgoe 2018), urban planning scholars (Legacy et al 2018) and human geographers (Ash 2017). Yet while these critical perspectives provide theoretically endorsed and valuable assessments of the current systemic and political landscapes in which AD is envisioned as participating, and the possible consequences of these visions, they less frequently create modes of intervention. Their engagements tend to be *about* rather than *with* the industry and policy actors concerned. Moreover they usually account for people through the notion of the 'social' or as 'publics' and thus neglect important questions concerning how the

DOI: 10.4324/9781003084471-10

experience of AD might plausibly be imagined to be part of future everyday lives. That is to say that their units of analysis tend to be sociological rather than phenomenological. Ultimately this lack of attention to the everyday and experiential means that the futures variously envisioned, contested and critiqued by dominant or scholarly narratives cannot account for how people always complicate futures predicted by economists, technology designers and policy makers. Conversely, design anthropologists (Pink et al. 2020) and media scholars (Markham 2020) argue that phenomenological understandings of everyday life have a pivotal role in underpinning ethical and viable routes to responsible future societal and individual ways of co-inhabiting the world with technologies.

In this chapter, we outline and demonstrate a way forward, shaped by design anthropology and rooted in ethnographic fieldwork. We take two steps beyond conventional anthropology: drawing on futures anthropology (Pink and Salazar 2017), our ethnographic research concentrates on revealing how the everyday present complicates dominant futures narratives; and drawing on design anthropology (Smith & Otto 2016, Smith 2022), we develop a mode of multi-stakeholder ethnography (Pink 2022), which is interventional not because it *impacts on* organisations, individuals or discourses, but because it *collaboratively engages with* them in a pedagogy of mutual learning, experimentation and creativity. Therefore, while we advocate for the critique and contestation of narratives of technological determinism, we also argue for intervention through collaboratively demonstrating the value of shifting future visions and subsequently the ambitions of policy makers and industry partners.

To develop our discussion, we draw on ongoing conceptualisation and research undertaken over a period of over six years. Our discussions about AD with research partners at Volvo Cars started a couple of years before our research projects commenced in 2016, first focusing on future mobilities through the prism of AD cars and later, from 2018, on MaaS. Our research has included ethnographic fieldwork in and around the Swedish cities of Gothenburg, Stockholm and Helsingborg and has been shared by a large and changing team of researchers, including ourselves. Here, acknowledging our colleagues, we bring together the findings to make a broader statement. We first discuss the trajectory of our future-focused ethnographies of AD in the present, undertaken from 2016, the critical response they generated to the solutionist innovation narrative and the implications of their future-focused ethnographic insights. By discussing research undertaken in 2020, adding to the collaboration municipal government partners, in the case discussed the City of Helsingborg in Sweden, we then show how, as AD cars become re-visioned as part of new solutions, anthropological analysis continues to complicate these new predictions. Significantly these examples emerged from research developed in partnership with our industry and city partners in order to elucidate and complicate the questions, contradictions and ambitions that were being discussed across these sectors, rather than as a distant critical response from the ivory tower.

This spatially and temporally expanded research site is akin to the *ethnographic place* (Pink 2022), a term used to describe the continually changing intensities of things, processes and experiences that configure relationally to each other during ethnographic research. Thus, a *design ethnographic place* is not a bounded or circumscribed set of activities. Rather, like place, as it is theorised by human geographers (Massey 1995), it is always in process, porous and continually changing in its composition with the movement of people, technologies, things and non-human organisms. We describe a site where theory, research design, fieldwork, analysis, discussion, workshops, dissemination occur, involving productive inter-disciplinary methods and dialogue. This is a site of collaborative and continuous learning, between stakeholders and researchers where ethnographic field working and the activities that surround it constitute an ethical and interventional mode of engagement.

## Ethnography as ethics

Futures anthropology is critical in its theoretical scholarship and in the sense that anthropological ethnography has a tendency to show up the complexities, contingencies, inequalities and modes of creativity that underpin social lives and experiences. Moreover, it reveals how these contest straightforward and often politically and economically invested visions of the present and future that are represented and projected by policy, industry and other powerful stakeholders in futures. Visual ethnography methods (Pink 2021) provide a powerful mode of revealing these inconsistencies between everyday experience and imagined everyday futures, and the visualisations of futures that are presented in industry, policy or other reports and campaigns. There is an ethics to this; should not ethical design and futures thinking be built through attention to the very elements of human experience and feeling that ethnographic research reveals? Indeed, investigating everyday experience and materialities of our relationships with AD cars brings to the fore ways of knowing not acknowledged in the dominant narratives of industry and policy. For example, with Thomas Lindgren we compared industry visions of how people would use future AD cars, with video and photographs made by participants in our ethnographic research into everyday imaginations of AD futures. Industry-derived concept-car visualisations of future AD cars show them as clean, used by well-dressed professionals in 'images of future automobilities … complicit in wider stories through which predictive visions are constituted and disseminated by science, industry, policy and media' (Pink, Fors and Lindgren 2018: 196). In contrast, cars used by the families who participated in our research were filled with 'stuff'. For our participants, driving a car involved feeling comfortable, and thus trusting that everything that might be needed for possible situations was at hand, such as carrying and leaving diverse things in the boot, whether or not 'really' needed.

Our ethnographic photographs and video stills of real-life situations of car use showed cars to often be messy and full of apparently unused things. They provide a stark contrast to images of future cars. Therefore, industry-produced images of future cars stand for a 'possibility', upon which subsequent clean and uncluttered imaginaries for future everyday mobilities can be built. In contrast, our ethnographic findings suggested that when we work from the other direction – to build our imaginaries of automobility futures on the idea that users of future AD cars will make them into sites which are cluttered with the complexities of their everyday lives – rather different visions emerge (Pink et al. 2019: 211). Thus, ethnographies of possible AD futures can serve as a corrective, which moderates the clean and clear visions produced by technologically determinist renderings of futures, ensuring that the mess of everyday life complicates those narratives.

Visual ethnography techniques do not only provide contesting visualisations but also offer a mode of getting under the surface of the everyday in such a way that makes evident the contingencies and modes of human improvisation through which it is lived out. They reveal the narratives or stories of participants in our research as they move through everyday environments, with technologies and other people and things. They show us how people learn, come to know, to trust, to bring technologies into their everyday lives and to move forward with them, improvising into uncertain futures. Our ethnographic practice is based on the principle of doing ethnography and learning *with* (Ingold 2008) participants as they move through their worlds. In such mobile ethnographies, researchers can traverse both everyday spaces during ride-alongs or self-recorded tours with participants, or imagined and remembered temporalities in performative or spoken encounters with them. We seek to create the circumstances (sometimes in collaboration with stakeholders) and ask the questions through which future technologies, situations and scenarios might be imagined, through which future experiences might be sensed, or through which to reflect forward to evaluate and assess the plausibility of dominant future visions. In doing so, the ethnographies discussed here had to be adaptive to the circumstances. This involved us coming to learn and know about participants as they moved. This included video recording and discussing with them as they drove or asking them to record, recount or describe their movement on video during our earlier projects.

Later we used video and audio calls through digital platforms or phone calls, as appropriate to different participants during the COVID-19 pandemic. This included participant's video recording of his own experiences in one case, and an extensive photo diary in another, both of which were integrated in the interviews with them.

The movement towards experimental ethnography in anthropology (Estalella & Sanchez Criado 2018) focuses on collaborative modes of practice. Acknowledging this, we advance a different practice, whereby our collaborations are with wider groups of stakeholders. We differ from traditional anthropologists in that: we work with research participants intensively, in ways that are to the point and aim for depth, but often short term (Pink & Morgan 2013); we undertake ethnography in teams, where different researchers play different roles (Pink 2022); we bring together findings from different but related projects (Pink 2022). The work discussed spans over six years and researchers have moved in and out of projects and between the partner organisations involved, as their own trajectories have evolved.

# Min väg till jobbet

Kattarp - Mariastaden - Drottninghög

07.10 Inga bilar i garaget men många cyklar och några motorcyklar.

**FIGURE 9.1** Part of a photo diary where a participant took photos of his 'way to work' (min väg till jobbet). This is the first picture in the diary with the caption: 07:10 No cars in the garage, but many bikes and a couple of motorbikes. Printed with permission from research participant

The other enduring relationships we build are with the stakeholders in our research, who like us are concerned to produce new, better understandings and more realistic and responsible visions of possible futures – that is futures that put people at the centre. Moreover we seek to shift the temporality of our research. Futures are always present in our research agenda, even when we do not explicitly ask about them. Our research design is shaped in relation to existing visions of futures that we are concerned about; in some cases, this informs how we investigate the present, and in others, it shapes how we ask people to show, perform and reflect with us on the possible futures they might experience. We also engage with people as they participate in experimental research set up by our research partners, whereby they might use simulations of possible future technologies that cannot be experienced in everyday life in the present. This involves researching with participants as they encounter possible futures and learn how to use simulated technologies that normally exist only in uncertain futures. As we show below, ethnography enables us to disrupt the narratives that our training has already prepared us to be critical of, and as a pedagogical device in our relationships with research partners.

## Autonomous driving cars

In 2015, AD cars were the most hyped emerging technology (Fortune 2015), they were already part of an awaited future, driven by the fantasy of science fiction. By the middle of the second decade of the twenty-first century, AD cars were discussed in terms of their participation in predicted futures, which (as we outline in Pink, Fors & Glöss 2018: 616) saw them as impacting on both society and individual lives (e.g. McKinsey & Company 2016), in ways such as: creating time for people to socialise, use infotainment and work while travelling by car (Kun, Boll, and Schmidt 2016); making automotive travel safer (Winkle 2016); supporting environmental sustainability as electric cars (Davila and Nombela 2012); or becoming part of new sharing businesses and economies (Lenz and Fraedrich 2016; Olson 2017). However, with some exceptions at the time, little research into human experiences or expectations of AD cars had been undertaken by social scientists in general and (with the exceptions of Wasson 2014; Vinkhuyzen and Cefkin 2016) by anthropologists in particular. Our work, developed as part of the Human Experiences and Expectations of Autonomous Driving (HEAD) project, an academic partnership with Volvo Cars in Sweden, sought to understand how people imagined and experienced AD cars, both through researching with them in the present to imagine AD futures, and engaging with them as they participated in testing simulated AD cars.

During the earlier years of our research, one story about AD cars tended to dominate academic, industry and policy environments and framed how much academic work subsequently addressed industry and policy makers. The narrative is as follows: AD cars were thought to be coming, and their societal benefits – in particular the guarantee of improved road safety and energy efficiency – were eagerly awaited by governments and illuminated by reports produced by consultancies and industry organisations. Technologically AD cars were possible, even if imperfect. However, this awaited future became moderated, as the regulatory, ethical and practical questions that their rollout would have entailed became increasingly acknowledged: philosophers (JafariNaimi 2018, Sparrow & Howard 2017) and geographers (Ash 2017) highlighted the ethical concerns; and regulators (although with some global variation) remained cautious about the rollout of fully AD cars on the roads.

However, while such discussions of ethics raise critical issues, they tend to be inextricable from an innovation process where engineering solutions create social and ethical questions that are sorted out in the aftermath by philosophers and regulators. The discussion of ethics and regulation of AD by philosophers is valuable; however, solving the ethical problems presented by AD by proposing future scenarios that would be ethically viable tends to only offer solutions to problems generated by technological innovation, rather than shifting the paradigm that creates these problems. As we argue below the intervention needs to be prior to this.

Our first ethnographic step into the field of AD car research was in 2016 in a study carried out by Sarah Pink, Vaike Fors and Mareike Glöss, which explored how people experienced driving in the present, how they experienced using automated features when their cars had them, how they used their smartphones and any modes of automation associated with apps in relation to their cars and how they imagined AD features and futures in relation to these experiences. We accompanied participants in their homes while they enacted their usual morning routines as they prepared to leave for work, and then took us on a drive to show us some or all of their daily commuting route, and discuss their experiences with us, while we video recorded.

At this point in our research trajectory, AD cars were predicted by some to be on the roads by 2020 and were largely represented in public discourses in terms of the societal benefits that they would bring if only publics would trust and accept them, and regulators allowed them. However, on the basis of our ethnographic encounters, we proposed a different argument. Our research showed that by putting human action at the centre of the question a different mode of thinking was possible, which meant we could imagine mobilities futures different to the model where the AD car was a discrete new product which could be launched into a society and subsequently beneficially impact on human lives and the environment. We argued that the question of how future technology innovation would change societal futures needed to be turned around, proposing that:

> the mobile future is likely to be one where smartphones, cars and wider transportation and mobilities systems might be vastly changed and/or not be what we currently know them to be. Therefore in order to grasp the principles of how this might play out (rather than predict its form) we need to research what people actually do and what really matters to them when they use cars and smartphones, and how everyday human interventions towards their interoperability are emerging.
>
> *Pink, Fors & Glöss 2018: 617*

While the final publication date of our work was 2018, the thinking behind it was developed from the moment we realised that the relationship between the car and the smartphone constituted a kind of hybrid technology rather than the two separately used discrete technologies. We were able to suggest that the idea of an AD car as a dominant form and a closed or independent product should be revised. While we would not claim to have predicted what has subsequently happened, events by the end of 2018 endorsed our point, as future mobilities began to be imagined increasingly as constituted through connected technologies and in particular smartphone apps.

Other ethnographic work we have developed has focused on how people experience and learn to use Wizard of Oz (WoZ) cars – cars in which the experience of being in an AD car (or a car with various levels of AD features) is simulated to the point where 'drivers' believe they are in a real AD car. Through this research, we have both developed understandings of how Human-Computer-Interaction (HCI) researchers in technology design disciplines and in the automotive industry conceptualise the way people trust and accept technologies (Osz et al 2018, Raats et al 2020). We do not address this question here due to space constraints, but note that, complicit in the narratives of technological solutionism discussed above, these trajectories of research and design seek to contribute to the success of technology solutions by designing and testing technologies that people will readily trust and accept. Our research has shown that trust and acceptance of new technologies however is much more circumstantial, and related not simply to the human-technology factor but to many other elements (Pink et al. 2020).

In summary our trajectory of research relating to AD cars has suggested that people use cars in ways not necessarily compatible with the vision of the future clean and shared AD car. People improvise to bring cars and other technologies together in ways that suit them and it is likely that they will do the same when encountering AD cars, and moreover it is likely that they will not trust or accept AD cars as envisaged in dominant narratives.

Since then, possible futures imagined for AD cars have diversified and the model of MaaS, of which AD cars might be an integral part, has become increasingly popular. Here the idea of an AD car as a technology that has leaky boundaries with other mobile and mobility technologies (Pink, Fors and Glöss in 2018) has become increasingly relevant in a context where AD futures are frequently conceptualised as part of and relational to other things, processes and services. Yet, the ways in which AD cars have been conceptualised in MaaS narratives – as part of a seamless system – are quite different to the leaky and relational technologies and blurred boundaries that we found in ethnographic research.

## Mobility as a Service

Towards the end of the first two decades of the century and into the 2020s, there has been a shift in emphasis in predictive narratives concerned with the future of transport mobilities, from AD itself to MaaS platforms and systems, in which AD plays a crucial role. MaaS can generally be defined as a vision of future intelligent transport platforms that integrate various modes of data and transport technologies with the aim of creating seamless, efficient and sustainable systems of mobility, by engaging modes of machine learning (ML), artificial intelligence (AI) and automated decision making (ADM). Of particular interest to us is the idea that within MaaS systems AD car and micro-mobility services will perform the necessary role of transporting people during the first and last miles of their journeys, since these portions of journeys are frequently not covered by other public or shared transport options.

As we enter the third decade of the twenty-first century, MaaS and other seamless digital platform-based mobility solutions have become frequently discussed components of the future of transport mobility. For example, a report by the influential consultancy McKinsey & Co. envisions that a shift 'from "vehicle as a product" to "mobility as a service"' which will create new consumer experiences and enable 'automotive players across the value chain to transform their business models into subscription models and lifecycle monetization' (McKinsey & Company 2020: 112).

MaaS has also been associated with mobility solutions for first and last mile travel. The first and last miles of travel have been framed as a 'problem', which when not well serviced by public transport encourages private car use. Therefore, AD cars and micro-mobility technologies – bike shares, electric bike shares, etc. – are discussed as first and last mile mobility solutions, to reduce the need for private car travel and ownership. For instance, McKinsey & Co. created a case study scenario for Frankfurt whereby: people would use shared micro-mobility technologies – electric scooters, bikes and mopeds – for daily commuting, and other leisure travel in the city, instead of cars; and this would be supported by the right regulatory frameworks, and urban infrastructures such as bike lanes, and hubs where people could seamlessly switch transport modes (Heineke et al 2019). AD cars are also suggested as last mile solutions by start-ups and in technology research disciplines. For example, a Singapore start-up QIQ Global (https://qiq.global/) is proposing to launch small two-seater electric semi-AD pods with self-parking and platooning features for last mile transportation (Abdulla 2020, August 12). Researchers have also explored the possibility of using AD cars for last mile transport in cities in the Netherlands (Scheltes et al 2017) and research into users of a last mile shuttle bus services has been focused on passengers' acceptance of these vehicles in relation to their feelings of safety and security (Soe et al 2020). A growing literature on such questions in engineering and transport research disciplines sees the AD shuttle or car as a first or last mile transport solution, alongside micro-mobility services. These first and last mile solutions are expected to contribute to the elimination of societal problems of car ownership, support the shift to electric vehicles and micro-mobility and to eliminate individual inconveniences. This, like earlier visions of AD cars as solutions to problems including environmental sustainability, traffic congestion and time poor quality of life issues (see Pink et al. 2018 for a critique of this) is consistent with the solutionist paradigm outlined above.

Yet, typically these proposals for new mobility solutions are not based on deep understandings of how people experience travel in diverse everyday life situations or the values that underpin this travel. Thus, we need to ask who are such solutions and conveniences made for? What everyday values do they suggest their users will have as they take up the personalised services offered by digital platforms informed by predictive data analytics? Whose first and last mile are they concerned with? And what do we find when we look at other peoples' first and last miles? As the geographer David Bissell eloquently puts it:

> Rather than imagining individual commuters as atom-like particles that mechanistically move from one point to another according to unchanging laws, we need to develop an appreciation of the richer suite of forces at play.
>
> *Bissell 2018: xix*

Our interest in first and last mile challenges was related both to the emerging industry and policy discourses surrounding them and to our research partners and stakeholders' interest in them. Moreover, first and last mile issues had already been raised as a key question for our (AHA) project during a workshop in 2018, where one of the groups had identified this as a topic to explore in relation to the future of AD pods and mobilities. Therefore, within our next project (AHAII) the possibilities of the first and last mile became a key question, which we addressed through a study of diverse communities in which we suspected these concepts would have different meanings. Here we discuss an example from this work: a preliminary 2020 study of how the diverse participants in the Drottninghög neighbourhood of Helsingborg city in the southwest of Sweden use their locality and the meanings of their first and last miles. Drottninghög is a socially and ethnically diverse working class neighbourhood, outside the city centre. It was built in 1967 as part of the Million Programme that aimed at providing Sweden with a million homes in ten years. The area is filled with identical apartment complexes, and there is a centre with social services and is surrounded by large grocery shops. It takes 15 minutes to take the bus to Helsingborg city centre and the area is undergoing a major transformation to densify and create both demographic and physical variation. Our Drottninghög participants are not intended to be a representative sample of future first and last mile mobility service users, rather our aim was to explore ongoing everyday practices, and reveal the implications of considering diversity.

In 2020 we interviewed five men and seven women living or working in Drottninghög, aged between 17 and 74. We found that for these participants the local environment and their family networks were a priority and were inextricable from how they moved and travelled. For them, accessing local shops, parks and community projects in the area was fundamental and they used local knowledge to know where and when to go. For instance: participants described how they worked out when to go to different shops to get the bargains, using the range of local shops rather than just one; one participant explained how he knew all the bus numbers and that their stops that were a short walk for him if he wanted to catch one into Helsingborg. Participants enjoyed walking through their local area near to their homes, making the first and last miles of their commutes or walks into the centre of Drottninghög not a problem to solve, make easier or eliminate with a mobility service. Rather the first mile was home, an environment they knew well and filled with the social, environmental, material and other resources that they needed and accessed on an everyday basis, through diverse experiences which included walking freely or with technological assistance for some older and disabled people. As one participant, A, who worked locally, expressed it, the social aspect and the feel of the neighbourhood were important:

> I work at Drottninghög's library so it is only walking distance, about 2–3 minutes depending. But sometimes it can take a little longer before I get to work because from home to work I meet a lot of people who might stop me on the road and then we start talking about one thing and the other. And it's just fun.

B has a car – a Mercedes – following from his first car, of the same make, which his grandfather had bought him. He loves his car and likes driving in this area, where participants told us a car was seen as a status symbol. Yet like other participants, he enjoys the local area for walking and meeting people and only uses the car if pressed

**FIGURE 9.2** One of the local shops in Drottninghög, a place to socialise on the way to work (Photo: Vaike Fors)

for time, stressing that 'if you just want to take a walk and shop at the same time, and talk to nice people, it takes quite a long time until you get home'. He told us:

> I both cycle in the area and go 'yes', when I have to shop something like that, which is nice when you walk, it really only takes me five to seven minutes togo to Maxi ..., but usually it takes so long because you meet so many nice people on the way when you stop and talk, 'how are you?', 'what are you doing now?', 'how are you?' and so on, so it can take a long time to ... go there and come back home.

These feelings were reiterated by other participants, for whom being in the local environment itself – rather than moving through and past it in a vehicle – was valued. Participants liked walking through the local streets near their homes, where they might bump into old neighbours or friends or just enjoy walking through, observing, relaxing. This included walking: with the dog; to the shops; or within their commute to Helsingborg.

For instance, C has lived in Drottninghög for 12 years and has 3 kids aged 9, 7 and 3 years. She works in preschools in Helsingborg and has one year left to finish her qualification as a preschool teacher at University. She and her husband are both refugees, have no other family in Sweden and have lived in two places in

**FIGURE 9.3** Walking through Drottninghög provides lots of opportunities to bump into people (Photo: Vaike Fors)

Drottninghög. C does not have a car, driving licence or bike so uses public transport and/or walking. She felt that driving would make her lazy and explained that walking was important to her in part because she has diabetes and needs to exercise, but also, she said:

> because it's more fun so when you walk you can get the opportunity to see a little more nature and take a little more air … But if you cycle, you have to go there in two or three minutes and you are back two or three minutes later.

She walks to the train station when she commutes to work by train. For C, ever since she arrived in Sweden using public transport has helped her to feel part of society.

When participants did use cars, this was most often not because they did not want to walk, cycle or get on public transport, but rather because their social identities, everyday family logistics, regimes of caring for others or timescales made it impossible to do anything else. Where cars were used they were often part of family relationships and used in contexts where they manifested modes of caring. For example, sharing the car among family members, families, friends and even neighbours was central to how participants coordinated everyday mobility. Sharing their cars, in a way, became the continuation of private car use, rather than something that could be provided by a mobility service. For instance, one participant used her car to drop off her kids to school during her commute, or to take her husband to the station when the weather was bad and he could not cycle.

Thus, as our ethnographic findings emerged, the proposition that the concept of the first and last mile represented a 'problem' and was filled with everyday inconveniences for individuals which MaaS might solve, appeared increasingly mismatched with the everyday experiences and routines of our participants. The ways people travelled were underpinned by the values and everyday ethics that are embedded in the socialities and economies of place and family.

## Intervention

During the journey of our research into AD cars and their possibilities for future mobilities we, with our co-researchers and research partners, have considered a series of scenarios, for example: that AD cars would be on the roads in Sweden by 2020; AD pods as first and last mile solutions; and AD cars within car sharing services. We will likely continue to co-create and investigate these and other such scenarios. Our anthropological task here is to participate in both the making of and the constructive critique of such scenarios, we are at once complicit in the constitution of narratives about possible mobility futures and in challenging them through our ethnographic research. The ethics of thinking about futures needs to be embedded in the diversity of the people whose futures we are concerned with, not only those people whose futures contribute to the narratives of digital capitalism and the services and products associated with it. We stress that as well as the diverse contexts of the global North, discussed here, as addressed elsewhere (Pink et al. 2018), it is also essential to collaboratively and critically respond to such questions from and with the global South.

Our approach acknowledges the uncertainty of any futures that we might wish to see as possible and that engages ethnographic investigation to unravel the elements that *complicate* such futures. One example of how we have done this is to make our ethnographic material produced in the AHAII project available and accessible in a catalogue format, which is iterated through the life of the project by adding materials as the project moves on. In the first iteration, we developed a workshop in which we invited the automotive company and city stakeholders connected to our project to engage with research themes developed from our ethnographic analysis of first and last mile mobilities in two neighbourhoods, including Drottninghög discussed above. In the catalogue, the themes were presented through stories told by the research participants, and the stories were used to reframe grand narratives and taken-for-granted concepts relating to how AD technologies are perceived as solutions to the 'first and last mile challenge' in people's everyday lives. The stakeholders were also asked to create worst- and best-case scenarios based on their engagement in the ethnographic materials, to inform the next prototyping phase in the project. One such worst-case scenario that emanated from this exercise was the 'Lonely and Excluding Pod Life' where

**Lonely and Excluding Pod life**

Everyone (kids, adults) has access to their own pod. The mileage of a pod is limited and when it runs out you have to e.g. walk or cycle. Wealthy families buy more pods to increase the amount of mileage they have. Family members trade their pod mileage with each other to maximise the use. Pods or shuttles provide solutions that target mainly high income families based on business travel needs. Oversized shuttles becomes a status symbol.

When travelling in groups pods connect together. This way each person is in their own pod and/or everything becomes delivered in automated delivery services. This limits the social interaction between the people travelling and the social interaction between people in shops etc.

**FIGURE 9.4** Worst-case scenario from the AHAII-catalogue (2022), printed with permission from the AHA II project

everyone travels in their own AD pod with no possibilities for social interaction (similar to today's privately owned car, but with the difference that each family member travels in their own single pod).

This involves a collaborative mode of working rather than a critical approach that simply pushes up against dominant narratives from the outside. Such interventions also require a nuanced understanding of transport mobilities, which echoes Bissell's proposal for 'an "ecological" approach to exploring transit life' which involves sensing 'how our everyday journeys to and from work are entangled in complex webs of relations with other people, places, times, ideas, and materials. … these webs of relations are kaleidoscopic. They are shape-shifting rather than static' (Bissell 2018: xix).

As we have shown through our ethnographic examples, transport mobilities are shaped by everyday practice, the values and priorities that underpin it and the contingent circumstances in which these evolve. It is important to bring these findings to the table where they can be debated alongside the ambitions and assumptions of industry partners and urban planners. Simultaneously the imagined futures of transport mobilities are also contingent and continually shifting, as are the organisations, industries and professionals who bring them to life. The future of AD cars continues to be reimagined, in dominant narratives as it emerges as a possible solution to evolving 'problems'. Our own work likewise shifts as we seek to re-shape these narratives. The key challenge for us to get ahead of the game, that is rather than only critically responding to dominant narratives, we need to put the ethics of attending to people at the forefront. Imagine a world where future mobility scenarios were led by a people-focused approach shaped through a design anthropological paradigm.

## Acknowledgements

We thank the many people who have participated in our research into future automated mobilities over the last decade, without whom our research would have been impossible. We also acknowledge and thank the academics and industry colleagues who have collaborated and partnered with us in the projects discussed in this chapter and the organisations who have funded our work: the Human Experiences and Expectations of Autonomous Driving (HEAD) project was undertaken by Vaike Fors and Sarah Pink, academic colleagues Martin Berg and Robert Willim, Post-Doctoral researchers Katalin Osz and Mareike Glöss, industrial PhD students Thomas Lindgren and Kaspar Raats, and our industry partners at Volvo Cars Annie Rydström, Robert Broström, Patrik Palo, Samuel Palm, Christoffer Kopp, funded by Swedish Innovation Agency VINNOVA (2016–2018), co-designing future smart urban mobility services – A Human Approach (AHA) and Design Ethnographic Living Labs for Future Urban Mobility – A Human Approach (AHA II), undertaken by Vaike Fors, Sarah Pink, Rachel Charlotte Smith, Jesper Lund, Esbjörn Ebbesson, Meike Brodersen, Peter Lutz, Thomas Lindgren and Kaspar Raats with Partners from City of Helsingborg – Susanne Duval Innings, City of Gothenburg – Suzanne Andersson, Volvo Cars – Patrik Palo, Casper Wickman, Robert Broström, Annie Rydström, Katalin Osz, Jan Nilsson, and transport companies Skånetrafiken and Västtrafik were through Drive Sweden by the Swedish Innovation Agency Vinnova, the Swedish Research Council Formas and the Swedish Energy Agency (2018–2022).

## References

Abdulla, A. Z. (2020, August 12). Singapore start-up QIQ aims to roll out shared electric microcars for last-mile trips. Channel News Asia. www.channelnewsasia.com/news/singapore/qiq-electric-microcars-last-mile-journeys-qiq-pods-13006284.

AHAII-catalogue. (August 2022). https://aha2.hh.se/.

Ash, J. (2017). *Phase Media*. London: Bloomsbury.

Bissell, D. (2018). *Transit Lives*. London: MIT Press.

Cohen, T., Stilgoe, J., Stares, S., Akyelken, N., Cavoli, C., Day, J., Dickinson, J., Fors, V., Hopkins, D., Lyons, G., Marres, N., Newman, J., Reardon, L., Sipe, N., Tennant, C., Wadud, Z., & Wigley, E. (2020). A constructive role for social science in the development of automated vehicles. *Transportation Research Interdisciplinary Perspectives*, 6: 2590–1982.

Davila, A., & Nombela, M. (2012). Platooning – Safe and eco-friendly mobility. In *SAE 2012 World Congress & Exhibition*. Detroit, MI: SAE International.

Estalella, A., & Criado, T. S. (Eds.). (2018). *Experimental Collaborations: Ethnography through Fieldwork Devices* (1st ed., Vol. 34). Berghahn Books. https://doi.org/10.2307/j.ctvw04cwb

Fortune. (2015). The most hyped emerging technology of 2015. http://fortune.com/2015/08/20/selfdriving-car-hype/.

Heineke, K., Kloss, B., & Scurtu, D. (2019, November 25). Micromobility: Industry progress, and a closer look at the case of Munich. McKinsey & Company. www.mckinsey.com/industries/automotive-and-assembly/our-insights/micromobility-industry-progress-and-a-closer-look-at-the-case-of-munich Accessed 28th Nov 2020.

Ingold, T. (2008). Anthropology is not ethnography. *Proceedings of the British Academy*, 154: 69–92.

JafariNaimi, N. (2018). Our bodies in the Trolley's path, or why self-driving cars must *not* be programmed to kill. *Science, Technology, & Human Values*, 43(2): 302–323.

Kun, A. L., Boll, S., & Schmidt, A. (2016). Shifting gears: User interfaces in the age of autonomous driving. *IEEE Pervasive Computing*, 15(1): 32–38. DOI: 10.1109/MPRV.2016.14.

Legacy, C., Ashmore, D., Scheurer, J., Stone J., & Curtis, C. (2018). Planning the driverless city. *Transport Reviews*, 39(1): 84–102.

Lenz, B., & Fraedrich, E. (2016). New mobility concepts and autonomous driving: The potential for change. In M. Maurer, J. C. Gerdes, B. Lenz and H. Winner (Eds.) *Autonomous Driving. Technical, Legal, and Social Aspects*. Berlin: Springer. 173–192.

Marres, N. (2018). What if nothing happens? Street trials of intelligent cars as experiments in participation. In S. Maassen, S. Dickel & C. H. Schneider (Eds.) *TechnoScience in Society, Sociology of Knowledge Yearbook*. Niimegen: Springer/Kluwer.

Markham, T. (2020). *Digital Life*. Cambridge: Polity.

Massey, D. (1995) *For Space*. London: Sage

McKinsey & Company. (2016). Disruptive trends that will transform the auto industry. www.mckinsey.com/industries/high-tech/our-insights/disruptive-trends-that-will-transform-the-autoindustry.

McKinsey & Company. (2020). *From no Mobility to Future Mobility: Where COVID-19 has Accelerated Change Compendium 2020/2021*. McKinsey Center for Future Mobility®. www.mckinsey.com/industries/automotive-and-assembly/our-insights/from-no-mobility-to-future-mobility-where-covid-19-has-accelerated-change

Morozov, E. (2013). *To Save Everything, Click Here: Technology, Solutionism, and the Urge to Fix Problems that Don't Exist*. London: Penguin Books.

Olson, E. L. (2017). Will songs be written about autonomous cars? The implications of self-driving vehicle technology on consumer brand equity and relationships. *International Journal of Technology Marketing*, 12(1). DOI: 10.1504/IJTMKT.2017.081506

Osz, K., Rydström, A., Pink, S., Fors, V., & Broström, R. (2018). Building collaborative testing practices: doing ethnography with WOz in autonomous driving research. *IxD&A Journal*, 37: 12–20.

Pink, S. (2015). *Doing sensory ethnography*. Sage, London

Pink, S. (2021) *Doing Visual Ethnography*. 4th edition. London: Sage.

Pink, S. (2022). *Emerging Technologies / Life at the Edge of the Future*. Oxford: Routledge.

Pink, S. & Salazar, J. F. (2017). Anthropologies and futures: Setting the agenda. In J. Salazar, S. Pink, A. Irving and J. Sjoberg (Eds.) *Anthropologies and Futures*. Oxford: Bloomsbury. 3–22.

Pink, S., Gomes, A., Zilse, R., Lucena, R., Pinto, J., Porto, A., Caminha, C., de Siqueira, G. M., & Duarte de Oliveira, M. (2018). Automated and connected? Smartphones and automobility through the Global South. *Applied Mobilities*, 6(1): 54–70. DOI: 10.1080/23800127.2018.1505263.

Pink, S., Fors, V., & Glöss, M. (2018). The contingent futures of the mobile present: Beyond automation as innovation. *Mobilities*, 13(5): 615–631.

Pink, S., Fors, V., Lanzeni, D., Duque, M., Sumartojo, S. & Strengers, Y. (2022) *Design Ethnography: Research, Responsibility and Futures*. Oxford: Routledge.

Pink, S., Fors, V., & Lindgren, T. (2018). Emerging technologies and anticipatory images: Uncertain ways of knowing with automated and connected mobilities. *Philosophy of Photography*, 9(2): 195–216. DOI: 10.1386/pop.9.2.195_1.

Pink, S., Osz, K., Raats, K., Lindgren, T., & Fors, V. (2020). Design anthropology for emerging technologies: Trust and sharing in autonomous driving futures. *Design Studies*, 69. DOI: 10.1016/j.destud.2020.04.002

Raats, K., Fors, V., & Pink, S. (2020). Trusting autonomous vehicles: An interdisciplinary approach. *Transportation Research Interdisciplinary Perspectives*, 7(100201). https://doi.org/10.1016/j.trip.2020.100201.

Scheltes, A., & Homem de Almeida Correia, G. (2017). Exploring the use of automated vehicles as last mile connection of train trips through an agent-based simulation model: An application to Delft, Netherlands. *International Journal of Transportation Science and Technology*, 6(1): 28–41.

Smith, R. C. (2022). Editorial: Design anthropology, special issue, design studies. *The Interdisciplinary Journal of Design Research*, 80. https://doi.org/10.1016/j.destud.2022.101081

Smith, R. C., & Otto, T. (2016). Cultures of the future: Emergence and intervention in design anthropology. In R. C. Smith, K. T. Vangkilde , M. G. Kjærsgaard, T. Otto, J. Halse and T. Binder (Eds.) *Design Anthropological Futures*. London: Routledge. 19–36.

Soe, R. M., & Müür, J. (2020). Mobility acceptance factors of an automated shuttle bus last-mile service. *Sustainability*, 12(13): 5469.

Sparrow, R. J., & Howard, M. (2017). When human beings are like drunk robots: Driverless vehicles, ethics, and the future of transport. *Transportation Research Part C: Emerging Technologies, 80*: 206–215. https://doi.org/10.1016/j.trc.2017.04.014

Stilgoe, J. (2018). Machine learning, social learning and the governance of self-driving cars. *Social Studies of Science*, 48(1): 25–56.

Vinkhuyzen, E., & Cefkin, M. (2016). Developing socially acceptable autonomous vehicles. In *Ethnographic Praxis in Industry Conference*. Minneapolis, US: Wiley Online Library, August 29–September 1. 522–534.

Winkle, T. (2016). Safety benefits of automated vehicles: Extended findings from accident research for development, validation and testing. In M. Maurer, J. C. Gerdes, B. Lenz and H. Winner (Eds.) *Autonomous Driving. Technical, Legal, and Social Aspects*. Berlin: Springer. 335–364.

# 10

# ECO-SENSORY TECHNOLOGIES AND THE SURREALIST IMPULSE

*Elizabeth de Freitas, Maggie MacLure and David Rousell*

## Introduction

Sensory experiences are newly reconfigured in a vastly expanded digital economy which is reshaping our relations to place and culture, and distributing data across widespread circuits of connectivity (Ruppert et al 2013). Sensing is now distributed across an increasingly complex array of digital devices, bodies, architectures, and built environments (Gabrys 2016, Tironi 2017). Digital sensors are 'emplaced' within buildings, embedded in smart phones, worn on bodies, mounted on rooftops, orbiting in satellites, submerged in soil, flying through air, and connected to plant and animal life. This redistribution of sensory relations goes well beyond the quantified self (Lupton 2016) and is occurring at a planetary scale, emblematic of what Rosi Braidotti (2013, 2019) has termed the 'posthuman condition', a convergence of technological and climatological disruptions that radically destabilises our understanding of sensory capacity. Under these conditions, the digital has come to be part of a 'general ecology' that commingles the 'natural' and the 'artificial' in new uncharted terrain (Hörl 2018). In terms of ethnographic research, this opens onto what Clough (2009) envisages: 'an *infra-empiricism* that allows for a rethinking of bodies, matter and life through new encounters with visceral perception and pre-conscious affect' (Clough 2009: 44; emphasis added).

Since 2015, our work in the Manchester Manifold Lab[1] has explored the creative potentials of a range of sensor technologies, including *environmental sensors* that detect invisible gases and particulate matter; *force sensors* that detect gravity and push/pull encounters; mobile *360 camera sensors* that can scan three-dimensional objects and environments; wearable *movement sensors* that detect a body's speed, acceleration, and orientation; and *biological sensors* that sense unconscious shifts in bodily temperature, heart rate, blood volume pulse, and electro-dermal skin activity (EDA). Recent developments in mobile technologies, affective computing,

DOI: 10.4324/9781003084471-11

neuro-marketing, movement and geo-location sensors, have made wearable digital devices increasingly accessible to corporations, governments, and the general public. The rapid movement of bio-eco-sensors and 'hand-held' technology, from the laboratory into the public domain, can be understood as a new stage in the relentless commodification of life through the algorithmic capture of sense data. By harnessing the otherwise invisible and asignifying play of affective intensity on the surface of the skin, for instance, the capture of biodata adds new subconscious dimensions to ubiquitous behavioural, geolocative, and predictive data profiling of individuals under corporate and governmental regimes. By tracking eye movements and micro-gestures, for instance, cameras capable of recording pre-conscious affect can fracture the 'moment' into molecular signals, while software sorts inhuman amounts of images for patterns in behaviour. In short, there is now the dangerous possibility – and current reality – that governments and corporations are 'mining' the intensive, unconscious, and affective dimensions of the body (de Freitas & Rousell 2021).

Our engagement with sensor technologies is driven by an interest in how digital devices might be repurposed to resist the clinical and pathologising discourses that have historically dominated the use of these technologies. We are interested in working with sense data as that which inheres in the relational environment (worldly sensibility) rather than the person (stimulus-response). This involves a complete retheorisation of sensors and data which contests the stimulus-response psychological model of perception studies (de Freitas 2018). The latter model, for instance, treats epidermal sensors (EDA) and the electrical conductivity of the skin as associated with intensity of affective response and the arousal of the sympathetic nervous system (Piccolini & Bresadola 2013, Platoni 2015). Typical scientific studies of skin conductance maintain the individual organism as the unit of analysis, attributing causality to an external stimulus triggering an internal response that materialises on the surface of the skin under controlled conditions (Hernandez et al. 2014). Our interest, on the other hand, is not in individual response or inter-subjective relations, but rather, in the fielding of impersonal atmospheric intensities that play across the wet surfaces of bodies, gathering transindividual sensitivities whereby the 'intensive atmosphere' carries within it the qualitative and quantitative ambivalences of worldly sensibility (de Freitas & Rousell 2021).

Might sensory technologies, as conceptualised and deployed through an ethnography of intensities, offer new possibilities for reactivating atmospheric blocks of sensation, while resisting the imperialist eye of conventional ethnography? Deleuze and Guattari (1987, 1994) argue that the human senses be reconsidered as part of an asignifying alliance, an eco-sensory ground on which the pyramid of representation is subsequently erected, its energy solidified into foundational 'bricks' of culture (signification). The task then is to try to follow the intensities and forces that still move, or might move, within the hierarchical structures of conventional representation. Our interest in the imperceptible forces that lie beyond or beneath human consciousness brings our work into contact with ethnography's recurring engagement with surrealism, as we describe below. Our focus in this chapter is therefore on sensor technologies as potential agents of surrealist ethnographic experimentation. We engage with digital devices as ecological agents, tracking intensive flows, layering affect, invaginating power, ramifying insight, and entangling concepts through playful inversion, pursuing a kind of surreal participation that avoids de-scription and conventional causal exegesis. Our approach builds on Deleuze and Guattari's important elaboration of 'sensation', and our own work which has contested the theorisation of sensation in perception studies (de Freitas 2016, 2020, de Freitas et al 2019).

We discuss here a project situated at the Whitworth Art Gallery in Manchester, UK, conducted in collaboration with the Young Contemporaries, a youth gallery programme. The gallery was approached as a public space and sensory milieu, structured, according to convention, to elicit perception and judgements of cultural value. We treated the gallery as a space for experimenting with the relational capacities of art, pedagogy, and collective forms of sensing, mobilising sensor technologies as part of a surrealist experiment. This approach was partially inspired by the work of Media theorist Mark Hansen (2015) who uses the concept of 'worldly sensibility' to describe a new 'radically environmental' distribution of sensation within computational material-cultures. Hansen defines worldly sensibility as a vast causal infrastructure of sensory activity that operates above, around, through, and below the thresholds of human sense perception and consciousness (Hansen 2015: 2). He argues that contemporary sensor technologies operate at speeds and scales that fall outside the bandwidth of human perception and thereby 'impact the environment – including our bodily environment – before impacting … our higher-order sensory and perceptual faculties' (Hansen 2015: 38). The micro-temporal speeds of digital algorithms, signal processers, camera mechanisms, and actuators operate so quickly that they literally feed sensory data 'forward', into the future, before we have a chance to catch up. Akin in some ways to early surrealist experiments with the non-conscious and autonomous tendencies of events, Hansen (2015) focuses on how digital sensors fold time in new ways, opening onto more than human temporalities. As sensory technologies stretch and package time below thresholds of human consciousness, we see the emergence of new forms of participation, labour, exploit, control, and surplus value arising within these 'augmented' posthuman milieus (Massumi 2018). This algorithmic capture of sensation to serve corporate, managerial, and governmental agendas makes critical and creative engagements with sensors increasingly urgent, a task that our project took up through a 'remixing' of sensory technologies and ethnographic surrealism.

## Ethnographic surrealism

Through its periodic encounters with surrealism, anthropology has found techniques for engaging with sensation, affect and more-than-human relations that exceed interpretation and rationality. Schwanhäußer and Wellgraf (2015) identify ethnographic surrealism as a 'minor' line or 'rogue tradition' in anthropology. They sketch the cyclical appearance of this surrealist impulse, from its inception in France in the 1930s, when the boundaries among surrealism, anthropology, and art were not yet consolidated (Clifford 1981).[2] Figures such as Michel Leiris operated across the boundaries of these disciplines: colonial explorer in the Dakar-Djibouti mission of 1931–33, contributor to the influential Surrealist journal *Documents*, author of the literary-ethnographic hybrid *Phantom Africa*, and member of the College de Sociologie, led by Bataille and Callois, which aimed to systematically document communal practices that reveal 'the sacred in everyday life'. Schwanhäußer and Wellgraf trace the subsequent appearances of ethnographic surrealism through its 'flirtatious liaison' with folklore, art, and social documentary in movements such as Mass Observation in the UK in the 1950s, the counterculture of the 1960s, its reappearance as avatar of postmodern sensibility embraced by James Clifford in the 1980s, the postcolonial surrealism of Michael Taussig, and recent explorations of the uncanny workings of affect in the work of Kathleen Stewart and Brian Massumi.

Schneider and Pasquolino (2014) also recount the use of avant-garde experimental film tactics within the history of anthropology, as do Estalella and Criado (2018) and Salazar et al (2017). Cinematic techniques have been used by anthropologists to disrupt the realist narrative, including superpositioning of images and jarring montage. Maya Deren's work (i.e. *Meshes of the afternoon*, 1943) foregrounds surrealist montage techniques in her study of trance-like feelings associated with ritual. The anthropologist Jean Rouch (i.e. *Les Maitres fou*, 1955) spoke of a 'ciné-trance' which used the camera and editing to bring the spectator into what Deleuze called the time-image (de Freitas 2015, 2016). These experiments were no less controversial in their reproduction of a colonial gaze, but they raised questions about how the scopic regime was structured through new media. More recently, Wanano (2014) describes how her ethnographic video work attempts to examine the role of the pixel (rather than the image) and thereby reckon with the role of software in the processing of video data.

The surrealists' fascination with inhuman affects, drugs, trance, dreams, ritual magic, and ghosts did not preclude a deep interest in science and technology. As Schwanhäußer and Wellgraf (2015) observe, their avant-garde experimentalism shared with normative science a commitment to a kind of objectivity that sought to bypass the proclivities of the authorial subject, in order to allow thought to manifest itself. Surrealism was experimental and speculative – aspiring to release the energies of the non-rational through experiments with automatic writing and photography, and innovative uses of film. Artists such as Ernst, Deren, and Duchamp for instance deployed the conventions of the magnetic or seismic trace in their art, in order to introject duration into the static scene of representations. Lomas and Stubbs (2012) describes automatism as practised by the surrealists as pre-eminently speculative: 'a research method, a set of investigative procedures that *organise and govern practice but do not determine outcomes*' (emphasis added). He notes how the surrealists appropriated early recording technologies, with the aim of transforming themselves into 'modest recording devices' capable of providing a graphic trace of 'forces and phenomena that do not themselves belong to a visual order of things'.

At the start of our project, the Whitworth Art Gallery was featuring *Thick Time*, an exhibition of five complex installations by South-African contemporary artist William Kentridge. Kentridge's bold architectural modification of the gallery radically transformed the museum space from an environment that traditionally conveys deference to dominant/hegemonic cultural value. The exhibition created a distinctive multi-sensory ecosystem of multi-channel sound, film, animation, sculptural, choreographic, and architectural components in a densely affective atmosphere. The artworks relayed disparate sounds, chants, atonal music, and polytemporal rhythms through non-linear imagery and obliquely positioned megaphones, altering the visual-sonic fabric of the space continuously. Rooms were also occupied by strangely altered antique media devices, large kinetic breathing and banging machines, which maintained a consistent pulse of rhythmic activity dissonant with surrounding audio and video screenings.

Our aim was to explore young people's sensory engagement with the gallery space during six workshops and an installation. The project attempted to mobilise a postcolonial surrealist impulse that we sensed in Kentridge's installation work, whose playful dynamic installations lured the eye, only to blast apart any unity of sense in the bombastic reverberating activity and incessant movement. His installations wove together re-imagined histories of colonialism with the philosophy of art, cinema, science, and technology. Kentridge (2014, min 12) has explained this approach simply as the way of going through the world; of going through the world making sense. There is no other way. 'We don't have complete information, and we cannot take it in'. Kentridge's work refuses the clarity of a single or coherent narrative of both coloniality and cultural revolution and produces monstrous and awkward machines, forging a polytemporal mix of imagery, sounds, and materials.

## Remixing thick time

Our workshops brought about 20 young people together for 3 hours at the gallery on each of six occasions. We were focused on the ways in which new media might be mobilised to alter the sense of time and participation, and how this altered form of engagement was linked to the themes and methods of Kentridge's *Thick Time*. We sought to experiment with various technologies, with the aim of sensing the affective atmospheres of the exhibition, plugging bodies into the liveliness, intensity, and multi-temporality of the artworks. More generally, we were interested in the sensory dimension of gallery experiences, noting that the senses become attuned to shifting compositions of light, sound, space, colour, movement, and form. We were also interested in how gallery time can feel surreally suspended, altered, slowed, quickened, or transfixed as bodies become affected by the particular atmosphere sustained within the built environment.

Our experimental techniques in the workshops included: (1) *The haptic eye*, which involved the use of hand-held and chest-mounted video-cameras as drawing tools for tracing the movement of Kentridge's art-media machines. These videos were subsequently cut into still images at half-second intervals, printed on paper, then traced onto wax paper, photographed, and reassembled as a form of stop-motion video. (2) *The sensing body*, which involved wearing biosensors that captured changes in electro-dermal activity, relayed via Bluetooth to a laptop. Participants moved together through the exhibition rooms while simultaneously watching the graphical rendering of the five biometrical responses in different colour codes on the computer screen. Later these devices were installed as part of a 'concept activation' game which further disrupted the biometric signals. (3) *Sounding time*, in which stereophonic headphones were plugged into a binaural audio-recorder and worn by participants as they circulated through the gallery space, multiplying and magnifying the tonalities and sonic atmospheres. (4) *Fugitive whispers*, which involved selecting particular places in the gallery, huddling in a small group, and then reading aloud, in a whisper, poetic texts about sensation and time.

Each of our workshops began by spreading 'concept cards' out on the table and inviting young people to pick one, including 'affect', 'sensation', 'sense', 'atmosphere', 'time', 'attunement', and 'intensity'. Discussions involved sense-making and sense-*breaking*, to the extent that a concept such as 'attunement' might travel from initial associations with 'listening', 'connection', and 'togetherness' into much darker associations with 'surveillance', 'predation', and 'death'. After a few visits, the skin conductance devices (EDA) were introduced, as playful gadgets, and different participants tried them on, and discussed how they operated. The EDA data generated during the discussion was then projected onto a screen in front of the group. This enabled everyone to witness the organic-electrical graphism, as it

**FIGURE 10.1** General view of the *Remixing Thick Time* exhibition

modulated over time, the group data drifting in and out of synchrony; ostensibly folding biosensory data back into the ethnographic site in an iterative feedback loop.

Drawing on the workshop experiments, we developed a set of installations, as part of a culminating public event at the gallery, titled *Remixing Thick Time*. For instance, the recorded 'fugitive whispers' made during the workshops were installed into small containers evocative of travel and departure, themselves installed within a dark inflatable dome of silence within the gallery. Exhibition visitors crawled into the dome with flashlights, seeking out these containers in the dark, and straining to hear these recorded whispers. We wanted to emphasise how whispers resist the urge to broadcast and refuse to fill the space, enticing bodies to come closer and stretch their senses beyond what might feel comfortable. Whispering in the gallery became a politics of counter-speech – quiet, intimate, proximal, close, secretive, opaque, not to be heard by all, without offering the comfort of contextual information, clarity of meaning or an identifiable speaker. We also created a 'Concept activation game' which included a set of cards with the key concepts on one side, and a set of surrealist commands on the flip side, offered as 'activations' of the concept. The game was meant to trouble ideas about stimulus-response in the sensory environment, destabilising the relationship among language, body, and milieu. To simulate the feeling of a game, we designed an embossed tablecloth, a set of game-like instructions, egg-shell timers for tracking time on task, and arranged the set of five EDA sensors on the table, with a projector streaming live biodata from the sensors (when worn) onto the gallery wall (Figure 10.2).

**FIGURE 10.2** Playing the 'Conceptual Activations' game in Whitworth's grand hall
Note: Concept Activiation Game designed by Laura Trafi-Prats, Elizabeth de Freitas, and David Rousell

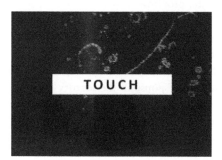

FIGURE 10.3 'Attunement' card, from the *Conceptual Activations* game

FIGURE 10.4 'Touch' card, from the *Conceptual Activations* game

People wandered into the great hall as part of their exploration of the gallery, and many people sat down at the table and began to play the game in a spontaneous, ad hoc fashion, while one member of the team – dressed in a lab coat – facilitated with the EDA sensors and helped clarify the instructions. Others stood by and watched the game play, commenting on the undulating waves of data projected onto the wall. As people started to activate concepts, enormous amounts of laughter were heard throughout the room. Each concept came with commands (Figures 10.3–10.5) which provoked the players to attend to the surreal relationship between sense and sensation, concept and meaning, language (as command) and action, under-scoring the ways in which causal agency is imagined or speculative. We were able to problematise language as timed demand, 'order words' and 'pass-words' (Deleuze & Guattari 1987), whilst situating the group as parlour-table spectators of their own playful layering of embodied rhythms.

Here 'attunement' becomes a kind of unwilled affirmation, a paradoxical move to form the affirmative word 'yes' when your tongue is unfree (Figure 10.3), whilst 'touch' involves imperceptible modes of contact with microscopic particles and affective memories (Figure 10.4), and 'atmosphere' has visitors fogging their mobile phone screens with their own breath, before taking fuzzy pictures of the hand of someone nearby (Figure 10.5).

As one plays and performs the designated task, the skin also signals its electrical activation to the group through the animated projected image. We emphasise how

1. Whisper to someone. Then walk away, while still facing them, and continue whispering until they cannot hear you.

2. Breath deeply on the screen of your phone as you take a picture of the hand of the person sitting next to you.

3. Go around the room actively sniffing. Come back and write a word that captures the smell of the room.

4.

5.

6.

**FIGURE 10.5** 'Atmosphere' card, from the *Conceptual Activations* game

the graphical output 'draws' the quivering charged periphery of the *conjoined* sympathetic nervous system for all players. In other words, the sympathetic nervous system becomes collective and shared, an expression of the affective ecology. The EDA sensory graphic fuses the five distinct signals, while smudging the gap between collective consciousness and collective sensation. Rather than framing this data as representing intensities that belonged to the individual human organism, the surrealist game scatters the signal into the atmosphere. We intended for our approach to resonate with Kentridge's darkly humorous exploration of the ways in which machinic media are mobilised in the making and unmaking of memory and history. The Conceptual Activations game used biosensors as atmospheric vital media to plug into intensive flows, exploring the surrealist underside of sensory data. Our game steals back the biodata and folds it into a graphical rendering that both affirms the body as electric-organic creature and yet undermines any claims to represent the individual as the singular agent of their sense and sensation.

Perhaps this playful event shows how ethnographic participant observation could become something akin to Stengers' 'immanent discrimination' (2018) or Cull's (2011) 'ontological participation', in which the opposition between participation and observation is dissolved or displaced, in favour of immersive, multi-sensory practices of *attention* to 'our ontological participation in immanence, change and movement' (Cull 2011:91). Reading Deleuze's philosophy of immanence in relation to the 'Activities' of performance artist Allan Kaprow, Cull suggests that ontological participation demands a kind of 'attention training' in order to sense the imperceptible movements of difference that compose events and subjects. Kaprow's Activities ask participants to enact seemingly banal or pointless actions; for instance:

> wetting a finger with saliva
> holding it up till dry
> calling out: now!
> Walking on
> 　　　*Kaprow, quoted in*
> 　　　*Cull 2011: 80*

Our Activations share with Kaprow's Activities the aim of bypassing the assurance of the discrete subject and its continuous calibration of meaning, purpose, agency, and self-certainty, in order to attend to the quiver of the inhuman. The notion of attention training amplifies Ingold's rethinking of participant observation as an 'ontological commitment' and 'an education for attention' to the indescribable and the inexplicable in human affairs (2014: 388).

## The missing half second

While strangers sat down to play the concept activation game, we projected a film titled *The Missing Half Second* onto another wall of the gallery and arranged a series of beach chairs for viewing. The film was composed in workshops with the Young Contemporaries using short videos made at the Kentridge show that were later split into 120 half-second still images. These images were printed and brought back to a subsequent workshop, where the images were redrawn, as black and white drawings on semi-transparent paper. These 120 redrawn images were then photographed and recomposed in layers and reanimated as a moving image, smudging the temporality of the event, to foreground the rich multiplicity and ghosting of the present moment. The film explores the idea of a missing temporal interval between sensation and conscious perception (Massumi 2002, Hansen 2006), by continuously interleaving and superimposing the disparate images.

The film is approximately 9 minutes in duration and can be viewed online at https://vimeo.com/326813533. The original video documents a participant as she herself videotaped a strange archaic set of machinic gears placed on top of a large wooden tripod mounted by Kentridge in the art gallery, moving her own camera in a circular fashion to animate the potential movements of this antique machine. In many frames of the video, we find that the gears of Kentridge's machine, the lens of the camera, and the face, arms, and hands of the young woman become indistinct (see Figure 10.6, top). They begin to circulate as an atmospheric body – the young woman's body disappears and reappears, slowly transformed into fragments of gears, fingers, wheels, etc (Figure 10.6, bottom).

The process of sampling and remixing media rendered a sense of being caught up in a maker's loop, which kept us switching back and forth between the still image and the moving image. Each of the original 120 drawn stills also lay along the gallery wall, on benches. The video was a moving image which relayed and proliferated the first images to such an extent, that it seemed to become the substance of an entirely different media, something more atmospheric, as though we had contaminated the gallery with the layerings of these cut-up and re-assembled images. The *Missing Half-Second* was further relayed through a reprogrammable sound system, which invited audiences to remix samples of sounds recorded by young people in the gallery, including the slamming sound of old machinery and the singing sounds of South African colonial-era music.

The use of the camera to follow the loudly slamming movements of industrial technology, and our collaborative subsequent redrawing of stills selected by the

**FIGURE 10.6** The *Missing Half Second*. Animated video. Rousell, de Freitas, Trafi-Prats, Still images #40–45 layered (top) and still images # 66–71 layered (bottom)

automated software, underscores how one can trouble ethnographic participant-observation, not by disabling vision *per se*, in a literal self-blinding that would allow the other senses to register more intensely; rather, it could involve an altered concept of digital vision, within ethnographic practices of sensing that are polyvocal, and synaesthetic, a vision in touch with all of itself at once (Grosz 2017, Ruyer 2017). Several authors have arrived at the notion of *haptic* vision (Marks 2002, Puig de la Bellacasa 2009, Deleuze 2003: 129; see also Massumi 2011) – a form of immanent sensing that has renounced the eye's transcendent position in the attempt to apprehend the abstract forces and intensities that compose events, destabilising standard ontological assumptions about the nature of perception (Cull 2011). Haptic vision works synesthetically across the boundaries that arbitrarily partition sensing into discrete senses and elevate some to more prominence than others. It also operates through registering rather than representation. In Hayward's term, haptic vision might be a matter of seeing with 'fingery eyes' (Hayward 2010). We mobilise here the notion of 'seeing without reading' sketched by Deleuze and Guattari in *Anti-Oedipus* as a practice of/for immanent or ontological participation (Cull 2011).

The eye that attempts to see without reading tries to avoid subjecting participants – human and non-human, virtual and actual – to observation's ambition to comprehend, and thereby consume, its objects. Seeing without reading is an *ambulant* practice (Deleuze & Guattari 1987) – a matter of attentively following and gathering the lines and contours of abstract yet intensive flows. Paradoxically, seeing without reading always demands a *jump* from the known to the unknown (Deleuze & Guattari 1983, Stengers 2008, James 1996). It involves acts of errant attunement, surreal disjunction, relayed attention, intensification and playful modulation. Seeing without reading implies that participation is fundamentally a matter of undergoing disjunctive movements of difference, and that participation 'comes first' before perception.

The *Missing Half Second* disperses the eye across a collection of drawn fragments, reassembled and transformed into the errant graphical trace of the haptic-eye. Leaning on anthropological studies of the relation of voice to the marking of the body (which they term a primitive 'graphism') in ritual and healing practices, Deleuze and Guattari assert that the eye was once a confederate in a 'magic triangle' of voice, body and eye: its function was not to perceive as representation but to register the relational milieu. Similarly, voice was not signifying, but rather oracular and declamatory; bodies similarly procured inscriptions of a localised graphism that was not yet writing but might still consist of 'a dance on the earth, a drawing on a wall, a mark on a body' (1983 188). The contribution of the eye was to grasp the 'terrible significance' of the asignifying relations amongst sensations. In order to do this, Deleuze and Guattari write, 'the eye jumps'. This jump establishes connections that are promiscuous, mobile, radial, and above all, *a*signifying. Deleuze and Guattari (1983: 204) write:

> the chain of territorial signs is continually jumping from one element to another; radiating in all directions; emitting detachments wherever there are flows to be selected; including disjunctions; consuming remains; extracting surplus values; connecting words, bodies, and sufferings, and formulas, things and affects; connoting voices, graphic traces, and eyes, always in a polyvocal usage.

Our software decomposition of the original gallery video into half-second intervals, the ink-jet printing, and then the detailed collective labour of redrawing each image on wax paper broke up the continuity of the moving image, only to then force a new unstable alliance amongst all these perspectives, by re-pixelating them, and using software again to achieve a soft merging and animated effect. This technique subordinated the representational quality of the ethnographic data, scrambling the camera eye into a more atmospheric registering, '*a way of jumping* that cannot be contained within an order of meaning, still less within a signifier' (Deleuze &

Guattar 1983: 204). The technique celebrated 'vision' as an ecological or atmospheric feature of an event, a kind of indigenising that forges unstable *alliances* or 'unnatural nuptials' (Deleuze & Guattari 1987). This experiment underscores how sensation is not about meaning, but *efficacy* – that is, effecting transformation. Our technique eschews the conventional coupling of sensation-proposition-explanation and tries instead to follow the abstract lines and intensities that connect events on the virtual plane, in a process of jumping that nevertheless keeps its feet grounded in what actually occurs, as the errant expression of those intensities.

## Concluding comments

We take it as axiomatic that ethnographic practices are inherently problematic, linked as they are to 'colonial specularity' (Bhabha 1994: 122) and its collusion in the 'humanising' projects of anthropology, even in the recent 'ontological turns' towards animism (Povinelli 2016) and pluriversality as ethnographic concepts (Blaser & de la Cadena 2018, Escobar 2020). The yoking of sensation to participation through multisensory ethnography can be understood as an attempt to democratise the asymmetrical relations imposed by the scopic regime of colonialism (Pink 2015). But we would argue that, despite these precautions, sensory ethnographic practice has tended to preserve the 'panoptic immunity' of the liberal subject (MacLure 2011), who exercises the prerogative to interpret the sensations of self and others by rendering them visible, transparent, and positioned without reciprocal obligation. Kirby (2011) also seeks to recast 'the question of the anthropological – the human – in a more profound and destabilising way than its disciplinary frame of reference will allow'. In other words, if sensory ethnography has a future as a posthumanist methodology, it may have to pass through the disciplinary thresholds of 'description' and 'interpretation' and become unrecognisable to itself, entering into new zones of confluence with experimental design research, non-rational modes of knowing, and speculative fabulation (Salazar 2020).

Mobilising the thought of Gilles Deleuze and Felix Guattari, this chapter pursued the ramifications of an ontological reconfiguring of sense and sensation, exploring surrealist practices of ethnography. In keeping with anthropological work associated with the ontological turn (e.g. Vivieros de Castro 2004, Salmond 2014, Holbraad et al 2014), we see this work as necessarily entailing transformation, deformation, and creative experimentation. We recruit digital technologies as confederates in this experimental work, in collaborative interventions in which humans, digital sensors, touch screens, video images, and physical artefacts are allied to bring forth flows of affect that engage and disrupt simplistic notions of participation and observation. This involved deforming or hacking or simply repurposing digital technologies, severing them from their predominant uses (such as surveillance, remediation or the tracking of human emotions or intentions) in order to harness their potential to bring forth new ethnographic insight into gallery experiences. Drawing specifically on Deleuze and Guattari's *Anti-Oedipus* (1972), we reconceptualise ethnographic writing as 'seeing without reading', a performative *graphism* that bypasses the mediations of explanation, description, and interpretation and aims to intervene directly in flows of eco-sensory affect. *Language here strikes the body as surrealist command, electrical pulse, whisper, and contracted memory.*

Our gallery experiments focused on the ways in which human sensations are caught up in, and transformed by, new forms of media, engendering new kinds of temporality and presencing. Deploying playful recuperations of sensory technologies, our approach considered sensibility outside the standards of perception studies, where stimulus-response experiments and human cognitive frameworks have dominated. By engaging with the monstrous media machines of Kentridge's installations, our ethnographic 'account' explores the potential of digital technology to open up 'participation without observation' (Grosz 2017, Ruyer 2017) and 'seeing without reading' (Deleuze & Guattari 1983), where bodies participate in a mutually consequential field of sensation.

We suggest that posthuman ethnography might revisit the surrealist impulses that have periodically animated anthropology, so as to map the circulation of intensive flows and material affect without submitting to the scopic regime of representation. The microtemporal speeds of the digital and sensory excitations that we have mobilised in our museum activations could be thought of as *speculation-made-concrete* – attempts to 'feed forward' (Hansen 2015) by folding and stretching time into futures that encompass us but remain uncanny, because they are never solely within our human grasp. We wish to emphasise, however, the distinctive political stakes of this theoretical move for an anthropology of futures, to the extent that State and corporate interests are increasingly using both speculative fabulation (Keeling 2019) and sensory technologies (Williamson 2020) to prefigure 'preferred' futures. Anthropologists and social scientists are enlisted in these efforts, and thus we see the need for a new convergence among critical ethnography, experimental art, and speculative design to reclaim sensory data from regimes of State and corporate control.

## Notes

1 Manifold Lab for Biosocial, Eco-Sensory and Digital Studies of Learning and Behaviour, www.themanifoldlab.com/
2 Clifford (1981: 117–8) summarised the political project of early surrealism thus: 'The sort of normality or common sense that can amass empires in fits of absent-mindedness or wander routinely into world wars is seen as a contested reality to be subverted, parodied and transgressed'. It is important to note however the complex relation that surrealism has always held to colonialism (Antle 2015) and to issues of race and gender (Keeling 2019). On the one hand, surrealist experimental projects responded directly to the threat of fascism and the subjugation of non-Western peoples, and surrealism continues to be part of decolonising and resistance aesthetics (Rousell et al 2020). Nevertheless, many critics have noted how surrealist opposition to colonialism often also replayed colonialist tropes, betrayed ambivalent attitudes to women, and adopted a problematic and exclusionary relationship to so-called primitivism (Rosemont & Kelley 2009).

# References

Antle, M. (2015). Dada and surrealism faced with colonialism. *South Central Review*, 32(1): 116–119.

Bhabha, H.K. (1994). In a spirit of calm violence. In G. Prakesh (Ed.), *After colonialism* (pp. 326–344). Princeton: Princeton University Press.

Blaser, M., & de la Cadena, M. (2018). Pluriverse: Proposals for a world of many worlds. In M. de la Cadena & M. Blaser (Eds.), *A world of many worlds* (pp. 1–22). Durham: Duke University Press.

Braidotti, R. (2013). *The posthuman*. Cambridge: Polity Press.

Braidotti, R. (2019). A theoretical framework for the critical posthumanities. *Theory, Culture & Society*, 36(6): 31–61.

Clifford, J. (1981). On ethnographic surrealism. In *The predicament of culture: Twentieth-century ethnography, literature and art*. Cambridge, MA: Harvard University Press.

Clough, P.T. (2009). The new empiricism: Affect and sociological method. *European Journal of Social Theory*, 12(1): 43–61.

Cull, L. (2011). Attention training, immanence, and ontological participation in Kaprow, Deleuze and Bergson. *Performance Research*, 16(4): 80–91.

de Freitas, E. (2015). Classroom video data and the time-image: An-archiving the student body. *Deleuze Studies*, 9(3): 318–336.

de Freitas, E. (2016). Re-assembling the student body in classroom video data. *International Journal of Qualitative Studies in Education*, 29(4): 553–572.

de Freitas, E. (2018). The biosocial subject: Sensor technologies and worldly sensibility. *Discourse: Studies in the Cultural Politics of Education*, 39(2): 292–308.

de Freitas, E., & Rousell, D. (2021). Atmospheric intensities: Skin conductance and the collective sensing body. In J. Fritsch, B. Thomsen, & J. Kofoed (Eds.), *Affects, interfaces, events*, pp. 221–241. Lancaster, PA: Imbricate! Press.

de Freitas, E., & Truman, S. (2020). Science fiction and science dis/trust: Thinking with Bruno Latour's Gaia and Liu Cixin's. *The three body problem*. Rhizomes: Cultural Studies of Emerging Knowledges. www.rhizomes.net/issue36/defreitas-truman.html

de Freitas, E., Rousell, D., & Jager, N. (2019). Relational architectures and wearable space: Smart schools and the politics of ubiquitous sensation. *Research in Education* [special issue on "biosocial imaginaries in education"], 107(1): 10–32.

de Freitas, E., Trafi-Prats, L., Rousell, D., & Hohti, R. (2022). A poetics of opacity: Towards a new ethics of participation in gallery-based art projects with young people. In Trafi-Prats, L., & Castro-Varela, A. (Eds.). *Visual Participatory Arts Based Research in the City* (pp. 126–142). London: Routledge.

Deleuze, G. (1994). *Difference and repetition* (P. Patton, Trans.). New York: Columbia University Press.

Deleuze, G. (2003). *Francis Bacon: The logic of sensation*. Minneapolis: University of Minnesota Press.

Deleuze, G., & Guattari, F. (1983). *Anti-Oedipus: Capitalism and schizophrenia* (R. Hurley, M. Seem, and H.R. Lane, Trans.). Minneapolis: University of Minnesota Press.

Deleuze, G., & Guattari, F. (1987). *A thousand plateaus: Capitalism and schizophrenia* (B. Massumi, Trans.). Minneapolis: University of Minnesota Press.

Escobar, A. (2020). *Pluriversal politics: The real and the possible*. Durham, North Carolina: Duke University Press.

Estalella, A., & Criado, T. S. (Eds.). (2018). *Experimental collaborations: Ethnography through fieldwork devices* (Vol. 34). Berghahn Books.

Gabrys, J. (2016). *Program earth: Environmental sensing technology and the making of a computational earth.* Minneapolis: University of Minnesota Press.

Grosz, E. (2017). *The incorporeal: Ontology, ethics, and the limits of materialism.* New York: Columbia University Press.

Hansen, M.B. (2015). *Feed-forward: On the future of 21ˢᵗ century media.* Chicago: University of Chicago Press.

Hansen, M. (2006). *Bodies in code: Interfaces with digital media.* Routledge.

Hayward, E. (2010). Fingeryeyes: Impressions of cup corals. *Cultural Anthropology,* 25(4): 577–599.

Hernandez, J., Riobo, I., Rozga, A., Abowd, G. D., & Picard, R. W. (2014). Using electrodermal activity to recognize ease of engagement in children during social interactions. In Proceedings of the 2014 ACM International Joint Conference on Pervasive and Ubiquitous Computing (pp. 307–317).

Holbraad, M., Pedersen, M., & Viveiros de Castro, E. (2014). The politics of ontology: Anthropological positions. *Cultural Anthropology Online,* January 13 2014, http://culanth.org/fieldsights/462-the-politics-of-ontology-anthropological-positions

Ingold, T. (2002). *The perception of the environment: essays on livelihood, dwelling and skill.* New York: Routledge.

James, W. (1996). *Essays in Radical Empiricism.* Lincoln, Nebraska: University of Nebraska Press.

Keeling, K. (2019). *Queer times, Black futures.* New York: New York University Press.

Kentridge, W. (2014). "How to make sense of the word". Interview. Filmed 2014. YouTube video, 30:24. Posted [October 2014]. www.youtube.com/watch?v=G11wOmxoJ6U

Kirby, V. (2011). *Quantum anthropologies.* Durham: Duke University Press.

Lomas, D., & Stubbs, C. B. J. (2012). *Simulating the Marvellous: Psychology–surrealism–postmodernism.* Manchester University Press.

Lupton, D. (2016). The diverse domains of quantified selves: self-tracking modes and dataveillance. *Economy and Society,* 45(1), 101–122.

MacLure, M. (2011). Qualitative inquiry: Where are the ruins?. *Qualitative Inquiry,* 17(10): 997–1005.

MacLure, M. (2013). Researching without representation? Language and materiality in post-qualitative methodology. *International Journal of Qualitative Studies in Education,* 26(6): 658–667.

Marks, L.U. (2002). *Touch: Sensuous theory and multisensory media.* Minneapolis: University of Minnesota Press.

Massumi, B. (2002). *Parables for the virtual: Movement, affect, sensation.* Duke University Press.

Massumi, B. (2011). *Semblance and event: Activist philosophy and the occurrent arts.* Cambridge, MA: Massachusetts Institute of Technology.

Massumi, B. (2018). *99 Theses on the revaluation of value: A postcapitalist manifesto.* Minnesota: University of Minnesota Press.

Piccolino, M., & Bresadola, M. (2013). *Shocking frogs: Galvani, Volta, and the electric origins of neuroscience.* Oxford University Press.

Pink, S. (2015). *Doing sensory ethnography.* London: Sage.

Platoni, K. (2015). *We have the technology: How biohackers, foodies, physicians & scientists are transforming human perception, one sense at a time.* New York: Basic Books.

Puig de la Bellacasa, M. (2009). Touching technologies, touching visions. The reclaiming of sensorial experience and the politics of speculative thinking. *Subjectivity,* 28(1): 297–315.

Povinelli, E. (2016). *Geontologies: A requiem to late liberalism.* Durham: Duke University Press.

Rosemont, F., & Kelley, R.D. (2009). Introduction: Invisible surrealists. In F. Rosemont & R.D. Kelley (Eds.), *Black, brown, & beige: Surrealist writings from Africa and the diaspora* (pp. 1–20). Austin: University of Texas Press.

Rousell, D., Hohti, R., MacLure, M., & Chalk, H. (2020). Blots on the Anthropocene: Micropolitical interventions with young people in a university museum. *Cultural Studies <-> Critical Methodologies*, 21(1): 27–40.

Ruppert, E., Law, J., & Savage, M. (2013). Reassembling social science methods: The challenge of digital devices. *Theory, culture, society*, 30(4): 22–46.

Ruyer, R. (2017). *Neofinalism* (Edlebi, A., Trans.). Minneapolis: University of Minnesota Press.

Salazar, J.F. (2020). Speculative fabulation: Researching worlds to come in Antarctica. In, J.F. Salazar, S. Pink, A. Irving, & J. Sjöberg (Eds.). *Anthropologies and futures: Researching uncertain and emerging worlds* (pp. 151–170). New York: Routledge.

Salazar, J.F., Pink, S., Irving, A., & Sjöberg, J. (Eds.) (2017). *Anthropologies and futures: Researching uncertain and emerging worlds*. New York: Routledge.

Salmond, A.J.M. (2014). Transforming translations (part 2): Addressing ontological alterity. *HAU: Journal of Ethnographic Theory*, 4(1). https://doi.org/10.14318/hau4.1.006

Schneider, A., & Pasqualino, C. (2014). *Experimental film and anthropology*. London: Bloomsbury Academic.

Schwanhäußer, A., & Wellgraf, S. (2015). From ethnographic surrealism to surrealist ethnographies. *Reconstruction: Studies in Contemporary Culture*, 15(3): 3.

Stengers, I. (2008). A constructivist reading of 'Process and Reality'. *Theory, Culture & Society*, 25(4): 91–110.

Stengers, I. (2018). The challenge of ontological politics. In M. de la Cadena &M. Blaser (Eds.), *A world of many worlds* (pp. 83–111). Durham: Duke University Press.

Tironi, M. (2017). Regimes of perceptibility and cosmopolitical sensing: The earth and the ontological politics of sensor technologies. *Science as Culture*, 27(1): 131–137.

Viveiros de Castro, E. (2004). Perspectival anthropology and the method of controlled equivocation. *Tipití: Journal of the Society for the Anthropology of Lowland South America*, 2(1). Available at: http://digitalcommons.trinity.edu/tipiti/vol2/iss1/1

Wanono, N. (2014). From the grain to the pixel, aesthetic and political choices. In A. Schneider & C. Pasqualino (Eds.), *Experimental film and anthropology* (pp. 183–198). London: Bloomsbury Press.

Williamson, B. (2020). New Digital Laboratories of Experimental Knowledge Production: Artificial Intelligence and Education Research. *London Review of Education*, *18*(2), 209–220.

# AFTERWORD

## Collaboration and experimentation

*Janet Roitman*

In their recent book, *Inquiry after Modernism* (2019), Paul Rabinow and Anthony Stavrianakis argue that modernist forms of anthropological knowledge and critique persist today despite changes in their conditions of production. Their point is that even though, for almost three decades, the "crisis of representation" has been the central topic of epistemology and the principal subject of critique in the social sciences (often indexed symbolically by the publication of *Writing Culture* in 1986), today anthropologists pursue and give credence to a realist mode of ethnography that takes representation to be quite unproblematic. The experimental moment was aborted (2019: 2). Rabinow and Stavrianakis focus on this shift in the status of critique, noting that during this prior period of experimentation, anthropology was the object, not just the lever of critique (2019: ix).

Their lament for the promise of the experimental moment finds redress in newfound attention to the conditions of production of anthropological knowledge. The chapters published herein pose questions about both the modes and the ends of anthropological inquiry. They address a quintessential anthropological problem: How does one delineate "the emergent?" This seemingly very general question has been articulated as a specifically *anthropological* question, denoted as "the anthropology of the contemporary," by Paul Rabinow (2003, 2008; for review, see Faubion, ed. 2016; Caldeira and Collier, eds. 2021; Roitman 2021).[1] It is taken up in various ways by the contributors to this edited collection through technologies – that is, through what are taken to be emerging technologies as well as through novel or unprecedented technological practices. Crucially, these interventions are not mired in technological determinism; nor do they profess pre-ordained conclusions about either a utopian or a dystopian view of digital platforms and the production and operationalization of data.

In that sense, these interventions generate potential insights into contemporary modes of problematization. Not merely a matter of inquiry into the ways that

DOI: 10.4324/9781003084471-12

people pose problems, problematizations entail epistemological and normative claims. In the words of Michel Foucault (1994: 670):

> A problematization does not mean the representation of a pre-existent object nor the creation through discourse of an object that did not exist. It is the ensemble of discursive and non-discursive practices that make something enter into the play of true and false and constitute it as an object of thought (whether in the form of moral reflection, scientific knowledge, political analysis, etc.).

In other words, the object of anthropological inquiry is not just a problematic situation, or the study of how novel phenomena, such as automated systems, ubiquitous sensors, and machine-learning algorithms unsettle human certainties. Instead, the objects of inquiry are the modalities through which problems are constituted. Anthropological inquiry generates insights into the fault lines of problematization: the emergence of forms and constellations of truth claims related to those forms.

As illustrated herein, this mode of inquiry ideally entails collaborative problematization. More than just interdisciplinary research, the present volume illustrates how collaboration is based on various forms of alliance and participatory observation with stakeholders, elucidating possible alternative scenarios, multi-engineering, co-visioning, co-sensing, and the aim to engender publics. This work, as Lanzeni and Pink (in this volume) note herein, "exceeds the convention of moving from the ethnographic encounter, to description, to abstraction." In contrast, a collaborative mode of inquiry involves what Rabinow and Bennett (2009: 266–267 and 280) term remediation, or the creation of interfaces between anthropologists and their various interlocutors that defines a new medium for articulating commonly defined problems. Remediation creates new configurations for inquiry; it hedges against the tendency to reach for long-standing metaphors in our attempts to delineate the emergent.[2] For Rabinow and Bennett, this configuration includes specific interlocutors: lab scientists, ethicists, and eventually those responsible for elaborating regulations and policies (see also Rabinow 1996, Rabinow and Bennett 2009). For the authors of the chapters herein, interlocutors include software engineers, coders, tech developers, tech entrepreneurs, product managers, investors, regulators, public administrators, and all the milieu in which socio-technological devices and operations are currently deployed or in stages of imagined deployment.

Ideally, anthropologists and their interlocutors become "epistemic partners" (Deeb and Marcus 2011). Ideally, a venue for shared knowledge production is established such that anthropology becomes less the application of tried-and-true foundational concepts (society, culture, state, capitalism) and more the exploration of emerging forms and the truth claims that instantiate – *or fail to instantiate* – those forms.

The work of establishing that venue potentially displaces the work of conventional critical theory, as the chapters in this volume indicate. Even when the aim of epistemic partnership remains elusive, the various projects described herein represent a movement away from the critique of existing relations and practices. On the one hand, a focus on emergent technologies incites that move, since the optic is the near future. But, at the same time, this work is committed to making visible the ways that new forms and practices are constituted; and that commitment is articulated in the form of propositions as opposed to critique. In other words, inquiry is not invested in, nor is it reduced to, a critical intervention based on an a priori understanding of how things "should" look or work. Likewise, and more profoundly, this mode of anthropological practice divests itself of the supposition that the guiding principle of our interventions is to unveil fundamental contradictions, or the bases of alienation (Cf. Roitman 2014) – a constant temptation for those who study emerging technologies in terms of a human/tech binary. It's also worth noting that the motivation to preclude this practice of unveiling contradictions as part of anthropological work is not inspired by the desire for an apolitical world – refraining from critique doesn't mean one gets to live in a utopian vacuum. To the contrary, impatience with perpetual critique inspires experimentation and hopefully the actualization of other modes of inquiry and politics. The commitment is to actualize a differential (cf. Roitman 2021).

This collection of collaborative and experimental work on emerging technologies demonstrates that research and scholarship cannot remain confined to text-based work and to writing texts in perpetual critique. Our worlds and forms of knowledge have always consisted of multiple media, and the move to experimentation enables us – and impels us – to apprehend novel and emerging media practices as modes of representation, on the one hand, and modes of knowledge production, on the other. *Anthropological knowledge can only account for the changes in its conditions of production by transforming the media through which it is practiced.* That is, through experimentation *in diverse media,* new forms can emerge.

We can see this practice of experimentation in the work of de Freitas, MacLure, and Rousell (this volume), who seek to avoid "conventional causal exegesis." Alongside the various contributors to this collection, they refrain from a priori assumptions about the nature of existing and emerging technologies (e.g. sensors, drones, automated mobility systems) as well as the methods and outcomes of data production and data operations (e.g. machine-learning algorithms, artificial intelligence). They thus avoid generalizations about technology and data, exploring instead concrete operations and pragmatic applications that generate particular effects. The latter include new categories of practice, new forms of value, new modes of judgment, and unprecedented questions for public debate.[3] Instead of generalizations about quantified human selves or totalizing surveillance regimes, instead of nostalgia for the past or euphoria about the future, collaborative and experimental research makes visible the fault-lines of alternative practices (cf. Dan-Cohen 2021a, 2021b; Rabinow and Dan-Cohen 2004). Not naïve to the deleterious effects of emerging technologies, this approach seeks to explore and to learn. It aims to better understand how the tech/human interface generates configurations, potentialities, and determinations that are best described and understood in terms of distributed agency.

Importantly, experimentation involves speculative labor: instead of decoding coherence and dissonance – success/failure or reproduction/breakdown or truth/alienation – it seeks changing forms, even entertaining "what if…?" propositions. Significantly, "what if" propositions are distinct from the "is/ought" propositions that are inherent to critical theory. In that sense, the experimental approach focuses on potential alternatives – the otherwise. And this mode of problematization and experimentation can be contrasted to a fixation on meaning, or on the (true) meaning of things (relations, behaviors, ideologies) and alienation from those (true) meanings (Roitman 2014).[4] Moreover, this form of experimentation is necessarily collaborative. Not a matter of bringing distinct disciplines into conversation, or mere interdisciplinarity, these collaborations are about how, not what. In that spirit, they are more concerned with "how we can think together than with the specific content of what we are thinking together."[5]

## Notes

1  For examples of this approach, see the contributions to Ong and Collier (2005), amongst others.
2  For example, a persistent metaphor mobilized in the social and human sciences is "social fabric." In contemporary studies of digital technologies, such metaphors are often mobilized to gloss or subsume what are in fact concrete and frequently indeterminant processes – for example, an alleged "algorithmic logic." On the last point, see Dourish 2017; Jaton 2021; Viljoen, Goldenfein and McGuigan 2021; Birch, Cochrane and Ward 2021.
3  See Jorgensen, Gad and Winthereik in this volume, who join calls for the problematization of AI as not overdetermined by the opposition between discriminatory and ethical AI. Read, for example, Jaton 2021 on ground-truthing.
4  Notably, Anthony Dunne and Fiona Raby have developed design practice that rejects the notion of design as a problem-solving modality. See Dunne and Raby (2013).
5  Quoted by The Labinar at the University of California, Berkeley (http://anthropos-lab. net/), which is now defunct. The Labinar was an example of this commitment, as part of the Anthropological Research on the Contemporary collaboration: For commentary, see Roitman (2021).

## References

Birch, K., D.T. Cochrane, and C. Ward. 2021. "Data as Asset? The Measurement, Governance, and Valuation of Digital Personal Data by Big Tech." *Big Data & Society*. Vol. 8, no. 1: 1–15. 20539517211017308.

Caldeira, T. and S. Collier. eds. 2021. "Preface: An Anthropologist of the Contemporary." Festschrift: Paul Rabinow. *HAU: Journal of Ethnographic Theory*. Vol. 11, no. 2: 713–714.

Clifford, J. and G. Marcus, eds. 1986. *Writing Culture: The Poetics and Politics of Ethnography*. Berkley, Los Angeles, London: University of California Press.

Dan-Cohen, T. 2021a. "The Future." 2021. Festschrift: Paul Rabinow. *HAU: Journal of Ethnographic Theory*. Vol. 11, no. 2: 754–756.

Dan-Cohen, T. 2021b. *A Simpler Life: Synthetic Biological Experiments*. Ithaca, New York: Cornell University Press.

Deeb, H. and G. Marcus. 2011. "In the Green Room: An Experiment in Ethnographic Method at the WTO." *PoLAR: Political and Legal Anthropology Review* 34 (1): 51–76.

Dourish, P. 2017. *The Stuff of Bits: An Essay on the Materialities of Information*. Cambridge, MA; London: MIT Press.

Dunne, A. and F. Raby. 2013. *Speculate Everything*. Cambridge, MA; London: MIT Press.

Faubion, J. ed. 2016. "On the Anthropology of the Contemporary: Addressing Concepts, Designs, and Practices." *HAU: Journal of Ethnographic Theory* 6 (1): 371–402.

Foucault, M. 1994. *Dit et ecrits. 1954–1988*. Paris, France: Editions Gallimard.

Jaton, F. 2021. *The Constitution of Algorithms: Ground-Truthing, Programming, Formulating*. Cambridge, MA; London: MIT Press.

Ong, A. and S. Collier, eds. 2005. *Global Assemblages: Technology, Politics, and Ethics as Anthropological Problems*. Maiden, MA: Blackwell.

Rabinow, P. 1996. *Making PCR: A Story of Biotechnology*. Chicago: University of Chicago Press.

———. 2003. *Anthropos Today*. Princeton, NJ: Princeton University Press.

———. 2008. *Marking Time: On the Anthropology of the Contemporary*. Princeton, NJ: Princeton University Press.

Rabinow, P. and G. Bennett. 2009. "Human Practices: Interfacing Three Modes of Collaboration" in Bedau, M. and E. Parke, eds. *The Ethics of Protocells: Moral and Social Implications of Creating Life in the Laboratory*. Cambridge, MA; London: MIT Press.

Rabinow, P. and T. Dan-Cohen. 2004. *A Machine to Make a Future: Biotech Chronicles*. Princeton, NJ: Princeton University Press.

Rabinow, P. and A. Stavrianakis. 2019. *Inquiry after Modernism*. Berkeley, CA. ARC Press.

Roitman, J. 2014. *Anti-Crisis*. Durham, NC. Duke University Press.

———. 2021. "Adjacency and secession." Festschrift: Paul Rabinow" *HAU: Journal of Ethnographic Theory*. Vol. 11, no. 2: 762–766.

Viljoen, S., J. Goldenfein, and L. McGuigan. 2021. "Design Choices: Mechanism Design and Platform Capitalism." *Big Data & Society*. Vol. 8, no. 2: 1–13.

# INDEX

Actor Network Theory 46
algorithms *see* artificial intelligence;
    automated decision-making
AlgorithmWatch report 80, 81, 83, 84, 86
anticipatory infrastructures 19
anticipatory practices 20
artificial intelligence (AI): anticipated
    proliferation of 93; disruptive aspirations
    receding 24–25; embedded authoritarian
    tendencies 93; expert systems in
    1980s and 1990s 96–97; explanation
    algorithms 102–103n2; hype and fear
    cycles regarding 97; imaginary of 23, 93;
    machine learning, shift of focus to 97;
    medical applications 96; situated action
    97, 101–102; *see also* Danish Tax and
    Customs Administration
automated decision-making (ADM):
    affective suitability as stabilizing force 87;
    data derivative 82; definition of 80;
    discriminatory models in credit scoring
    decisions 79–80, 81, 82; fact-checking
    and dialogue, crucial in assessment of 89,
    90; general bias against underprivileged
    individuals and communities 81;
    industrial horizons of efficiency and
    optimization 85–86; legal redress against
    discrimination 79–80, 82; resisting
    naturalization of 87; socio-technical
    complexity of 80, 83, 90; use of
    spreading 81–82; violations of privacy
    in personality assessment 84–85, 86,
    87–89

autonomous driving (AD) cars: car–
    smartphone relationship as hybrid
    technology 144; as first-and-last-mile
    transport 'solution' 145–150; growth of
    ethical and regulatory concerns 143;
    Human Experiences and Expectations
    of Autonomous Driving (HEAD) 143;
    as leaky boundaries technology 145; in
    Mobility as a Service (MaaS) systems
    138, 139, 145–150; phenomenological
    analysis, lack of 139, 143; as socially
    isolating pods 150–151; solutionist
    paradigm, framed within 138, 139,
    144, 146; sterile commercial visions vs.
    cluttered, adaptive reality of car use
    140–141, 145; technologically
    determinist narratives 138, 143; utopian
    vs. dystopian visions of 138; Wizard of
    Oz cars 144; *see also* Mobility as a Service

broken world thinking 83, 86, 87, 90
brownfield 26
bubble tech 26

care, thinking with 83–84, 86, 87–88, 89, 90
child protection social work during
    COVID-19 pandemic: digital exclusion
    69; digital intimacy, successful generation
    of 69–70, 71; digital wayfaring 73–74, 75;
    everyday embodied ethics 74–75; home
    visits, difficulty of substituting for 69,
    71–73; limited pre-pandemic use
    of digital technologies 66–67; rapid